THE THEORY OF EXCHANGE

THE THEORY OF EXCHANGE

PETER NEWMAN
Visiting Professor of Political Economy
The Johns Hopkins University
Baltimore, Maryland

PRENTICE-HALL, INC. *Englewood Cliffs, New Jersey*

Library of Congress
Catalog Card No.: 65-10334

PRENTICE-HALL INTERNATIONAL, INC., *London*
PRENTICE-HALL OF AUSTRALIA PTY., LTD., *Sydney*
PRENTICE-HALL OF CANADA, LTD., *Toronto*
PRENTICE-HALL OF INDIA (PRIVATE) LTD., *New Delhi*
PRENTICE-HALL OF JAPAN, INC., *Tokyo*

Printed in the United States of America
91377-C

To My Parents

PREFACE

This book presents a comprehensive account of the elementary theory of the exchange of commodities, and has been written out of my conviction that existing discussions of this important topic in economic treatises reflect neither the richness nor the rigor of which modern economic theory is capable. Apart from the chapter on demand, the book represents a return to the tradition of Jevons, Edgeworth, and Walras in its focus on exchange *systems* rather than on the theory of the individual consumer. In this regard, it could be viewed as an introduction to the wider study of general systems of allocation, including production.

Little in the book is completely new, except possibly for the method of approach. This proceeds by postulating a unified set of axioms for the preferences of the typical individual and then erecting the whole of exchange theory on this axiomatic base. The derivation of the theory from the postulates is leisurely and informal but rigorous, and should give those unfamiliar with it some idea of the power and limitations of the axiomatic method.

In principle, the book is self-contained both economically and mathematically, but the reader will probably move faster if he has already had two or three years' training in economic theory, as well as a background of reasonably sophisticated college algebra; essential use of the differential calculus is made only in the last part of Chapter 6. As a text, the book could serve as a supplement for the upper division or graduate price theory course, and as introductory to courses on mathematical economics and on international trade theory.

My main debts are to my former student Bruce Gensemer for his critical reading of several versions of the manuscript and to L. J. Savage for mathematical advice concerning Chapter 6; I am grateful also for the careful prepublication reading of the final draft by Lionel McKenzie,

University of Rochester, and by Edwin Mills, The Johns Hopkins University. But I alone am responsible for the (possibly null) set of errors that remain. I would like to thank the Center for Research on Economic Development at the University of Michigan for providing secretarial assistance and Elizabeth Carrico for being an excellent and cheerful typist.

PETER NEWMAN

CONTENTS

1

INTRODUCTION

In these few program notes, we set the scene for what is to follow in Chapter 2 and beyond by outlining the role that the theory of exchange plays in general economic analysis. Some degree of methodological self-consciousness now will help to prevent confusion later on, and these informal remarks are meant to help provide just that.

A. ANALYSIS OF SYSTEMS AND OF INDIVIDUALS

Anyone sufficiently interested in abstract theory to have read beyond the preface will not need to be reminded of the very insubstantial nature of apparently hard facts. One does not have to go to the extremes of Conrad's *Lord Jim* ("They wanted facts. Facts! They demanded facts from him, as if facts could explain anything") to realize that we can only hope to observe phenomena systematically if we have a set of instructions that tell us what to look for. These different sets simply *are* different theories; some ways of looking at "reality" are useful and fruitful, others are not; and the whole situation is complicated by the difficulty of ascribing meanings to such terms as "useful" and "fruitful" that are any less ambiguous than the concept of "a fact" itself.

Over the last two centuries, economists have devised many different ways in which to approach the study of the vast mass of economic "reality." Purely for the purposes at hand, it is useful (!) to divide a large part of these theories into two classes, those whose main focus is on the behavior—possibly the optimal behavior—of *individuals* in the reality, and those which concentrate on the *interactions* among a group of individuals forming a *system* within the reality. An example of the former class is the theory of the individual monopolist, as developed by Cournot; and of the latter, the theory of aggregative short-period equilibrium devised by Keynes in his *General Theory*.

Mention of aggregative theories may lead the reader to think that the distinction which is being made corresponds to the fashionable dichotomy between micro- and macro-economics, terms introduced thirty years ago by Ragnar Frisch. But, as these phrases have gained popularity, they have also gained ambiguity—a common fate of popular ideas—and they are now used in so many different senses as almost to have lost any meaning at all. In common parlance, micro-economics seems to refer to the study of firms and households, and macro-economics to the study of synthetic aggregates such as national income and national consumption; the basis for the distinction appears to be relative size, as the words themselves indicate.

But in a world in which the net profits of a single firm, General Motors, are larger than the entire national incomes of scores of countries, this basis of relative size loses much of its justification. Much more importantly, the micro-macro distinction does not specify to what *end* firms and households and aggregates are being studied. If it is the characteristics of the individual firm or household, or of the individual aggregate, that are at issue, then the theory falls into our first class. If, however, the study is of the *system* of firms, or of households, or of aggregates, then it is of the second class. The division according to apparent "size" has very little economic meaning or relevance in this context.

Nor does the common antithesis between partial and general equilibrium analysis correspond to the distinction that is being drawn here. As used by its originator, Marshall, the device of partial equilibrium analysis was a self-conscious method by which one examined a small chunk—such as an industry—of a general economic system, in isolation from the rest of the system; this trick was "justified," if at all, by an appeal to hypotheses about the ways in which the component parts of the given system interlocked or failed to interlock. It is easy to understand how, over time, this distinction gradually merged into the idea that dealing with individuals *qua* individuals was partial equilibrium analysis, and that analyzing systems was general equilibrium analysis; but that was a later interpretation. For Marshall, it was a simplified way of studying parts of *systems.*

Incidentally, the use of General Motors as an illustration emphasizes the dangers of thinking even of firms as *individuals*, for that firm certainly is not an economic unit. Probably many nations, certainly the more sovietized economies, are each more of an economic entity than is G.M., which means in turn that the apparently "hard" concepts of a firm's profits and outputs need not be less metaphysical (even in this regard) than a more aggregative concept such as national income. I see no reason, in general, why the one type of concept should be regarded as any more "real" than the other, though in particular instances this may turn out to be the case.

The attentive reader will probably be wondering how, if even firms (and households) can themselves be regarded as systems, we can draw a valid distinction between the study of systems and the study of individuals. The

answer to this is simply that, for the purposes at hand, we *choose to regard* the firms and households as individual entities and do not probe more deeply into their structure. For other purposes we might wish to do so, but then we would probably have to *dis*regard the "fact" that the multilayered firm operates within a system of such firms. Doubters of the cogency of this argument may draw comfort from the assurance that such hierarchies of theories often exist in other sciences, for example in physics, where the poor atom has been—fruitfully—analyzed at many levels since the days of Democritus.

As we emphasized at the beginning, there are many potentially useful ways of looking at the same reality. The best that we can do is to accept this state of affairs as right and natural, but always to remember what theory is currently under discussion and not confuse it with other, perhaps related, theories, for these will usually possess different aims, different methods, and different assumptions. To quote the dramatist Harold Pinter:

> Because "reality" is quite a strong firm word we tend to think, or to hope, that the state to which it refers is equally firm, settled and unequivocal. It doesn't seem to be, and in my opinion, it's no worse or better for that.

B. THE ROLE OF UNCERTAINTY

In addition to the distinction that we have just drawn, and quite apart from it, there is another twofold division of economic theories, according to the role played by *uncertainty* in the theory. We can assume that each individual acts as if he were quite sure both of his data and of the consequences of his actions, in which case we would be dealing, by definition, with *behavior under certainty*; or we can assume that this is not the case, that the individual knows that his actions have unforeseen consequences and that the data on which he bases them are not fully revealed to him; then we would be dealing with *behavior under uncertainty*. An example of the first kind of theory is Cournot's theory of perfect competition, and of the second, many parts of the theory of oligopoly, which also originated with Cournot.

Notice that this division does not correspond to the common distinction between statics and dynamics, i.e., between those theories that do not involve *time* explicitly and those that do. The uncertainty of which we have spoken may arise in several ways, of which that induced by the contemplation of the unknown future is merely one of the most important. Uncertainty may also arise in such problems of conjectural interdependence as are typified by the chain of reasoning: "He knows that I know that he knows . . . that I know that if I cut price, he will cut even more. What should I do?"

Perhaps a sufficiently deep philosophical investigation would discover that these various sources of uncertainty in economic theories all have a common origin; indeed, perhaps one already did. But at least to a first approximation we may regard them as different, and so issue a warning against confusing the present dichotomy with the static-dynamic division that is itself so often misinterpreted. Several economic theories that involve time in an essential way, but *not* uncertainty, have in fact been constructed and these have proved very fruitful; an example would be the major part of the theory of capital. Conversely, several useful theories exist which meet the uncertainty problem full on, but do not involve time in any but a formal sense; the theory of two-person constant-sum games of strategy is an outstanding example of this.

C. A CONVENIENT CLASSIFICATION OF ECONOMIC THEORIES

We can now put together our two analytical distinctions between types of theories and consider a two-way classification based on them that will be of some use to us. It will save time and space if we set this up as a two-way table of the kind beloved by methodologists of the taxonomic school and put in the vacant cells of the table some of the suitable candidates for the relevant positions. No great precision or completeness is claimed for this allocation, and we will not take space to defend it; that would be tedious and unnecessary at this stage, especially since many of the theories—such as the theory of capital—are not monolithic and should have parts of them tucked away in other corners of the table. But the general picture should be of some help, particularly to those with earlier acquaintance with several of the theories.

Focus of Interest	*Certainty*	*Uncertainty*
Individual Units	*Alpha*, which includes theories of the individual: 1. firm, including monopoly 2. producer, including most of linear programming 3. consumer, including the supplier of factor services	*Beta*, which includes theories of optimal behavior under uncertainty, such as 1. optimal capital accumulation by firms 2. inventory policy, including portfolio decisions 3. optimal savings patterns 4. theory of speculation
Systems of Units	*Gamma*, which includes theories of systems concerned with 1. allocation, including exchange and production theories 2. welfare economics 3. economic growth, including capital accumulation 4. classical theory of money	*Delta*, which includes such systems of optimizing units as those in 1. theories of oligopoly, and in models of conflict 2. theory of games 3. stochastic analyses of economic systems, including queuing theory 4. Keynesian short- and long-run theory

Let us review these cells very briefly:

Alpha: These theories are very useful as a pedagogic introduction to the more general types *Beta* and *Gamma*, but pushed beyond a certain range they tend to become rather scholastic, except insofar as they serve as a theoretical basis for econometrics, as in the case of consumer theory. If we wish to study optimal behavior of firms *as such*, then it is usually quixotic not to recognize that the firm almost always operates in an uncertain environment; and then we are led to *Beta*-type theories. If, on the other hand, our chief ultimate aim lies in systems theory, then the difficulties of analyzing the behavior of large groups of individuals mean that we must keep the theory of the component units *simple*, if we are not to exceed both our grasp and the requirements of theoretical simplicity.

Beta: Many of these theories hardly belong to economics any more, having been removed into the capacious maw of the ill-assorted set of disciplines known as *operations research*. This was only to be expected, since many of the problems they deal with are eminently practical in character. Let us note, incidentally, that—logically speaking—this cell is also the present home of the theory of statistics, although recent developments by de Finetti and Savage suggest that eventually it may come to rest in the cell below.

Gamma: The emphasis here is on the behavior of the whole *system*, without worrying too much about a detailed theory for the component parts. The loss of information that this entails is compensated for by the quite different perspective, and the correspondingly different results, that can be obtained from a systematic adoption of this—systematic—viewpoint. Consider, for example, the elementary fallacy of composition concerning the burden of the public debt, which so bedevils public economic discussion in the United States, and which is at bottom mainly a failure—or an unwillingness—to make a distinction between the mode of analysis appropriate for individuals and that appropriate for systems.

The theory of this book belongs to a branch of type *Gamma*, as shown by Item 1 in that cell. It forms part of the study of allocation systems and is limited by its self-imposed condition that no production is allowed, so that all allocation and distribution is of *fixed stocks of commodities*. In production theory we widen this situation, first by considering production of commodities from other commodities and from fixed resources in general, and then by analyzing what happens when resources themselves are mobile between uses and, to some extent, over time. The theory of allocation systems that involve production is more complicated than that of exchange systems only and is held over, together with a detailed discussion of the interrelations between the two types of system, for another volume.

Delta: This is the most difficult of all branches of economic theory, and therefore comparatively little headway has been made with it. Of the four examples cited, the first is in an unsatisfactory state, and the next two do not really belong to the central core of economics at all but lie at its boundaries with other disciplines. The uncertainty component of Keynesian short-period theory is relatively minor, and that for the long run is hardly developed yet. One of the chief difficulties with *Delta* is, indeed, that we really do not know what a satisfactory theory of this type would, or should, look like. Would we recognize a fully satisfactory theory of oligopoly if we saw it? The example of the *General Theory of Employment, Interest and Money* suggests that the answer is probably "yes," but there does exist a lingering doubt, at least in my mind.

Much of the actual analysis of this book is of type *Gamma*, and *all* of it is directed primarily to that end. But in Chapter 2 we first have to construct a theory of type *Alpha* for the individual's preference structure, which is then used in Chapter 3 to prove the existence of equilibrium prices as an *intrinsic* property of the exchange system. Mechanisms for obtaining these prices are analyzed in Chapter 4, and generalizations of the whole theory, including some very recent work on *viable* allocations, are discussed in Chapter 5.

To many people a book on exchange theory without a large section on demand would be Hamlet without the Prince, and in Chapter 6 we return to *Alpha* analysis to construct a theory of demand, based on the theory of choice behavior, or of "revealed preference." Throughout this chapter we shall stress the many interconnections of demand theory with the theory of exchange, though actually the theories are basically distinct. In the final chapter we shall consider what are, in effect, some problems of converting *Gamma* theory into *Alpha* theory; and, not surprisingly, we shall discover that most of these problems are almost insuperable.

The "Notes on the Literature," which are placed at the end of each chapter except this, are not mere bibliographies but are an integral part of the book and should be read as such. They serve to put the general exposition, which is usually free from references, firmly into the context of past and present economic analysis. This is particularly true of the Notes to Chapters 3 and 4, which deal with several problems of exchange theory whose interpretation in existing literature is far from clear.

2

THE PREFERENCE STRUCTURE OF AN INDIVIDUAL

A. INTRODUCTION

This chapter employs a short series of carefully stated axioms to build a model of an individual's preference structure, and the book will then deal mainly with a world inhabited entirely by such synthetic people. Our *model* men are always just that—and no more. The set of axioms which animates them is designed solely for the analysis of exchange systems and only has relevance in that context. It cannot be carried over to other types of theoretical system without much further justification.

Reality is seldom so definite that one can be sure that the assumptions of any theory are closely met in practice. So it is fortunate—but not fortuitous—that the theory of exchange developed here is very robust, in the sense that its basic structure changes little with moderate alteration in almost any one of its axioms. This warrants our concentration on the *simplest* set of axioms that will serve to set into motion a reasonably complete analysis of exchange. As the Notes at the end of this chapter indicate, greater "realism" can often be secured by adopting different axioms, though usually at the cost of complicating detail; and this cost is not justifiable in the central exposition, whose chief concern—apart from relevance—is with simplicity and clarity.

This concern also makes it desirable that the treatment be informal and discursive, though rigorous within its own limits. Thus, for example, no formal attempt is made to prove the fact that the set of axioms constituting the model is logically consistent and independent, while time *is* taken to set out each concept fully, to relate it to what has gone before and to make clear the exact role of each axiom. Later chapters will normally proceed at a less leisurely pace, in part just because the foundations are laid down here with some care.

B. BASIC CONCEPTS

(i) The Field of Choice

The theory takes for its basic situation that some individual (whom we shall always call Adam) is confronted with a set of "alternatives" from among which he must select one, which he then receives.* Unless otherwise stated, everything is assumed to happen *within* one time period, so that quantities do not need to be dated. Within this period, the set of alternatives actually available to Adam (which we shall call his *attainable set*) will not be the set of all the alternatives among which he could conceive of exercising his choice. For if it were, there would be no scarcity and hence no need for a logic of choice; this would probably be a very pleasant state of affairs (if only because it would obviate the need for economists), but it does not seem an urgent prospect.

In the theory of exchange, an "alternative" is simply a collection (or "basket" or "batch") of goods and services, a concept for which we will usually reserve the name *commodity bundle.* Now the "set of all commodity bundles among which Adam could conceive of exercising his choice" is a distressingly vague concept, and for the moment we can do no more than say that in any given problem there will be a well-defined *field of choice* (denoted always by X), which is such a set of commodity bundles. The role played by these sets will gradually become clearer as the analysis proceeds.

Notice that by stating that the field of choice is simply a set of commodity bundles, the theory implicitly assumes that Adam's preferences (though not his choices) are influenced only by the commodities that he himself might receive. It follows that changes in *anything* else cannot alter his preference structure, whether they be in general environmental factors, or in factors much more specific to the exchange situation, such as the choices of other traders and the prices of relevant commodities. In the first case we assume that background changes take effect slowly enough to be negligible in a short enough period, while the second type is excluded because if it were not so, the analysis of exchange would be much more complicated. If Adam's preferences did change in this latter fashion, then the model preference structure would be a useless tool of analysis, since it would have to be "redrawn," as it were, after every change in the trading situation.

(ii) The Preference Relation

In any axiomatic theory with empirical meaning such as ours, it is necessary to have terms that are undefined. No matter how careful we are to obtain logical economy in our system of postulates, there will always exist

* For this reason that branch of decision theory to which the present chapter belongs is sometimes called the *theory of choice under certainty*, to be contrasted with the theory of choice under *un*certainty. The latter theory is now extensively studied and has enormous ramifications; its most typical (if tawdry) example is that of the selection of the "best" bet in a gambling situation.

primitive notions not definable by means of the other terms in the system. The main primitive notion in our theory of preference structures is the idea of preference itself. The idea that an individual *prefers* one commodity bundle in the set X to another such bundle is one that we assume has an immediate intuitive meaning, and so one which will receive no further discussion. Notice that no statements are made about how much Adam prefers one bundle to another; it is enough to take account only of the existence of the preference itself.

Actually it is logically more elegant, and indeed easier, to take as our primitive notion not "preference" but a slightly more generalized relation. Before introducing this, however, it is convenient to describe some of the notation which will be used throughout the book. A commodity bundle in the field of choice X will be denoted always by the generic symbol x, and different bundles will be distinguished by superscripts, e.g., x^0, x^1, x^2. It is important to realize that these x's are not numbers but will usually signify whole *lists* of numbers. For example, the bundle x^0 might consist of 3 pounds of white, vitamin-enriched bread, 2 pounds of brown, no-essential-vitamins-removed bread, 6 scoops of chocolate nut sundae with whipped cream and hot fudge sauce, and 2 cartons of strawberry-flavored yoghurt. Whatever else this collection might be, it is certainly not a quantity of any one commodity; and therefore we cannot carry out the usual algebraic operations, such as multiplication and division, on the symbol x^0. In Chapter 6 we will describe an algebra for manipulating such symbols, but now it is sufficient merely to warn against treating them as ordinary real numbers.

We can now describe our generalization of the idea of preference. If Adam *either* prefers a bundle x^0 to another bundle x^1, *or* considers the two bundles to be equally satisfactory, we say that he considers x^0 to be *at least as good* as x^1, or to be *no worse than* x^1. It is unfortunate that the English language does not appear to possess just one word that would describe this generalized preference relation, and mainly because of this linguistic inadequacy some authors use the word "preferred" where we use "at least as good as"; they reserve the term "strictly preferred" for the case where Adam believes x^0 to be actually *better* than x^1. But this terminology violates the accepted English usage of "preferred," so we will stick to the clumsier expression given above. In any case, we can attain linguistic economy by using the symbol R_A to denote the relation of being "at least as good as," the subscript referring to our individual, Adam. Thus if we write down the trio of symbols $x^0 R_A x^1$, this is shorthand notation for the phrase "the individual, Adam, considers that the commodity bundle x^0 is at least as good as the commodity bundle x^1."

In order to introduce this primitive notion R_A, we began with the idea of (strict) preference. But this was only for purposes of exposition; and once we have R_A we can dispense with the earlier notion entirely; the treatment can be turned around and "preference" defined in terms of R_A itself. To see this, observe that if x^0 is preferred to x^1, then this must mean that x^0 is at least as good as x^1, *and* that x^1 is *not* at least as good as x^0. We can write this down compactly in symbols if we add two more pieces of notation. Let P_A stand for the relation "preferred to," so that $x^0 P_A x^1$ reads "Adam prefers x^0 to x^1"; and let the symbol $\sim$ stand for the negation of any relation, so that $\sim(x^0 R_A x^1)$ signifies that x^0 is *not* at least as good as x^1 (as far as Adam is concerned), while $\sim(x^0 P_A x^1)$ means that, for Adam, x^0 is *not* preferred to x^1. Then we can write down

DEFINITION 1 (OF P_A): $x^0 P_A x^1$ means $((x^0 R_A x^1)$ and $\sim(x^1 R_A x^0))$.

In the same way, we can define the idea that two bundles x^0 and x^1 are *equally satisfactory* to Adam. This can occur only if he considers x^0 to be at least as good as x^1, and x^1 to be at least as good as x^0. Although the rather lackluster connotations of the word make it not altogether appropriate, long usage in economics sanctions the phrase "x^0 is *indifferent* to x^1" to denote this situation of equal satisfaction. Accordingly, we write $x^0 I_A x^1$ to mean that Adam ranks x^0 and x^1 equally; formally, we have

DEFINITION 2 (OF I_A): $x^0 I_A x^1$ means $((x^0 R_A x^1)$ and $(x^1 R_A x^0))$.

C. GENERAL AXIOMS

The axiom system is composed of two conceptually distinct parts. The first three axioms refer to very *general* aspects of the preference structure, and hence they (or others rather similar) are likely to occur in *any* formulation of individual choice under certainty. The remaining four postulates are tailored to a more specialized situation, which is that of the classical theory of pure exchange. These are naturally more restrictive than the others, and by suitable variations on their theme one can construct many models, all of which would have a strong family resemblance; we deal only with the simplest.

(i) The Axiom of Comparability

The first general axiom seems of such breathtaking scope that it is wise to introduce it first in a very simple situation. Let us imagine Adam establishing a preference structure over a field of choice X consisting of only three commodity bundles. We can conceive of him doing this in the following curious way: he considers two identical fields of choice, takes one bundle at a time from each, and for each pair of bundles so obtained states which batch is at least as good as the other. Since any bundle from X can be matched with any bundle from its "mirror image" which is the other X (implying that *any* bundle can be matched with itself), it follows that in order to give complete information on his preference structure over this "small" X, Adam would have to make *nine* such "paired comparisons."

The first axiom postulates that, no matter how large X may be in any problem, whether small, medium-sized or—infinitely—large, Adam can always pronounce on the relative merits of each bundle in each pair that it is possible to form from X and its mirror image. Formally, we write

Axiom I (Axiom of Comparability). For any pair of bundles x^0 and x^1 in the field of choice X, *either* $x^0 R_A x^1$ *or* $x^1 R_A x^0$.

Two points about this axiom should be noticed at once. First, the word "or" is used in what logicians call the inclusive sense. The axiom asserts that *at least* one of the statements is true, and leaves open the possibility that both may be so, in which case $x^0 I_A x^1$, by Definition 2. Secondly, there is no restriction that x^0 and x^1 need be different bundles, so it follows that either $x^0 R_A x^0$ or $x^0 R_A x^0$, which is to say that both occur and hence that always $x^0 I_A x^0$, a reasonable enough proposition.

Essentially, Axiom I is both a restriction and an idealization. It is restrictive in that it obviously could not apply to those bundles concerning which the individual has no information. I, for example, do not know whether I would prefer a month's vacation in the Vale of Kashmir to a similar period in Kyoto, because—alas—I have had no experience of either. But for just that reason such conundrums are of little relevance for my everyday conduct; if they were, I would soon make it my business to learn about the relative attractions of both places. Thus this axiom brings into relief the importance of delineating carefully just what the field of choice is in any particular problem.

The idealization postulated by Axiom I is that there are no "holes" within the field of choice, these holes consisting of groups of bundles about whose relative merits the individual is ignorant. It is difficult to see how a static theory of preference such as ours could usefully be developed without such an axiom, for the alternative is to postulate ignorance, and from ignorance on the part of the individual can come little but ignorance on the part of the theorist. If we deal with a dynamic theory of preference, however, in which *learning* is possible, then we have another story altogether, and some interesting work has been done on this.

(ii) The Axiom of Consistency

The next axiom is also a serious affair, although intuitively very reasonable. It is essentially a requirement that Adam's preferences be consistent, in the sense that they should not be such that a skillful questioner could trap Adam into contradicting himself. Unlike Walt Whitman, our Adam would not be prepared to shrug off such a situation with: "Do I contradict myself? Very well then, I contradict myself." He would take steps to revise his preference structure in order to make it consistent.

Specifically, Axiom II will require of Adam that for every triple of bundles x^0, x^1, x^2 in the field of choice, if he considers x^0 to be at least as good as x^1, and x^1 to be at least as good as x^2, then he must regard x^0 as at least as good as x^2. In logical terms, we are asserting that the relation R_A is *transitive*. Formally, we have

Axiom II (Axiom of Consistency). For any triple of bundles x^0, x^1, x^2 in the field of choice X, the statement ($x^0 R_A x^1$ and $x^1 R_A x^2$) implies that $x^0 R_A x^2$.

Many objections have been made against axioms such as Axiom II, even by those who stay within the framework of a static theory of preference. Here we mention only two main lines of criticism, the first of which stems from the idea of "threshold" effects, and which is actually normally used to criticize the similar idea of transitivity of indifference, though it can easily be extended to deal with Axiom II. Adam might consider a bundle x^0 to be at least as good as x^1 merely because he lacked the power to discriminate between the two bundles; and for similar reasons x^1 might be held to be no worse than x^2. But the preference "gap" between x^0 and x^2 might be much larger than that between x^0 and x^1, or between x^1 and x^2, so that Adam might say that x^2 is better than x^0, his rather coarse standards of calibration being able to judge *their* relative standing. The combination of two "gaps," each of which is below the individual's threshold of (preference) perception, might itself be above that threshold. Regarded in this light, Axiom II seems to be an idealization of reality which is appropriate for simple theories of exchange systems, although needing considerable scrutiny before use in analysis whose main interest is individual behavior as such.

A more telling objection concerns the difficulties of being consistent when the relevant bundles contain numerous commodities, especially when the commodities themselves possess many criteria in terms of which preferences are formed. A common example of such seeming irrationality when manifold criteria are present is where a man announces that he prefers one motorcar *A* to another car *B*, on the apparently trivial ground that he likes *A*'s color better than that of *B*. What he usually means by this is that he has compared the engines, performances, comfort, style, and other features of the two cars and found them equal in each respect. His preference is then based on the relative scores of the lesser criteria, such as color. This man, on being questioned, might then well forget the earlier major comparisons and simply announce the result of his ranking of the cars by the last—and possibly rather trivial—criterion; but it would then be most misleading to draw conclusions about his irrationality from this reply. Similar apparent irrationalities in entrepreneurial choices of industrial location can sometimes (though by no means always) be explained on analogous grounds.

An amusing illustration of the actual *in*consistency of preferences in such multiple-criteria situations has been provided in an experiment conducted by Kenneth May. He hypothesized three potential marriage partners, and endowed them with various qualities. The first (labeled x) was said to be "very intelligent, plain looking, and well off"; the second (y) was "intelligent, very good looking, and poor"; the third (z) was "fairly intelligent, good looking, and rich"; each was "described as acceptable in every way, none being so poor, plain or stupid as to be automatically eliminated." Some 62 American college students were then asked to rank these potential partners in order of preference. The nature of the difficulty involved in the ranking may be shown by the following table, where each partner is thought of as a little bundle of criteria:

		Criterion		
		Intelligence	*Looks*	*Wealth*
	x:	Excellent	Poor	Medium
Bundle	y:	Medium	Excellent	Poor
	z:	Poor	Medium	Excellent

It turned out that, on a comparison of x with y, there were 39 for x and 23 for y, y beat z by 57 to 5, but z beat x by 33 to 29; so that the group, considered as a whole and going by majority vote, displayed inconsistency. Although this result *could* have been due solely to the results of majority voting (see Chapter 7), in fact seventeen individuals displayed the cycle of preferences xPy, yPz, and zPx, which would contradict Axiom II.

Such examples lend weight to the objection that the consistency axiom will be violated sometimes in practice. On the other hand, one might take the view that such inconsistencies are merely temporary, to be erased by the individual when they are discovered, either by himself or others. In any event, it is clear that Axiom II is a powerful tool, ruling out many types of preference structure, so that we should be able to derive powerful conclusions with its help; and so it will turn out.

(iii) The Construction of a Preference Ordering

With Axioms I and II, we have all the ingredients for Adam to be able to establish what is called a preference ranking. The force of Axiom I is to require Adam to have a *complete* coverage of the field of choice with R_A, with each bundle in X being as good as itself, while it is common (though not universal) in logic to call any relation R_A which satisfies Axiom II an *ordering*. Therefore in logical terms we have constructed what is often known as a *complete weak ordering* R_A of the field of choice X.*

* The ordering is called *weak* because it allows the possibility that for any two bundles (not necessarily different) we might have $x^0 R_A x^1$ *and* $x^1 R_A x^0$. A set which was *strongly* ordered by a relation S would be one for which this possibility was ruled out, e.g., when the positive integers are ordered by the relation "less than".

For the record, and in order to avoid ambiguity, it will be useful to frame the following formal

DEFINITION 3. An individual's *preference ranking* of a field of choice X is a relation R_A which satisfies Axioms I and II.

Because of Axiom I, every bundle in X is connected with every other bundle in X by means of R_A, and it is often possible, on the basis of this fact and Axiom II, to formulate statements that must be true about Adam's preference concerning a pair of bundles when we are given other information about these bundles. Thus if we are told that x^0 is preferred to x^1, and that x^1 is preferred to x^2, then x^0 *must* be preferred to x^2. This means that P_A is a transitive relation, while a similar statement is true for I_A. Since these results are important, let us prove them:

(a) *P_A is a transitive relation in X.*

PROOF: We have to show that the statement ($x^0P_Ax^1$ and $x^1P_Ax^2$) implies $x^0P_Ax^2$. Since by the definition of P_A, $x^0P_Ax^1$ implies that $x^0R_Ax^1$, and $x^1P_Ax^2$ similarly implies $x^1R_Ax^2$, it follows from Axiom II that $x^0R_Ax^2$. It remains to show that $\sim(x^2R_Ax^0)$. Suppose this to be false, so that $x^2R_Ax^0$. Then $x^2R_Ax^0$ and $x^0R_Ax^1$ imply by Axiom II that $x^2R_Ax^1$, contrary to the hypothesis that $x^1P_Ax^2$. Hence $\sim(x^2R_Ax^0)$, and therefore $x^0P_Ax^2$.

(b) *I_A is a transitive relation in X.*

PROOF: We have to show that $x^0I_Ax^1$ and $x^1I_Ax^2$ together imply that $x^0I_Ax^2$. From the definition of I_A, we have $x^0R_Ax^1$ and $x^1R_Ax^2$ which, by Axiom II, give $x^0R_Ax^2$. Similarly, the original hypothesis by definition implies that $x^2R_Ax^1$ and $x^1R_Ax^0$ which, again by Axiom II, imply that $x^2R_Ax^0$. Hence $x^0R_Ax^2$ and $x^2R_Ax^0$, which by definition are equivalent to $x^0I_Ax^2$.

The relations P_A and I_A have other important properties, proofs of which are given below:

(c) *If $x^0I_Ax^1$, then $x^1I_Ax^0$.*

PROOF: This statement asserts that I_A is a *symmetric* relation, and the proof is obvious from the definition of I_A.

Note that (c) and (b) state, respectively, that I_A has the properties of being symmetric and transitive in X, while we have already shown that always $x^0I_Ax^0$, a property known as *reflexivity*. Logicians call relations having these three properties *equivalence* relations, so that the relation of indifference has, by Axioms I and II, implicitly been assumed to be such an equivalence relation.

(d) *For all* x^0 *in* X, $\sim(x^0 P_A x^0)$.

PROOF: This asserts that P_A is an *irreflexive* relation in X. Suppose this were false, so that $x^0 P_A x^0$ for some x^0. But then, by very definition of P_A, we have both $x^0 P_A x^0$ and $\sim(x^0 P_A x^0)$, which are obviously contradictory statements. This proves the result.

(e) *If* $x^0 P_A x^1$, *then* $\sim(x^1 P_A x^0)$.

PROOF: This asserts that P_A is *asymmetric* in X. If it were false, then we would have $x^0 P_A x^1$ and $x^1 P_A x^0$ which, by property (a) already proved, imply $x^0 P_A x^0$; but this contradicts property (d) above.

In addition to these "individual" properties of R_A, P_A, and I_A, we can raise questions about the way in which they "gear" together. Thus if x^0 is at least as good as x^1, and x^1 is preferred to x^2, what can we say about the relation between x^0 and x^2? There are six possible couplings, namely $R_A P_A$, $R_A I_A$, $I_A P_A$, and their converses $P_A R_A$, $I_A R_A$, and $P_A I_A$. We give proofs only for the first three, leaving the exactly analogous proofs of the others to the reader.

(f) *If* $x^0 R_A x^1$ *and* $x^1 P_A x^2$, *then* $x^0 P_A x^2$.

PROOF: From the definition of P_A, the hypotheses imply that $x^0 R_A x^1$ and $x^1 R_A x^2$, which, by Axiom *II*, yield $x^0 R_A x^2$. Suppose $x^2 R_A x^0$. Then since $x^0 R_A x^1$, again by Axiom II, we would have $x^2 R_A x^1$, contrary to hypothesis. Hence $x^0 R_A x^2$ and $\sim(x^2 R_A x^0)$ or, equivalently, $x^0 P_A x^2$. Notice that property (a) is contained within this result (f), and hence is redundant, in the sense that the same proof does for both.

(g) *If* $x^0 R_A x^1$ *and* $x^1 I_A x^2$, *then* $x^0 R_A x^2$.

PROOF: Obvious from the definition of I_A and from Axiom II.

(h) *If* $x^0 I_A x^1$ *and* $x^1 P_A x^2$, *then* $x^0 P_A x^2$.

PROOF: From the definition of I_A, we have $x^0 R_A x^1$. Hence from (f) above we can conclude that $x^0 R_A x^1$ and $x^1 P_A x^2$ together imply $x^0 P_A x^2$.

It follows from these results that combinations of pairs of our preference relations yield only the same class of preference relations, so that there is no need to go on to consider trios, quartets, or other groups of relations, since their study can always be reduced to that of couples. Thus, working from left to right, we have from result (f) that $R_A P_A I_A$ implies $P_A I_A$, which is the converse of (h); similarly, from (g), $R_A I_A I_A P_A$ implies $R_A I_A P_A$, which from (h) implies $R_A P_A$, which is (f). These conclusions are a relief, for they enable the analysis of the logical connections between the preference relations to be called complete.

(iv) The Axiom of Selection

In any given choice situation, Adam will be limited (by definition) to his attainable set, which is a *subset* of his field of choice X. Since Axioms I and II provide him with a preference ranking, each bundle can be compared with every other, and it follows that in *any* subset Y of X—and in particular for the currently attainable set—we can often* isolate a nonempty class of bundles each of which is highest in his preference ranking of Y. (Sometimes, of course, this class will have just one member, in which case there is a unique bundle in Y, preferred to all the others in that subset.) We shall call this "superior" class of batches in Y the *maximal class of* Y (to be denoted by Y_M) and the "rest" of Y will be denoted by $(Y - Y_M)$, i.e. $(Y - Y_M)$ is the subset Y minus the maximal class. We formalize these ideas by

Definition 4. The *maximal class* Y_M of any subset Y of the field of choice X is the set of bundles x^M such that (a) for any pair of bundles x^{M1} and x^{M2} in Y_M, $x^{M1} I_A x^{M2}$, and (b) for any x^M in Y_M and any x in $(Y - Y_M)$, we have $x^M P_A x$.

Now it seems very reasonable to suppose that, in any choice situation, Adam will always select an element from the maximal class of the attainable set. For unless he had some such guiding principle in mind, why go to all the bother of constructing a preference ranking of X? This leads us to adopt the formal

Axiom III (Axiom of Selection). Given a field of choice X, and an attainable set Y which is a subset of X, the individual will always select a bundle from the maximal class Y_M of Y.

Axiom III plays the same role in modern systems such older ideas as "economic man," "rational man," "maximizing utility," and "maximizing satisfaction" have played in earlier theories of individual behavior. There has been such futile logomachy on this subject in the past that little needs to be said here.† "Rational behavior" is a term which will be avoided as much as possible but which, when it is used, means precisely behavior in accordance with Axioms I–III and *nothing* else. Rational behavior in our

* We have to use the word "often" rather than "always," for there are pathological cases where *no* maximal class exists; but in most economic contexts the existence of such a class is ensured by other assumptions.

†Much of that small part of this debate which has meaning turns out, on examination, to be critical of the realism of the earlier axioms (especially the first) rather than of Axiom III as such.

model is neither good nor bad, foolish nor wise, beautiful nor monstrous; it is simply behavior which obeys the axioms. Different axiom systems, therefore, carry with them their own interpretations of rational behavior.

If it is objected that this approach is really rather an emasculation of such a profound subject as rationality, a simple defense is to point once more to the aims of the whole theory of exchange; these do not include meta-economic discussions of rationality. Just for the record, we repeat our definition formally as

DEFINITION 5. An individual is said to display *rational behavior* in our system if (and only if) he acts in accordance with Axioms I–III.

D. SPECIAL AXIOMS

(i) The Commodity Space

So far the fields of choice X that we have dealt with have been very general indeed. Each has consisted of a set of commodity bundles, where each bundle of this set in turn was a "collection of various amounts of goods and services." Actually, we could have been even more ambiguous than that; there is no need for the commodity bundles to consist of actual quantities of goods and services in the usual sense of that term. For example, the field of choice could be a cake, where the various commodity "bundles" would be all possible pieces which could be removed from the cake. If the cake were a rather fancy affair, such pieces would be highly inhomogeneous in composition, containing varying mixtures of eggs, flour, sugar, fruit, nuts, and icing, and it would probably be inappropriate (at least where children are concerned) either to consider such a cake as one commodity or to attempt to characterize each slice by a finite series of criteria, such as the ingredients mentioned. The "bundles" are now, in effect, *subsets* of the cake X. Yet Axioms I–III can still be applied to this field of choice and a preference ranking of the pieces of cake so obtained.

For most problems, however, and in particular for the classical theory of exchange, it proves appropriate to specialize the field of choice considerably. We do this first by stipulating that there exists some finite number, say n, of commodities, and that this number remains constant throughout the analysis. This number n can (and will, in most modern economies) be very large, but it makes for great ease of exposition if we take the very simple case of $n = 2$; in point of fact, it is true that almost all of the main conclusions of the theory are exhibited even in this simple case. Very little that is essential is lost by this restriction, and we shall be careful to point out at the appropriate times just what is special to the two-commodity case.

Since we want to keep matters simple, it will prove convenient to suppose also that our two commodities are each available in *any* nonnegative amount, which implies that each of them is continuously divisible. This idealization is not so restrictive as it sounds, since we are interested in "typical" individuals—who are in a sense scaled-down versions of the whole exchange market—rather than in actual individuals. Any actual individual might find indivisibilities of some importance, as in the purchase of cars; to the market as a whole, however, such indivisibilities are often much less important, as when several million cars are sold each year. If we are primarily interested in the behavior of the market, therefore, such divisibility assumptions appear less absurd. But in any case, the assumption is one of convenience only and is completely inessential to the basic logic of the exchange system.

Since these assumptions mean that the field of choice can now be illustrated by a diagram of the type used in plane analytical geometry, it would be nice if we could give names to our two commodities corresponding to the x-axis and y-axis of those diagrams. Unfortunately, English is a language very poor in names for commodities beginning with these two letters, and unless we are prepared to indulge in the study of such exotic phenomena as the exchange of xylophones for yashmaks, this avenue is closed to us. It seems natural to turn to the other end of the alphabet and denote the two axes by a and b, respectively, though even here English has fewer plausible commodities than one might imagine. The names we have chosen, "ale" and "bread," are purely mnemonic, and if the reader objects to them, he may substitute any other alliterative commodities he fancies.

We can now formulate our definition of the field of choice in this special situation; since it is specialized, we give it a different name—"commodity space"—but retain the same symbol X as before.

Definition 6. The *commodity space* X is a field of choice consisting of all possible bundles of two commodities, where each commodity can be obtained in any nonnegative amount.

(ii) The Axiom of Dominance

With this definition of a commodity space, all bundles become pairs (a, b) of quantities of commodities. Since these are pairs of numbers, it is not immediately obvious what one might mean if one said that a bundle x^0 (consisting of the pair (a^0 of ale, b^0 of bread)) were *larger* than another bundle x^1 (consisting of [a^1 of ale, b^1 of bread]). It seems obvious that if a^0 is larger than a^1, and b^0 is larger than b^1, then x^0 should be held to be larger than x^1; but it also seems reasonable to say that if a^0 equals a^1, but b^0 is larger than b^1, then x^0 is still larger than x^1, since after all it contains no less of one commodity (ale) and more of the other (bread). Similarly if a^0 is larger than a^1, and b^0 equals b^1, then x^0 is held to be larger than x^1. Actually, it is more convenient to use not the ambiguous word "larger" but different terms, defined by the following definitions, in which we use the familiar symbol $>$ to mean "greater than" and the not so familiar $\geqq$ to mean "greater than or equal to."

DEFINITION 7. A bundle x^0 is said to *dominate* a bundle x^1 if either (i) $a^0 \geqq a^1$ and $b^0 > b^1$ or (ii) $a^0 > a^1$ and $b^0 \geqq b^1$.

DEFINITION 8. A bundle x^0 is said to dominate x^1 *strictly* if $a^0 > a^1$ and $b^0 > b^1$. Clearly, if x^0 strictly dominates x^1, it dominates x^1. This leads to

DEFINITION 9. If x^0 dominates x^1 but does not strictly dominate x^1, then we say that x^0 *weakly dominates* x^1.

If Adam considers the commodities to be positive goods and not actual nuisances (or dis-commodities), he would implicitly be saying that if a bundle x^0 dominates x^1, he prefers x^0 to x^1. In another terminology that is often used, if he is not *saturated* or *satiated* with a commodity, he will by definition actually prefer a larger quantity of it. This leads us to formulate

AXIOM IV (AXIOM OF DOMINANCE). If two bundles x^0, x^1 in X are such that x^0 dominates x^1, then x^0 is preferred to x^1 (i.e., $x^0 P_A x^1$).

This axiom is sometimes referred to as the axiom of nonsaturation or nonsatiation; we give it the present name partly because of similar usage in other branches of decision theory, and partly because positive words like "dominance" sound better than essentially negative terms such as "nonsaturation." This axiom plays an extremely powerful role in the theory, essentially because it enables us often to forecast a person's *preferences* among bundles solely from the observable and measurable *quantities* of which the bundles are composed. Although powerful, however, it is not basic to the type of theory we are dealing with, and theories not using it have been constructed. One alternative way of looking at it is that, in effect, it cuts down the commodity space from the general positive part of the plane to that subset in which the axiom holds.

We can use the axiom immediately to provide a good deal of information on the preference structure of Adam, information that is best conveyed graphically.

In Fig. 2.1 we draw the commodity space X for the first time, consisting of all bundles composed of nonnegative amounts of ale and bread. Once we have chosen a system of units for both ale and bread, there is a one-to-one relation between any commodity bundle x and a point in the AOB plane. Such a point is our arbitrary bundle x^0, which has an "ale" coordinate a^0 and a "bread" coordinate b^0. We now inquire: What is the set of bundles x which are at least as good as x^0? And what is the set of bundles x

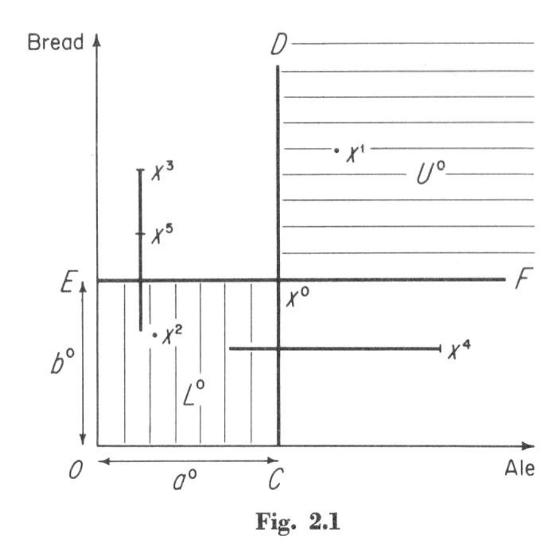

Fig. 2.1

such that x^0 is no worse than any bundle in the set? We formalize the description of these two sets by

DEFINITION 10. For any bundle x^0 in X, the *better set associated with* x^0 (denoted by B^0) is the set of all bundles x such that xR_Ax^0; and

DEFINITION 11. For any bundle x^0 in X, the *worse set associated with* x^0 (denoted by W^0) is the set of all bundles x such that x^0R_Ax.

It follows from these definitions and Axiom I that x^0 is in both sets,* and from the definition of I_A that if any other bundle x is in both sets, then x^0I_Ax. Because of Axiom I also, the sets B^0 and W^0 together fill the whole commodity space X.

Now how far can we get, on the basis of our present axioms, in identifying these sets B^0 and W^0? From Axioms I–III we know that x^0 belongs to both, and that is *all* we know about the sets. But the addition of Axiom IV enables us to take matters much further. To see this, look at the area shaded with horizontal lines in Fig. 2.1. In this area bounded by and including the lines Dx^0 and x^0F, it is true that, for any point x (such as x^1), we have that x dominates x^0; by Axiom IV this means that xP_Ax^0, so that all points in the area are members of B^0. Any point (such as x^0) in X has such an area associated with it, and for convenience we frame the following definitions concerning such areas:

DEFINITION 12. For any bundle x^0 in X, *the upper wedge associated with* x^0 (denoted by U^0) is the set of all bundles x which dominate x^0.

DEFINITION 13. For any bundle x^0 in X, *the lower wedge associated with* x^0 (denoted by L^0) is the set of all bundles x which x^0 dominates.

* We use "better" and "worse" for the sake of euphony, though strictly speaking we should refer to the "no worse than" set and the "no better than" set, respectively.

Thus the upper wedge U^0 of x^0 is a subset of B^0, because of Axiom IV; and for exactly the same reason, the lower wedge L^0 of x^0 (shaded with vertical lines in Fig. 2.1) is a subset of W^0. It is obvious from Definitions 12 and 13 that the two wedges, unlike B^0 and W^0, *cannot* overlap; the point x^0 belongs to neither U^0 nor L^0, though belonging to both B^0 and W^0.

So Axiom IV by itself wipes out two large areas of ignorance concerning Adam's ranking of x^0; all bundles in U^0 are better, and all those in L^0 are worse. But it cannot throw light on the remaining two areas, one lying "northwest" of x^0, contained by (but not containing) the lines Ex^0 and x^0D, and the other lying "southeast" of x^0 bounded by Cx^0 and x^0F. We cannot say *a priori* whether bundles such as x^3 and x^4 are better or worse than x^0. Such information can come only from detailed knowledge of Adam's preference structure; information on quantities alone, in these areas of ignorance, is of no help. On the other hand, if we *did* know that some bundle, such as x^3, was better than x^0, we could say immediately that all the bundles lying in the upper wedge U^3 of x^3 were better than x^0; and many of these bundles would be in the original areas of ignorance.

But this would require *preference* information on at least one such bundle x^3 and, failing that, it would appear that we can make no further statements about Adam's preference structure from quantities alone. Actually this is not the case; Axiom IV does enable us to say substantially more about the structure of the sets B^0 and W^0. It is true, for example, that neither set can be disconnected into a series of component subsets, separate from each other; both B^0 and W^0 must be "all of a piece," or in more technical terms, each must form a *connected* set, a fact which is best discussed in the graphical terms of Fig. 2.1. In order to prove the result, let us assume that it is false, so that W^0 consists of at least two unconnected subsets.

Notice that because of Axiom IV, W^0 must contain the lower wedge L^0 of x^0. Now let that (connected) part of W^0 which includes L^0 be denoted by W^{0L}, and consider any bundle in W^0 not belonging to W^{0L}. Such a bundle must exist, by hypothesis, and it cannot be in U^0, because of Axiom IV, so let us suppose one such point to be x^3, lying northwest of x^0. Drop a perpendicular from x^3 into the interior of L^0, and hence of W^{0L}, an operation that can clearly always be carried out for "northwestern" points such as x^3. Then there will exist a point on this perpendicular, say x^5, which lies in B^0, for otherwise the whole line from x^3 into W^{0L} would belong to W^0. If this latter proposition were so, however, then x^3 would be *connected* to L^0 by a series of bundles each of which belongs to the (by hypothesis) connected set W^{0L}, so that x^3 would also belong to W^{0L}, contradicting our initial supposition.

Therefore there must be at least one bundle x^5 lying on the line and belonging to B^0, which means by definition that $x^5R_Ax^0$. In addition, x^3 (weakly) dominates x^5, which by Axiom IV implies that $x^3P_Ax^5$ and $x^5R_Ax^0$ together imply $x^3P_Ax^0$, and hence $\sim(x^0R_Ax^3)$, contradicting our hypothesis that x^3

is in W^0. The reader should carry out a similar proof for a bundle such as x^4, lying "southeast" of x^0, this time drawing a horizontal from x^4 into L^0.

Thus our sets B^0 and W^0 each consist of one connected set, and these two components together exhaust the commodity space X. Moreover the two sets cannot overlap except possibly along a curve; for it is a simple matter to show (using Axiom IV again) that if there were an *area* of overlap, the individual would display inconsistency. In Fig. 2.2, suppose that B^0 and W^0 intersect in the area V^0. Choose any bundle such as x^1, lying in the interior of V^0; then there will exist another bundle x^2 lying in the interior of V^0 and also in the lower wedge L^1 of x^1. Since x^1 is in W^0, then $x^0 R_A x^1$; and since x^2 is in B^0, then $x^2 R_A x^0$; and these two statements together, by Axiom II, imply that $x^2 R_A x^1$. But since x^1 dominates x^2, then by Axiom IV we have $x^1 P_A x^2$, which implies $\sim(x^2 R_A x^1)$, and hence gives a contradiction.

This proof demonstrates that there can be no point in the interior of V^0, which therefore cannot be an area. If the two sets B^0 and W^0 do have any points of overlap (i.e., bundles x such that $x I_A x^0$), then these points must, at most, lie along a curve. But we have *not* shown that such a curve exists. It is true that the set V^0 of points of overlap is not empty, since x^0 always belongs to both B^0 and W^0, by Axiom I. But nothing in our axiom system so far enables us to say that V^0 has any other points. It is true that there must be an upper boundary curve of W^0, above which all points of X belong to B^0; and a lower boundary curve of B^0 must exist, below which all points of X are also in W^0; and our analysis has shown that these two curves must coincide in one curve through x^0. But it does not follow that all the bundles in this boundary curve belong to V^0. It might be, for example, that they are all preferred to x^0, or x^0 might be preferred to each of them; one can easily imagine many weird possibilities, each consonant with the definition of the curve as an upper boundary for W^0 and a lower boundary for B^0.

In the next section this problem will be discussed further, but first let us prove another result by using the powerful Axiom of Dominance. This result

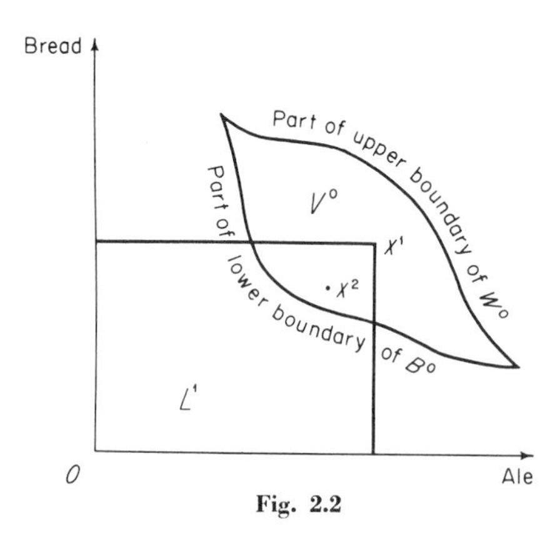

Fig. 2.2

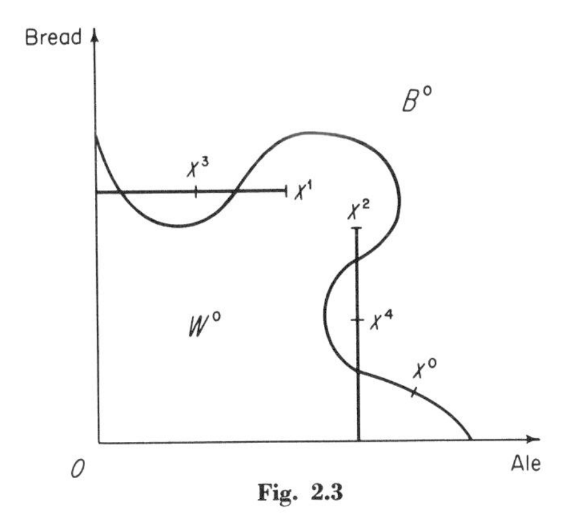

Fig. 2.3

states that it is a corollary of our axiom system so far that the boundary curve we have just described must slope downwards from northwest to southeast; the proof of this is illustrated in Fig. 2.3.

Suppose that the boundary curve sloped "upwards" from southwest to northeast over some range, and pick a bundle, such as x^1, close to this part of the curve and inside W^0. Draw a horizontal from x^1 to the "bread" axis. Then this line must pass through B^0, and there will therefore exist at least one point (*e.g.*, x^3) on the line, such that $x^3R_Ax^0$. But x^1 (weakly) dominates x^3, so that by Axiom IV, $x^1P_Ax^3$. Then $x^1P_Ax^3$ and $x^3R_Ax^0$ imply $x^1P_Ax^0$, contrary to the earlier statement that x^1 is in W^0. A similar proof utilizing bundles such as x^2 and x^4 in Fig. 2.3, would rule out the possibility of the curve sloping "down" from northeast to southwest. But clearly one of these two proofs would be redundant, since we cannot have one type of slope without the other.

(iii) The Axiom of Continuity of Preferences

We have just shown that there is no reason so far for believing that the boundary curve through x^0 will always consist entirely of bundles x which are such that xR_Ax^0 and x^0R_Ax, i.e., which are all indifferent to x^0. A statement that such a curve always exists can only be made by introducing a specific axiom to that effect.

In order to see this more clearly, suppose that Adam were a complete dipsomaniac, with an ungovernable passion for ale. By assumption he will prefer any bundle x^1 which contains more ale than x^0, *irrespective* of the relative quantities of bread contained in the two bundles. However, if two bundles did each contain the same quantity of ale, we may suppose that Adam is sufficiently sober to obey Axiom IV and prefer that bundle which contains more bread. A complete picture of our drunkard's preference structure is drawn in Fig. 2.4.

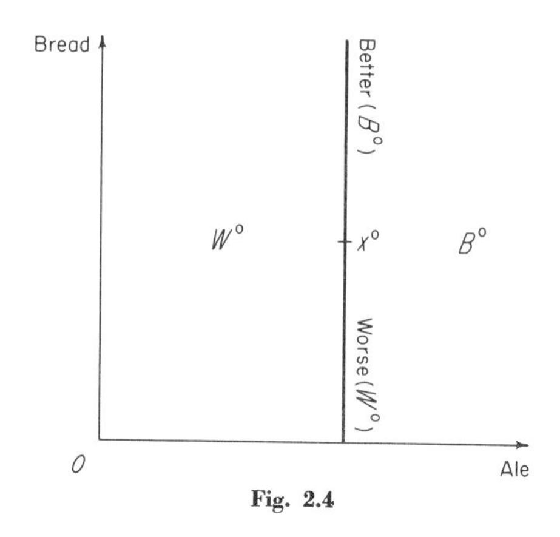

Fig. 2.4

For any point x^0, all bundles to the right of x^0 are in B^0, and all bundles to the left are in W^0; all points (vertically) above x^0 are in B^0, and all points (vertically) below are in W^0. The lower boundary of B^0 is the vertical line through x^0, which is also the upper boundary of W^0. Given this monomania for alcohol, the preference structure is very simple and may be based on quantity information alone; yet the reader may easily verify that Axioms I—III are each satisfied, so that Adam's preferences are "rational" in terms of our system, although perhaps irrational in the everyday sense (which illustrates the dangers of bandying about words like "rational" without careful prior definition).

The point of this example is that for *any* bundle x^0, the only batch indifferent to x^0 is itself; the idea of "indifference curves"—i.e., boundary curves composed entirely of bundles belonging to both B^0 and W^0—is a completely vacuous concept in this example. Now the reader may object that this ranking, although admittedly a perfectly possible complete weak ordering, is also a highly unlikely situation; and so it is, in this extreme form. But clearly less violent examples of this type can occur, in which indifference curves would fail to exist over some parts of X.

Such apparently bizarre preference orderings are in fact analogous to the way in which words are ordered in dictionaries; "azure" comes before "baby" in English dictionaries because a precedes b in the alphabet (as for our alcoholic "ale" precedes "bread"), even though the later letters *a* and *b* of baby much precede the later letters *z* and *u* of azure. For this reason, such rankings are known as *lexical* or *lexicographic* orderings. As Georgescu-Roegen in particular has pointed out, when a commodity is considered as a bundle of attributes (as in our automobile and marriage partner examples in Section C (ii)), it might make a good deal of sense to have an ordering which is lexical in character, even though not necessarily of the extreme lexical type of Fig. 2.4.

This failure of indifference curves to exist does not affect the main development of the theory very much, provided one or two other minor and very reasonable assumptions are made; but it is a great convenience, at least for the geometrical method of exposition that we shall use here and in the next chapters, to adopt an axiom which does ensure their existence and so implies the continuity of Adam's preferences. There are many ways in which this might be done; we shall employ the most brutally frank—and simplest—version:

Axiom V (Existence of Indifference Curves). All bundles x represented by the lower boundary of B^0 (or, equivalently, the upper boundary of W^0) are such that $x^0 I x$.

As we have just indicated, this axiom is equivalent in this context to several other seemingly unrelated assumptions concerning the "continuity" of the preference ranking R_A of the commodity space X. For example, it may be shown that it is equivalent (even without Axiom IV) to the following assumption: For each pair of bundles x^0 and x^1 such that $x^0 P_A x^1$, there exists a set of points N^0 around x^0, and a set of points N^1 around x^1, such that all the points in N^0 are preferred to x^1, and x^0 is preferred to all the points in N^1. The reader should check (by means of a counterexample) that this assumption is not satisfied in Fig. 2.4.

Given Axiom IV, however, Axiom V is also equivalent to another and perhaps simpler continuity assumption introduced by Wold and illustrated in Fig. 2.5.

Let x^0, x^1, and x^2 be any three bundles in X such that $x^0 R_A x^1$ and $x^1 R_A x^2$. Then this form of the continuity assumption states that there should always exist, on the straight line joining x^0 to x^2, a point x^3 such that $x^1 I_A x^3$. If we were prepared to confine ourselves to a commodity space consisting only of *positive* (i.e., excluding zero) quantities of commodities, then an even simpler

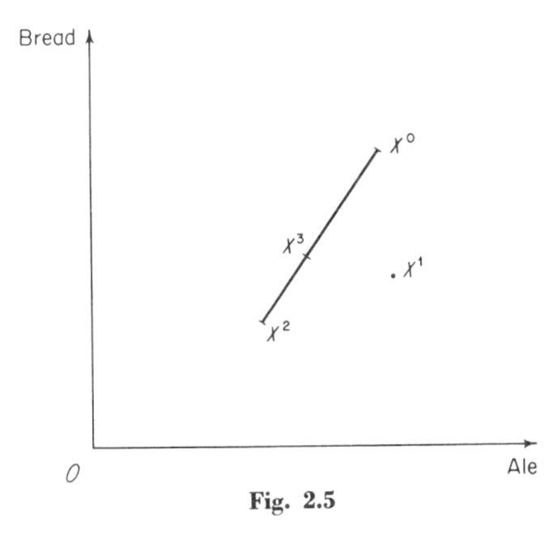

Fig. 2.5

assumption is equivalent (given Axiom IV) to Axiom V. This reads as follows: For all x^0 and x^1 such that $x^0 P_A x^1$, there exists a bundle x^3 in the interior of the lower wedge L^0 such that $x^3 I_A x^1$, and a bundle x^4 in the interior of the upper wedge U^1 of x^1, such that $x^0 I_A x^4$. Again the reader should verify that neither of these assumptions is fulfilled in Fig. 2.4.

It is not necessary here to go into the rather complicated proofs which demonstrate the equivalence or near-equivalence of these various conditions (and others like them) to our Axiom V. It is sufficient merely to emphasize the necessity of *some* explicit axiom on the continuity of Adam's preferences. In particular one must be careful not to fall into the trap of believing that since the commodity space X is "continuous" (i.e., divisible), so must the preference ranking R_A of X; our dipsomaniac example disproves this. Continuity of the commodity space in no way implies continuity of preference.

Once we do have such an axiom, however, then the same rather complicated proofs enable us to deduce that there will always exist a continuous real-valued function of the commodity bundles, which may be used to *represent* the preferences of Adam,* in the following sense:

DEFINITION 14. Let a real-valued function u_A be defined on the whole of the commodity space X, so that its value for any bundle x (i.e., for the pair of numbers $(a, b,)$) is denoted by $u_A(a, b)$. Then the function u_A is said to *represent the preference ranking R_A of X* if, whenever the statement $x^0 R_A x$ is true, the statement $u_A(a^0, b^0) \geqq u_A(a, b)$ is true, and conversely.

It is useful to add the further

DEFINITION 15. The function u_A of the last definition is called a *representation* of R_A.

Thus if we have a representation u_A, and its value for one bundle x^0 is no less than its value for another bundle x, then x^0 must be at least as good as x. The proofs referred to above show that Axiom V implies that a *continuous* representation will always exist. Since for all bundles x on the indifference curve through x^0, it is true that $x^0 R_A x$ and $x R_A x^0$, then it follows from Definition 14 that we must have both $u_A(a^0, b^0) \geqq u_A(a, b)$ and $u_A(a, b) \geqq u_A(a^0, b^0)$, so that $u_A(a, b) = u_A(a^0, b^0)$. Hence all bundles on the same indifference curve have the same representational value, and these curves can accordingly be looked upon as the contours, as it were, of the representation u_A, since for any such curve through x^0, we have $u_A(a^0, b^0) = c^0$, where c^0 is some constant depending only on x^0 and u_A.

Notice that the representation u_A is by no means unique; if one representation of R_A exists, then infinitely many do so. Suppose that we formed the new function u_A^1 defined by $u_A^1(a, b) = u_A(a, b) + k$, where k is any positive

* A real-valued function is simply one whose values are real numbers, as opposed to functions whose functional values are complex numbers, or matrices, or any other sorts of object, such as cows.

constant. Then it is easy to check, from Definitions 14 and 15, that u_A^1 is also a representation of R_A. The same would be true if the function were taken to be u_A^2 or $\sqrt{u_A}$ or $\log u_A$ or e^{u_A}, or indeed any continuous function of u_A which has the property that *its* value increases when the value of u_A increases; each such function would be a continuous representation if u_A were a continuous representation. We will see that such representations, and especially such continuous representations, are not necessary to the analysis of preference structures; but they do make for simplicity of treatment, which is one of our main aims.

Although we cannot give here a complete proof that (given Axioms I–V) at least one continuous representation—and hence infinitely many such—will always exist, we can indicate the extremely plausible nature of this statement, using a construction of Wold.

In Fig. 2.6, let x^0 be any bundle in X, and let OE be the line through the origin O which makes an equal angle (45°) with each axis. Then a perpendicular from x^0 to OE will cut the latter at a point x^1, which will dominate x^0 and hence, by Axiom IV, be such that $x^1 P_A x^0$. For similar reasons, the point x^2 where the horizontal from x^0 cuts OE will be such that $x^0 P_A x^2$. Then, by the assumption of Wold mentioned earlier (see Fig. 2.5), which we have asserted to be equivalent to Axiom V (given Axioms I–IV), there must be a bundle x^3 on OE and between x^1 and x^2 such that $x^0 I_A x^3$. Now this is true for any x^0, so that for any bundle there is a point on the line OE indifferent to it. Since for each point x^3 on OE, it is true that $a^3 = b^3$ (by construction), we can represent x^3 by the number a^3 (or b^3); and we can assign this number a^3 to any bundle x^0 indifferent to x^3. In this way each bundle in X receives a number which represents its relative ranking. To prove that this representation is continuous is another and more difficult matter, but in view of the "continuous" nature of the representation along the line OE, the statement is very plausible.

In many discussions of preference theory, the representation u_A is called a

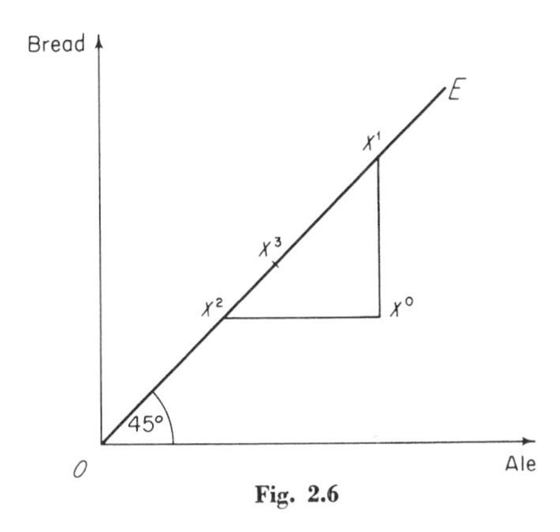

Fig. 2.6

utility function, which is why it is denoted here by the letter u. Almost as much ire and confusion has been aroused over "measurability of utility" as over the meaning of rationality, and most of this is just as irrelevant to our main line of inquiry as was the former discussion. For the analysis of exchange, nothing appears to be gained by adding axioms which will permit only those representations which imply the usual meaning of "measurability." The situation, however, may be quite different in the analysis of *other* types of systems. In the analysis of individual behavior under uncertainty, in particular, it has turned out that some apparently highly reasonable axioms do result in the existence of such representations *of preferences among risky situations*. Von Neumann and Morgenstern have shown that, given obedience to a set of these reasonable axioms applicable to preferences among "gambles," then it follows that the individual behaves as if he were maximizing a representational function (a "utility indicator") which is unique, apart from choice of origin and measurement units. This has been interpreted by some economists to mean that "utility" is "measurable" as height or weight is measurable, and to identify this "utility" with the satisfaction from commodities implicit in the idea of a preference ranking over "sure" alternatives. But it should be clear that the two situations are quite different, and that comparison of them is really not appropriate. Although the use of the term "utility" by von Neumann and Morgenstern was perhaps unfortunate, it now seems best to abandon the term "utility" in the analysis of choice under certainty and to reserve it entirely for situations of choice under uncertainty, keeping the colorless but accurate word "representation" for the former situation (a self-denial which, logically, would require us also to drop the notation u_A; but force of habit is too strong to make the change worth while, especially since we need the letter r for something else).

Finally let us stress that we do not have to use a representation, even if it is available. In many circumstances it may be more elegant *not* to use it. Thus we could reinterpret Axiom III (the Axiom of Selection) in representational language by saying that the individual will always select a bundle which maximizes the value of the representation, provided the bundle lies within the attainable set. This may or may not be a more appropriate way of expressing the axiom, depending on the problem at hand. But one use of an axiomatic formulation is that it enables us to see that we do not *have* to have a representation in order to express the basic idea lying behind the phrase "maximizing satisfaction"; our poor sot of Fig. 2.4 can still obey Axiom III, even though he does not have a representation of his preference ranking.

(iv) The Personal Rate of Substitution

At last we have arrived at that stage in the development of our theory at which many presentations of the general subject are apt to begin. What follows consists of answers to the question: What shape does the typical indifference curve have (apart, that is, from its general and already deduced slope from northwest to southeast)? If Adam does not obey Axiom V, he may not have any indifference curves at all, but we could still ask analogous questions about the "shape" of his preference structure; however we will stick—or, more precisely, require Adam to stick—with our five axioms throughout this section.

There is implicit in the whole concept of a preference ranking of a field of choice the idea that there is, as it were, more than one path to Rome, more than one bundle of commodities which will enable Adam to attain a given level of satisfaction. Indeed the assumptions so far imply that there are infinitely many bundles that will do so, consisting of all the points of the indifference curve corresponding to this level of satisfaction. By substituting ale for bread, or bread for ale, Adam can move along any indifference curve by choosing bundles which will just maintain his preference level. This leads to the important idea of compensation, which is made precise in the following:

DEFINITION 16. The bundle x^1 is said to *compensate* the individual for the loss of the bundle x^0 if (and only if) $x^1 I_A x^0$, and

DEFINITION 17. In the above definition, if $a^1 > a^0$, then the amount $(a^1 - a^0)$ is called the *compensating variation in ale* for the loss of $(b^0 - b^1)$ of bread. If $a^1 < a^0$, then $(b^1 - b^0)$ is similarly called the *compensating variation in bread* for the loss of $(a^0 - a^1)$ ale.

Before proceeding further, let us introduce some notation which will be used, wherever relevant, throughout this book. The generic symbol Δ will mean a *change* in the level of the variable written after the symbol; thus, Δb signifies any change—small or large—in the level of b. Notice that the symbols Δb by themselves do not specify the *direction* of the change; an increase in b corresponds to a positive Δb, and a decrease in b to a negative Δb.

We can now formulate the first part of Definition 17 by saying that if x^1 compensates x^0, then if Δa^{01} (i.e., $(a^1 - a^0)$) is positive, it is called the compensating variation in a for the loss of Δb^{01} (where Δb^{01} is $(b^1 - b^0)$ and negative). Notice that Δa^{01} depends on x^0 and on the magnitude of the "loss" Δb^{01}. Given the continuity of the preference ranking expressed by Axiom V, the compensating variation in a for any loss Δb will always exist: without Axiom V, exact compensation may not be possible but only under- or over-compensation (think of our dipsomaniac).

Now suppose that we asked Adam the question: If we "withdrew" an amount Δb^{01} of bread from your present bundle x^0, how much ale would you require in compensation? His answer would of course be: "The compensating variation in a at the point x^0," an amount denoted by Δa^{01}. If he had had another initial bundle, say x^2, and the same amount of withdrawal of b, $\Delta b^{23} (= \Delta b^{01})$, had been proposed, the relevant compensating variation in a, Δa^{23}, would in general have been different from Δa^{01}. If we proceeded in this way for the bundle x^0 and every possible amount of withdrawal Δb, we could discover the whole of one side—the "right" side—of his indifference curve through x^0; and if we then tried taking ale away from him, compensating him with bread, and testing every possible withdrawal of ale, we could find the other side—the "left" side—of his indifference curve through x^0. We could then switch attention to another bundle x^2 not on the indifference curve through x^0, and test that by means of withdrawals and compensating variations. Proceeding in this way until all the infinitely many indifference curves had been completely delineated, we would then have a complete picture of Adam's preference structure.

The purpose of describing this ridiculous procedure is not to propose it seriously as a method of empirical verification of a preference structure but to drive home the fact that the size of the compensating variation in a (or b) at any point depends entirely on Adam's preference structure. Its magnitude for any bundle x^0 tells us at what rate a person is prepared to *substitute* commodity a for commodity b, given that he is to stay at the same level of satisfaction, and that he is initially at the point x^0.

This leads to an important definition, but first we must clear up a rather delicate matter. Under the present assumptions, both a and b are continuously divisible, so that Δb and—because of Axiom V which asserts continuity of preferences—therefore Δa, can be made as small as we please. So no generality is lost by making the "withdrawals" of a commodity always equal to one unit, since we can always choose measurement units appropriately. We now formulate

DEFINITION 18. The *personal rate of substitution of ale for bread at point* x^0 is the compensating variation in ale for the loss of one unit of bread at that point. This magnitude is denoted by ${}_{ab}r^{A0}$, and has the dimensions "quantity of a per unit quantity of b."

The superscript ^{A} stands for Adam, and ^{0} for the bundle x^0. Notice that, unless Axiom V holds, ${}_{ab}r^{A0}$ may fail to exist, since exact compensation may not be possible. Given that axiom, however, ${}_{ab}r^{A0}$ always exists,* is unique, and depends only on x^0 and not at all on Δb, since it is only *defined* for standard unit decrements in b. Notice further that it is a concept defined solely in objective, measurable terms; although derived from consideration of the individual's preference structure, the personal rate of substitution itself is measured in terms of commodities. Because of this, although its magnitude will change if the commodities are measured differently, it will clearly not change if we alter the representational function. By working through the discussion which led to Definition 18, the reader may verify that nowhere was any assumption made concerning the actual representation employed.

* In the case of boundary points this statement may need careful interpretation; this problem is discussed in detail in Section D(vi).

To make matters complete, we add the analogous

Definition 19. The *personal rate of substitution of bread for ale at the point* x^0 is the compensating variation in bread for the loss of one unit of ale at that point. This magnitude is denoted by ${}_{ba}r^{A0}$, and has the dimensions: "quantity of *b* per unit quantity of *a*."

These definitions are not standard in the literature on these matters (see the Notes), and some words of explanation to those accustomed to other conventions seem in order. The usual term is not "personal" but "marginal rate of substitution"; but this has two disadvantages. First, and the more important, the word "marginal" in the usual phrase is completely redundant. Substitution of one commodity for another can take place *only* at the margin, and the size of that margin which is applicable in our definitions is indicated by the word "rate," which signifies the standard convention that the withdrawal of bread (or ale) is always by one unit at a time.

In case doubt still remains, consider the other standard economic concepts to which the word "marginal" has been applied, such as cost, revenue, product, and utility. In these cases we also constantly use such terms as *total* cost and *average* cost; but we do not have a concept corresponding to "total rate of substitution," and seldom do we refer to the "average rate of substitution"; this should put us on our guard that there is something odd about the use of the word "marginal" in this context. It was probably introduced because what we have called the personal rate of substitution was first conceived of as a ratio of *marginal* utilities; but that is no reason for retaining it in a theory based on preference orderings.

Thus there are strong grounds for dropping "marginal," yet there is an important reason (our second disadvantage) for adding a word such as "personal." In work on the theory of production, it is common to introduce the idea of a marginal rate of substitution between inputs in productive uses. Then when both consumption and production are discussed together, as in full general equilibrium theory, it is necessary to distinguish between marginal "subjective" rates of substitution and marginal "technical" rates of substitution. By dropping "marginal" and introducing "personal" right at the start, however, one is able to give a compact but complete description of the concept throughout the analysis. The word "personal" is preferable to "subjective," both on grounds of euphony and because it harmonizes with recent usage in basic work on general decision theory, where Savage has introduced the term "personal probability."

(v) The Axiom of Convexity

The next axiom places a severe but reasonable restriction on Adam's preference structure, and just because it is stringent it allows very powerful conclusions to be derived from the complete axiom system. It would take us much too far afield to discuss its historical origins and development, but it is fundamentally based on the venerable idea that one's desire for a commodity generally becomes less "urgent" the more one has of it. In the present context this basic idea develops into the hypothesis that, as more and more withdrawals of unit quantities of bread are made, the more and more does Adam miss his bread, so that the ever larger become the compensating variations of ale that must be given to him. In the same way, if withdrawals of ale were made, Adam would demand greater and greater compensations of bread.

We now formalize this assumption as the extremely important

AXIOM VI (INCREASING PERSONAL RATE OF SUBSTITUTION). The personal rate of substitution of any commodity a for any other commodity b *increases* as a is substituted for b.

Notice that there is no need to add "along a given indifference curve," since the personal rate of substitution is only defined for movements along indifference curves; it is not defined for any other type of movement.

There are two main (but, of course, intimately connected) ways in which Axiom VI may be expressed in geometrical terms, and we shall discuss both, since each is very useful. Let us first look at Fig. 2.7.

Suppose that we start at the point x^0, "withdraw" one unit of bread, and pay the compensating variation in ale, Δa^{01}. Then the new bundle $x^1 = (a^0 + \Delta a^{01}, b^0 - 1)$ lies on the indifference curve through x^0, by definition of the compensating variation in ale. Now withdraw one unit of bread from x^1 and add the compensating variation in ale, Δa^{12}. The new point $x^2 = (a^1 + \Delta a^{12}, b^1 - 1)$ will be on the indifference curve through x^0, and it follows from Axiom VI that Δa^{12} is greater than Δa^{01}. In the same way, x^3 is found to be on the same indifference curve, and Δa^{23} is larger than Δa^{12}, which in turn is larger than Δa^{01}. Thus the shape of the indifference curve must be

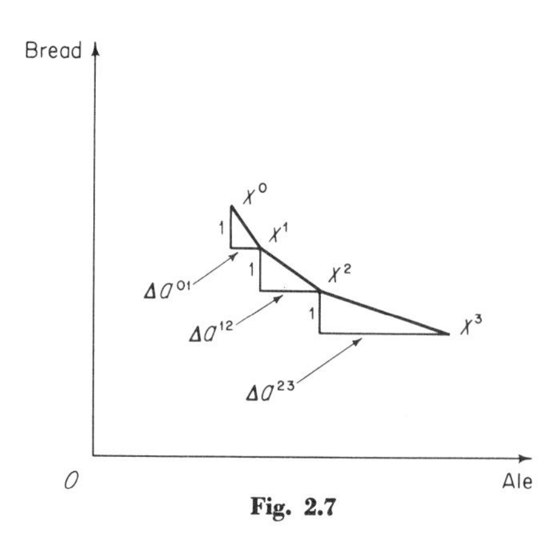

Fig. 2.7

such that, as we proceed along it to the right from x^0, unit decrements of b must correspond to ever larger increments of a. Similarly, if we proceed along it to the left from x^0, unit decrements of ale must be accompanied by ever increasing compensating variations in bread.

It follows from this that each indifference curve must be *convex* towards the origin. The reader may want to take this statement on trust, but it is instructive to prove the equivalence between convexity and Axiom VI. First, let us recall the definition of a convex curve:

DEFINITION 20. A curve in the plane (a, b) is *convex* if, given *any* two points x^0, x^1 on the curve, the chord joining x^0 and x^1 touches the curve only at these two points.*

In Fig. 2.8, let x^0 and x^1 be any two bundles such that $x^0 I_A x^1$. Then our assertion that Axiom VI implies that the indifference curve through x^0 is convex becomes, in the light of Definition 20, equivalent to the assertion that the section of the indifference curve between x^0 and x^1 lies entirely below the line x^0x^1. Incidentally, it will be convenient here, and even more in the next chapter, to have a notation for the indifference curve through any bundle x^0. We will employ the symbol C^0 to mean such a curve through x^0, C^1 to mean the indifference curve through x^1; and so on. The set of points represented by C^0 is the same as the "overlap" set V^0 of Fig. 2.2.

Now the compensating variation in ale for the withdrawal Δb^{01} is the amount Δa^{01}. Consider now withdrawing not Δb^{01} but *half* that amount,

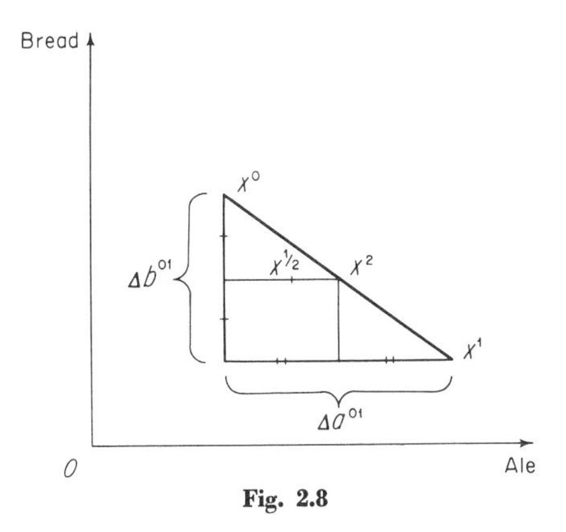

Fig. 2.8

* Some writers use the words "strictly convex" to describe this situation, reserving "convex" to cover the situation where some or all of the chord might coincide with the curve. The latter situation would correspond to the personal rate of substitution being *constant* over the relevant ranges, as the reader will readily perceive from the following proof. Of course, only if the units of the commodity can be chosen indefinitely small will the indifference locus be a "curve" in the everyday sense; otherwise it will consist of linear segments and not be strictly convex.

$(\Delta b^{01})/2$. If we denote the new compensating bundle by $x^{1/2}$, where can $x^{1/2}$ lie? Suppose that it was coincident with the point x^2 on x^0x^1. Then it would follow, by the geometry of similar triangles, that the compensating variation in ale for the withdrawal $(\Delta b^{01})/2$ would be exactly one-half of Δa^{01}. But this would imply that the personal rate of substitution were constant over this range, contrary to Axiom VI. Similarly, we may rule out points lying above the line x^0x^1 which would imply a decreasing personal rate of substitution. Therefore the unique bundle $x^{1/2}$, such that $x^0 I_A x^{1/2}$, must lie on the horizontal line through x^2 and below the line x^0x^1. This must remain true for any withdrawal in the range from 0 to Δb^{01}, so that all points on C^0 between x^0 and x^1 must lie below x^0x^1. Since x^0 and x^1 were any two bundles on C^0, and C^0 was itself arbitrary, the result is proved for the whole commodity space X.

Let us next turn to the second aspect of the geometrical representation, having just demonstrated the first aspect that all indifference *curves* are convex. Since each C^0 is the lower boundary of the "better set" B^0, it follows that B^0 is a set of points with a convex lower boundary. We now formulate the important definition:

DEFINITION 21. A set of points Z is said to be a *convex set* if, given any two points x^1 and x^2 in Z, all points lying on the straight line joining x^1 and x^2 are also in Z.

Examples of convex sets are lines, triangles, rectangles, circles, and parabolas (the first and last types being *unbounded* convex sets, the others *bounded*). It follows immediately from Definition 21 that the commodity space X is an unbounded convex set, while it may be easily proved (and this is our second aspect) that the same is true of B^0 as well. For in Fig. 2.9 let x^1 and x^2 be any points in B^0, and suppose that x^3 is a bundle on the line joining x^1 and x^2 which is in W^0, so that B^0 is not convex.

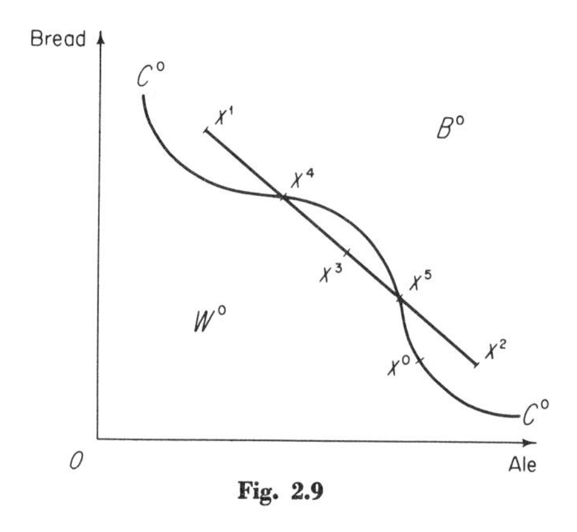

Fig. 2.9

Then, since $x^1 R_A x^0$ and $x^0 R_A x^3$, it follows from Wold's continuity condition (equivalent to Axiom V) that there must be a batch, say x^4, on the line joining x^1 and x^3 such that $x^0 I_A x^4$. Similarly, since x^2 is in B^0, we have $x^2 R_A x^0$, which, together with $x^0 R_A x^3$, implies that there exists a batch, say x^5, on the line $x^2 x^3$ such that $x^0 I_A x^5$. Now x^3, x^4, and x^5 all lie on the same line $x^1 x^2$, and x^3 lies between the "indifferent" points x^4 and x^5. It therefore follows from the result illustrated in Fig. 2.8 that x^3 must actually be preferred to x^4 and to x^5, and hence to x^0. But this contradicts the assumption that x^3 is in W^0. Hence B^0 is a convex set, and because of Axiom IV it is obviously unbounded as well. The proof may easily be modified for the case where C^0 has linear segments, which corresponds (as we have seen) to a constant personal rate of substitution.

This "Axiom of Convexity," as we may now call it, is very powerful, and perhaps the most essential of the whole set of seven. It can be modified a little by substituting the words "does not decrease" for "increases", and the same general type of conclusion still holds. But we cannot allow *de*creasing personal rates of substitution (abbreviated hereafter to *prs*) without seriously damaging most of the results of the theory of pure exchange.

We must not bewail the necessity of this axiom too much; it seems very reasonable and leads to consequences we should be quite happy to explore. One never gets out of a theory what is not put in, and indeed we are unusually lucky if the mechanical efficiency of our theorizing is anywhere near unity; so it is essential to have interesting, nonvacuous axioms if we are to get interesting, nonvacuous results.

(vi) The Axiom of Continuity of Substitution

The last axiom is the least essential of all, serving only to keep matters as simple as possible. The convexity axiom states that the personal rate of substitution (*prs*) increases as we move round an indifference curve but does not stipulate how this increase occurs, whether smoothly or by a series of discrete jumps. The problem is best illustrated by a figure which takes any indifference curve, say C^0, and "stretches" it to form a segment of the x-axis of an ordinary Cartesian diagram. Since C^0 is convex, no two points on it have either the same ale-coordinate *or* the same bread-coordinate. It follows that a simple way to accomplish the stretching is to assign each point on C^0 a number which is its a-coordinate (or b-coordinate, it makes no difference), and then to mark off along the abscissa a length equal to this a-coordinate. In this way we construct a one-to-one "mapping" of C^0 into the x-axis which preserves its direction. This is illustrated in Fig. 2.10, where 2.10(a) depicts the original curve C^0 extending from S on the bread-axis to T on the ale-axis, and 2.10(b) shows the corresponding segment ST of the abscissa onto which C^0 is mapped. It is appropriate to label this segment of the abscissa "Distance along C^0" (measuring from S), since any point x^0 on C^0

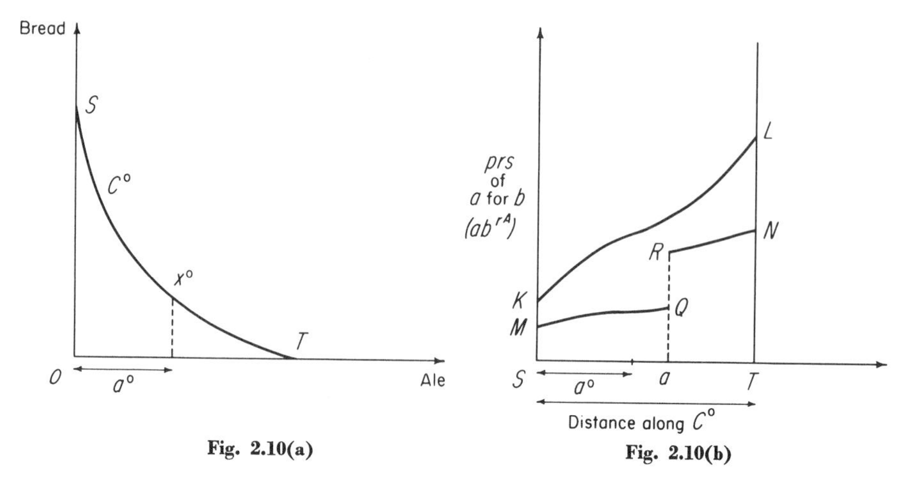

Fig. 2.10(a) **Fig. 2.10(b)**

with a-coordinate a^0 has the "length" a^0 on the abscissa of 2.10(b). Points to the left of x^0 on C^0 have corresponding distances less than a^0 in 2.10(b).

Since the *prs* of *a* for *b* is defined (i.e. unique) for each bundle on C^0, we can consider this *prs* as a function* of the points belonging to C^0, and so of the "distance" of any such point along C^0. The graph of this function is plotted in 2.10(b), where its argument values are the distances measured along the abscissa from S to T, and its functional values (Adam's *prs* of *a* for *b*) are measured along the ordinate. By Axiom VI, these functional values must increase monotonically as we move from S to T, but they can do so either smoothly (as with the curve KL) or with one or more discontinuities (as with the "simply" discontinuous curve $MQRN$).

Now consider the economic meaning of the latter case. Suppose we approached the point at which the discontinuity occurs (its ale coordinate being *a*) from the right; then we would conclude that the *prs* there is R. If we had approached from the left, we would have deduced that the *prs* was Q; and Q is quite different from R. This means that at the point *a* the *prs* is not well defined, since there are infinitely many values of the *prs* (all those between Q and R), to which *a* corresponds. This means in effect that there is *no prs* at *a*, a state of affairs which tends to complicate the analysis. Therefore we adopt the following axiom, the force of which is to rule out curves such as $MQRN$ and so to ensure that the behavior of the *prs* along any indifference curve is always represented by continuously rising curves such as KL.†

Axiom VII. (Axiom of Continuity of Substitution). For every x^0 in X, the personal rate of substitution of one commodity for another at x^0 is always well defined (i.e., unique).

* Except, strictly speaking, for the boundary point T; this problem is discussed later.

† By inserting the word "continuously" after "increases" in Axiom VI the same effect could have been obtained without a separate axiom; but it seems worthwhile to separate quite clearly the role of "convexity" of substitution from that of continuity of substitution.

This axiom naturally places a further restriction on the shape of the indifference curves themselves, and in order to elucidate just what this restriction is, we must investigate the relation between the *prs* and the *slope* of an indifference curve at any point. In Fig. 2.11, let mm' be the tangent to a point x^0 on C^0, and let the distance ux^0 measure one unit of ale, and rx^0 one unit of bread.

Then, by definition, the *prs* of bread for ale at x^0 is measured by the distance uw, and the *prs* of ale for bread at x^0 by rt. The slope of C^0 at x^0, with respect to the a-axis, is the slope of the tangent mm' at x^0 and is measured by $\tan \alpha$, which is equal to uv/ux^0. The "dimensions" of this slope are best found by considering C^0 to be the curve of a function f relating the bread coordinate to the corresponding ale-coordinate (i.e., $b = f(a)$). Then analytic geometry tells us that the slope of C^0 at x^0 measures the rate of change of b with respect to a, and therefore has the dimensions "units of b per unit of a;" similarly, the slope of C^0 at x^0 with respect to the ordinate is equal to $\tan \beta$ (the ratio $rs:rx^0$) and has the dimensions "units of a per unit of b." Thus the "a-slope" at x^0 has the same dimensions as ${}_{ba}r^{A0}$, and the "b-slope" there has the same dimensions as ${}_{ab}r^{A0}$.

Let us elaborate on this "dimensional" problem*. If we increased the size of the units in which bread is measured, meanwhile keeping those for ale fixed, then ${}_{ba}r^{A0}$ would fall, since fewer *units* of bread (although the same actual quantity) will be required for compensation. Similarly, if we increased the units in which ale is measured, keeping those for bread fixed, then ${}_{ba}r^{A0}$ would rise, since larger units mean that there is more loss of ale to be compensated for. Using the terminology of dimensional analysis, we express this by saying that the "dimension" of b (written V) enters *negatively* into the

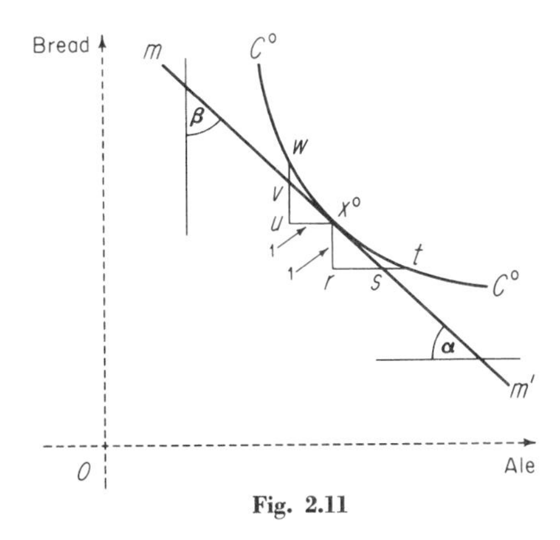

Fig. 2.11

* It is unfortunate that scientific usage employs the word "dimension" in two related contexts, namely in this meaning and in the more common geometrical meaning of spatial dimension.

dimensions of ${}_{ba}r^{A0}$, while that of a (written U) enters *positively*; the dimensions of the "derived" concept ${}_{ba}r^{A0}$ are accordingly represented by $V^{-1}U$. It is easy to check that the dimensions of ${}_{ab}r^{A0}$ may similarly be written $U^{-1}V$, so that the dimensions of the *product* of the two *prs* will be $(V^{-1}U)(U^{-1}V)$; these dimensions will cancel each other, and the product have no "dimensions" at all, which means that it is a pure number, independent of any units. For similar reasons the product of the "a-slope" and the "b-slope" of C^0 at x^0 will also be a pure number. These results may be paraphrased by saying that although a change in measurement units will usually change each *prs* and each slope, it will not change the product of the two *prs*'s at x^0 or of the two slopes there.

Consideration of Fig. 2.11 shows that since $uw > uv$, ${}_{ba}r^{A0}$ is greater than the a-slope at x^0, and similarly for ${}_{ab}r^{A0}$ and the b-slope, since $rt > rs$. Now the units in which a and b are measured are arbitrary, and since each commodity is assumed to be completely divisible, each unit can be made arbitrarily small. As these units are shrunk (not necessarily in fixed proportion to each other), each *prs* will change and so will each slope, but clearly each *prs* will continue to be larger than the corresponding slope. From the diagram it appears highly plausible to argue that, as this shrinking goes on, ${}_{ba}r^{A0}$ approaches arbitrarily closely to the a-slope at x^0, and similarly for ${}_{ab}r^{A0}$ and the b-slope. Not only is this statement plausible, but it is also true, being essentially one of the main theorems of the differential calculus; unfortunately, its rigorous proof requires tools of mathematical analysis whose knowledge is not assumed here.

Thus the a-slope of C^0 at x^0 measures the "limiting" *prs* of b for a there, while the b-slope measures the "limiting" *prs* of a for b at the same point. Moreover these two slopes are obviously reciprocal (since $\tan \alpha \equiv 1/\tan (90^\circ - \alpha) \equiv 1/\tan \beta$), which implies that the limiting *prs*'s are reciprocal as well.

If we therefore adopt the convention that the measurement units are always arbitrarily small, we can identify the slope of an indifference curve at any point with the corresponding *prs* at that point. It follows that, if the *prs* changes discontinuously at some points as we move round C^0, the *slope* of C^0 at each such point must change discontinuously also. This is illustrated in Fig. 2.12, where C^0 is "pointed" or "kinked" at x^0 in such a way that all lines between mm' and nn' are tangent to C^0 at x^0.

Therefore the implication of Axiom VII for the shape of the indifference curves is that such "corner tangencies," as they may be called, are ruled out. Each curve must have a continuously turning, unique tangent at every point.

An important case that has not yet been analyzed at all is the one in which x^0 is not a bundle in the *interior* of the commodity space but lies on the boundary, as in Fig. 2.13. Here there are infinitely many "tangents" to C^0

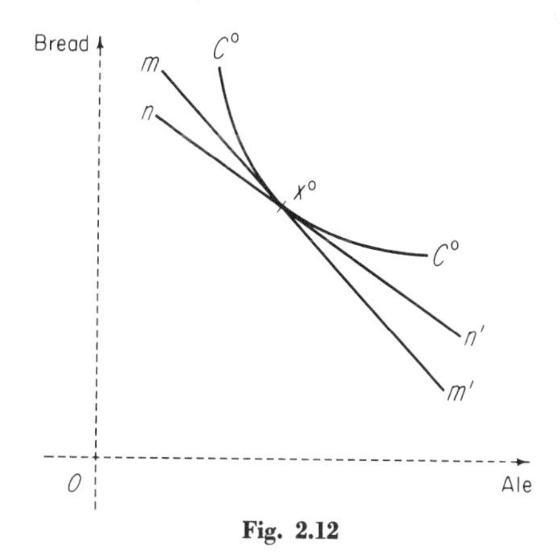

Fig. 2.12

at x^0, since all the lines (such as nx^0) between the abscissa and the "tangent" mx^0 (whose b-slope has the "minimal" value $\tan \beta$), are in contact with C^0 only at x^0.

Consideration of these boundary points brings to light an actual inconsistency in the present structure of the model. For it is obvious that at x^0 further substitution of ale for bread cannot be made, so that by Definition 18 the *prs* of ale for bread cannot exist there; it is literally *undefined* at x^0. Yet Axiom VII states that for all bundles in X, the *prs* of one commodity for another is *well* defined; and x^0 certainly belongs to the commodity space.

The way we resolve this conflict is to adopt a *convention* by which each boundary point such as x^0 in Fig. 2.13 (and each "bread-axis boundary point") is endowed with a rate of substitution which, strictly speaking, it does not possess. The conventional value that we shall adopt for the *prs* of ale for bread at x^0 is the value ($\tan \beta$) of the slope of the "minimal tangent" mx^0; the *prs*'s of bread for ale of bundles on the b-axis are defined in an exactly

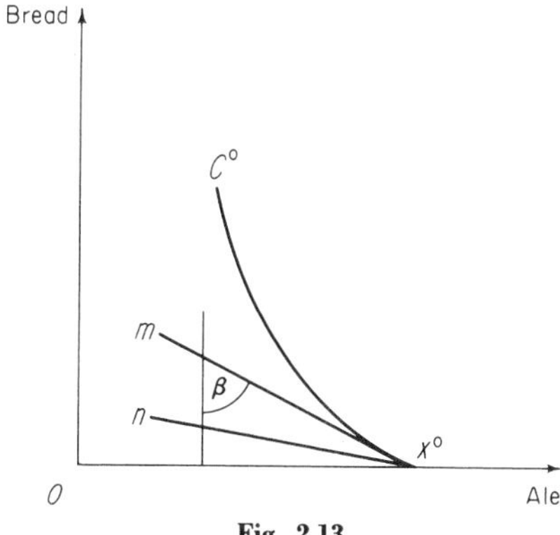

Fig. 2.13

similar way. By construction, all the *prs*'s of points belonging to C^0 are below $\tan \beta$, and because they increase (by Axiom VI) in a continuous manner (by Axiom VII) toward $\tan \beta$, it seems reasonable to take this *b*-slope of mx^0 as actually the *limiting* value of the "genuine" *prs* belonging to points of C^0 in its immediate neighborhood.*

If we adopt this convention, then we can safely talk about the *prs* in *either* direction at any boundary point. Thus it provides a retroactive justification both for the procedure in Fig. 2.10(b), which assigned a definite *prs* of value LT to the boundary point T, and for our even earlier assertion, after Definition 18, that the magnitude ${}_{ab}r^{A0}$ always exists.

In a two-dimensional commodity space, these problems of what happens at the boundaries may not seem to be very important, but great care must be taken in more realistic situations. For if the number of commodities involved is large, then it is most unlikely that the individual would hold something of *every* commodity; but then, if some holdings are actually zero, this means that the individual is indeed at a boundary point of the commodity space. This in turn greatly reduces the applicability of some mathematical tools (such as the differential calculus) to the model, for these devices are often only effective—or at least simple—for positions in the interior of the commodity space, where all quantities are strictly positive.

These considerations are not criticisms of the model as such (boundary points are in fact usually easier to analyze), but simply mean that we must be careful to choose the appropriate mathematical tools with which to analyze it. For two-dimensional situations, geometry and simple logic are perfectly satisfactory on almost all counts; in more general cases, the relevant tool kit is provided by algebra and topology, especially by the theory of convex sets.

(vii) The Pathology of Substitution

The axiom system is now complete, and ensures—in accordance with our program of simplicity—that all the variables are "well behaved" and continuous. However, before going on to use the axioms to analyze exchange, it will be useful to glance at some extreme cases that are ruled out by the postulates, but which are instructive in helping us to grasp fully the nature of the model. In the same way that we had a dipsomaniac illustrate the extreme case where no indifference curves exist, so it is useful to take another faddist—this time about food, not drink—to illuminate these pathological cases of substitutability.

Suppose that Adam was concerned only with food consumption and

* In technical terms, $\tan \beta$ is the *supremum* of the *prs* of points of C^0, and also the *infimum* of the *b*-slopes of the "tangents" to C^0 at x^0. This convention cannot usefully be generalized to three or more dimensions, as we shall see in Chapter 6.

insistent on maintaining a diet that, for any given level of well-being, was *nutritionally balanced.* Purely for the sake of geometrical illustration, we shall confine the analysis to the unrealistic case of two nutrients, say protein and starch, whose quantities are denoted by n_p and n_s respectively. Then nutritional balance is taken to mean that Adam, following the advice of his current dietitian, insists on these nutrients being consumed in some fixed, desired ratio $n_p^* : n_s^*$, a ratio dependent only on the units in which the nutrients are measured. To simplify matters further by unrealistic assumptions, suppose that there are only two foods available, say meat and bread, and that meat contains only protein (in the quantity m_p units of protein per unit of meat), while bread contains only starch (with b_s units of starch to one unit of bread).

Then the requirement of nutritional balance means that the two foods themselves must always be consumed in fixed proportion. For to obtain n_p^*, Adam must consume n_p^*/m_p $(=m^*)$ units of meat, while to obtain n_s^*, he must consume n_s^*/b_s $(=b^*)$ bread units. So the fact that Adam's preferences *fix* the ratio n_p^*/n_s^*, together with the "technical" facts that m_p and b_s are fixed, mean that the ratio $m^*/b^*(=(n_p^* b_s)/(n_s^* m_p))$ is also fixed. In order to obtain a preference ordering over the whole commodity space, we add the assumption that Adam can always dispose of food in excess of his requirements at no cost to himself. Then we can represent his preference structure over the commodity space of meat and bread in Fig. 2.14.

Each of the commodity bundles x^1, x^2, x^3, x^4, and x^5 lies on a line through the origin (such lines are often called *rays*), whose slope K (tan α) is equal to the desired commodity ratio $m^* : b^*$. Since surplus can always be freely disposed of, an excess of any one commodity is no burden. Thus, if the diet ratio were 2 : 1 and the foods were held in the ratio 3 : 1, Adam would throw away meat costlessly until the actual ratio was brought to the desired level of 2 : 1. So every bundle in X can be compared consistently with every other,

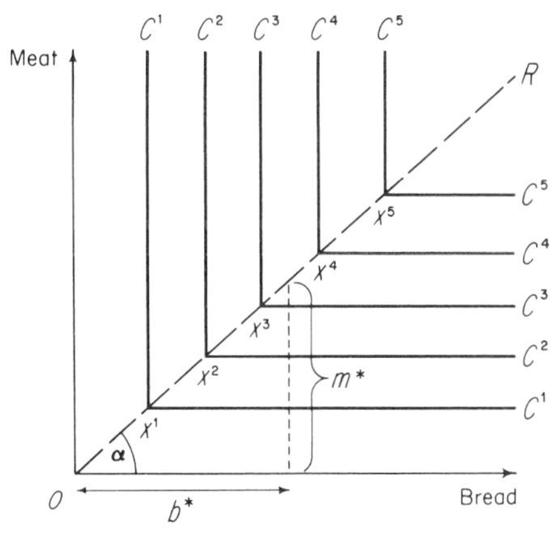

Fig. 2.14

and the indifference "curves" exist, having the rectangular form of those few shown in the diagram.*

This preference structure therefore obeys Axioms I, II, III, and V, but "just" fails to satisfy Axioms IV and VI, as the reader should verify. It gives a thumping violation of Axiom VII; for along any indifference curve such as C^1, the *prs* of bread for meat at each point above x^1 is zero, while for each bundle to the right of x^1 on C^1 it is plus infinity. At x^1 itself the *prs* takes every value from zero to plus infinity, giving the largest possible jump discontinuity of substitution; and this is true for every point on OR.

Now suppose we introduced a third commodity—say rice—which also contained only starch, this time in the proportion r_s of starch per unit of rice. Then since b_s units of rice contain $b_s r_s$ units of starch, one unit of bread has the same nutritive value as b_s/r_s units of rice. If this were Adam's only criterion of comparison, then rice and bread would be complete substitutes for each other, and his indifference "map" between the two would have the appearance of Fig. 2.15, being determined entirely by "technical" considerations.

Since the *prs* of rice for bread is constant at b_s/r_s (and the *prs* of bread for rice accordingly fixed at r_s/b_s), the indifference "curves" are now straight lines of slope $\tan \beta$ (with reference to the bread-axis), which is equal to b_s/r_s. If rice were combined with bread always in the ratio $b_s : r_s$, then each unit of this "composite" commodity would have the same nutritive value and hence be equally satisfactory to Adam. It could, therefore, be regarded simply as an ordinary commodity, at least for him.

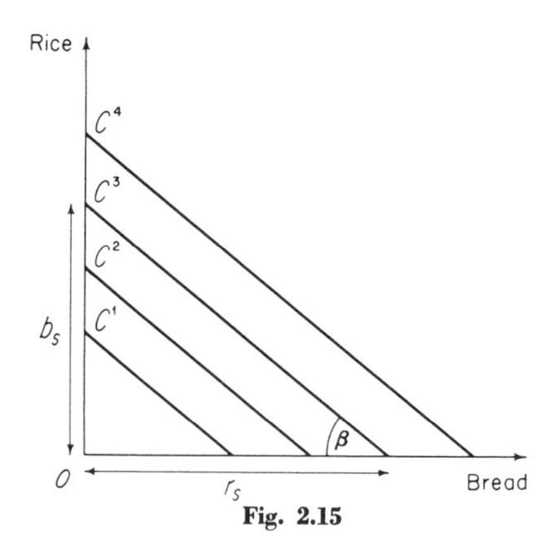

Fig. 2.15

* In all diagrams involving indifference curves, it must be remembered that they are merely *samples* from the preference structures concerned, just as contour lines on a map represent only a few selected altitudes and are not in themselves a depiction of the whole topography. Since preferences are not assumed to be measurable as height is measurable (i.e., uniquely except for origin and scale), *distances* between indifference curves, unlike those between map contours, have no meaning in terms of preferences. In Fig. 2.14, for example, the higher OR the indifference curves cut, the higher the level of preference; but the actual *magnitudes* of the distance between curves have no significance in Adam's preference structure.

Thus our two pathological cases illustrate two polar cases of substitutability, the first demonstrating an extreme lack of it, and the second showing complete substitutability. Neither is compatible with the axiom system (the second contradicting Axiom VI), but each throws light on the structure of the model.

E. CONCLUSION

(i) Generalization to More than Two Commodities

It is an excellent exercise (if only in three-dimensional geometry) to rework the whole of part *D* for the case of three commodities.* Almost the whole analysis remains valid in this more complicated case. An indifference "curve" becomes a bowl-shaped surface between, say, ale, bread, and cheese, the better set B^0 lying on and above the surface, the worse set W^0 lying on and below. A further generalization takes us to four or more commodities, but now geometrical illustrations fail, and we have to employ the algebra of n-dimensional geometry; but the same basic structure still applies.

The only major change required is to broaden the definition of dominance to cover the case of three or more commodities. We take advantage of this to introduce a notation which will be used often. Instead of depicting different commodities by different initial letters, let us index them by number. Specifically, let x_1 stand for the quantity of the first commodity, x_2 for the quantity of the second commodity, and so on. A commodity bundle x is now a so-called *n-tuple* of numbers $(x_1, x_2, x_3, \ldots, x_n)$, and a particular bundle x^0 consists of quantities $(x_1^0, x_2^0, x_3^0, \ldots, x_n^0)$. We now formulate

DEFINITION 7A. A bundle x^0 is said to *dominate* a bundle x^1 if (1) each of the following inequalities holds:

$$\begin{aligned} x_1^0 &\geqq x_1^1 \\ x_2^0 &\geqq x_2^1 \\ x_3^0 &\geqq x_3^1 \\ &\vdots \\ x_n^0 &\geqq x_n^1 \end{aligned}$$

and (2) if strict inequality holds in at least one of these n relationships above. If x^0 dominates x^1, we write $x^0 > x^1$ (where x^0 and x^1 are not ordinary numbers but bundles of commodities).

* A particularly instructive example is to visualize what the indifference "map" between the three commodities of D(vii) (bread, meat, and rice) would look like, under the conditions assumed there.

DEFINITION 8A. A bundle x^0 is said to dominate x^1 *strictly* if each of the following inequalities holds:

$$\begin{array}{c} x_1^0 > x_1^1 \\ x_2^0 > x_2^1 \\ x_3^0 > x_3^1 \\ \cdot \quad \cdot \\ \cdot \quad \cdot \\ \cdot \quad \cdot \\ x_n^0 > x_n^1 \end{array}$$

If x^0 strictly dominates x^1, then we employ the symbols $x^0 \gg x^1$.

DEFINITION 9A. If x^0 dominates x^1 but does not strictly dominate x^1, then we say that x^0 *weakly dominates* x^1, but do not use a symbol different from "$>$."*

Apart from the new notation, Definition 9a is the same as 9. With these reinterpretations of the "dominance" relationships, the analysis can be carried through with little change. Permissible variations can now consist of adjustments in all but the good which has been withdrawn, but the definition of *prs* is still required to run in terms of two commodities only, so that the appropriate compensating variation is made only in one commodity.

(ii) Recapitulation of the Axioms

In many modern research papers, the axioms that we have been at such pains to spell out are laid before the reader like food in a cafeteria, and in this way are made to occupy only a paragraph or so. But it is as well in an expository treatment to make clear just what the role of each axiom is, how all the axioms mesh together, and how alterations might be effected, leaving nothing to be taken on trust. All this we have tried to do (at the cost of many pages of exposition), but now we permit ourselves the luxury of bringing all the axioms (though not definitions) together. Collectively, they define what we shall mean by the preference structure of an individual. Formally, we write

DEFINITION 22. The *preference structure of an individual A* is a ranking R_A of the commodity space X, which obeys the following seven axioms:

AXIOM I (AXIOM OF COMPARABILITY). For all x^0, x^1 in X, either $x^0 R_A x^1$ or $x^1 R_A x^0$.

AXIOM II (AXIOM OF CONSISTENCY). For all bundles x^0, x^1, x^2 in X, $x^0 R_A x^1$ and $x^1 R_A x^2$ together imply $x^0 R_A x^2$.

* If we know that condition (1) of Definition 7a holds, but are not sure that (2) holds (i.e., it is possible that x^0 actually *equals* x^1), then we write $x^0 \geqq x^1$.

Axiom III (Axiom of Selection). Given an attainable subset Y of X, the individual will select a bundle from the maximal class Y_M of Y.

Axiom IV (Axiom of Dominance). For all x^0, x^1 in X, if x^0 dominates x^1, then $x^0 P_A x^1$.

Axiom V (Axiom of Continuity of Preferences). For all x^0 in X, all bundles x on the lower boundary of B^0 are such that $x^0 I_A x$.

Axiom VI (Axiom of Convexity). The personal rate of substitution of any commodity a for another commodity b increases as a is substituted for b.

Axiom VII (Axiom of Continuity of Substitution). For all x^0 in X, the personal rate of substitution of one commodity for another at x^0 is always well defined (i.e., unique).

In the next three chapters we shall use individuals' preference structures in order to analyze the exchange of commodities between persons.

NOTES ON THE LITERATURE

A. The first treatment of preference theory along axiomatic lines appears to be that in the neglected paper by Ragnar Frisch: "Sur un problème d'économie pure," *Series Norsk Matemisk Forenings Skrifter*, Serie I, Nr. 16 (1926), 1–40 (since reprinted in *Metroeconomica*, 9, 1957, 79–111), although Irving Fisher's much earlier discussion in Chapter 1 of *Mathematical Investigations in the Theory of Value and Prices* (New Haven, 1892, reprinted by Kelley, New York, 1961) is very suggestive, especially since we know that Frisch was influenced by this work of Fisher (see R. Frisch: *New Methods of Measuring Utility*, Mohr, Tübingen, 1932, p. 3).

Two papers which carried forward the axiomatic method were those by N. Georgescu-Roegen ("The Pure Theory of Consumer's Behavior," *Quarterly Journal of Economics*, 50, 1935–6, 545–93), and H. Wold ("A Synthesis of Pure Demand Analysis," I–III, *Skandinavisk Aktuarietidskrift*, 26, 1943, 85–118 and 220–63, and 27, 1944, 69–120). But the most influential modern treatment has been that by Kenneth Arrow. See his *Social Choice and Individual Values* (Wiley, New York, 1951), 11–17. A thorough statement is contained in the advanced work of G. Debreu: *Theory of Value* (Wiley, New York, 1959), Chapter 4, while easier treatments are to be found in D. W. Bushaw and R. W. Clower: *Introduction to Mathematical Economics* (Irwin, Homewood, Ill., 1957), Chapter 5; J. R. Hicks: *A Revision of Demand Theory* (Oxford U.P., 1956), Part 1; and H. Wold: *Demand Analysis* (Wiley, New

York, 1953), Chapter 4. Useful books on logic dealing with relevant material are P. Suppes: *Introduction to Logic* (Van Nostrand, New York, 1957), Chapter 10; and A. Tarski: *Introduction to Logic* (2nd ed., Oxford U.P., New York, 1946), Chapter 5.

B. *Section (i)*

(a) Excellent treatments of axiom systems for individual behavior under uncertainty are to be found in D. Ellsberg: "Classic and Current Notions of 'Measurable Utility'," *Economic Journal*, 64, 1954, 528–56; W. Baumol: "The Cardinal Utility which is Ordinal," *Economic Journal*, 68, 1958, 665–72 (reprinted substantially as Chapter 17 of his *Economic Theory and Operations Analysis* (Prentice-Hall, Englewood Cliffs, N.J., 1961); and in H. Markowitz: *Portfolio Selection* (Wiley, New York, 1959), Chapter 10. On a higher level of mathematical (though not necessarily economic) sophistication are the treatments by L. Savage: *The Foundations of Statistics* (Wiley, New York, 1954), Chapter 5; I. N. Herstein and J. Milnor: "An Axiomatic Approach to Measurable Utility," *Econometrica*, 21, 1953, 291–97; and R. J. Aumann: "Utility Theory Without the Completeness Axiom," *Econometrica*, 30, 1962, 445–62. These all stem from the basic work by J. von Neumann and O. Morgenstern: *The Theory of Games and Economic Behavior* (2nd ed., Princeton U.P., Princeton, N.J., 1947), 617–32, to a large degree anticipated (in this regard) by earlier work of Frank Ramsey, which appears in his posthumously published collection of papers, *The Foundations of Mathematics* (Routledge, London, 1931), 156–211.

(b) Some economists, such as Veblen, have attached considerable importance to the dependence of individual preferences on others' choices, and some attempts have been made to deal with various aspects of this situation. Early examples are A. C. Pigou's two articles: "Some Notes on Utility," *Economic Journal*, 13, 1903, 58–68, and "The Interdependence of Different Sources of Demand and Supply in a Market," *Economic Journal*, 23, 1913, 19–24. A stimulating modern discussion is in J. S. Duesenberry: *Income, Saving and the Theory of Consumer Behavior* (Harvard U.P., Cambridge, Mass., 1949), while a very sophisticated treatment of the general equilibrium aspect is that by L. W. McKenzie: "Competitive Equilibrium with Dependent Consumer Preferences," *Second Symposium on Linear Programming* (National Bureau of Standards, Washington, D.C., 1955), 277–93.

Other economists (e.g., T. Scitovsky: "Some Consequences of the Habit of Judging Quality by Price," *Review of Economic Studies*, 21–22, 1943–5, 100–105) have tried to construct theories to deal with the case where preferences are assumed to be in part dependent upon changes in prices, either present prices or those expected to rule in the future.

B. *Section (ii)*

The reader is referred to the works cited for A, especially those by Arrow and by Suppes, for further practice in the handling of these concepts.

C. *Section (i)*

An interesting discussion of what happens when the individual is assumed to be ignorant about the field of choice is contained in N. Georgescu-Roegen: "The Theory of Choice and the Constancy of Economic Laws," *Quarterly Journal of Economics*, 64, 1950, 125–38. Recent work by psychologists interested in learning theory is of relevance in this context. See, for example, R. D. Luce: *Individual Choice Behavior* (Wiley, New York, 1959), and the series of papers in Part 3 of *Mathematical Methods in the Social Sciences, 1959* (ed. by K. Arrow, S. Karlin, and P. Suppes, Stanford U.P., Stanford, Calif., 1960).

Section (ii)

The problem of "threshold" effects is discussed fully in J. Rothenberg: *The Measurement of Social Welfare* (Prentice-Hall, Englewood Cliffs, N.J., 1961), Chapter 7, while the problems of choices with multiple criteria are well discussed in K. May: "Transitivity, Utility and Aggregation in Preference Theory," *Econometrica*, 22, 1954, 1–13 (this contains the marriage partner example), and in N. Georgescu-Roegen: "Choice, Expectations and Measurability," *Quarterly Journal of Economics*, 68, 1954, 503–34.

D. *Section (i)*

Theories have been constructed which deal with preferences over a "discrete" commodity space, where one or more commodities are available only in integer amounts. See, for example, J. R. Hicks, *op. cit.*, Chapter 5; R. Stone: *The Measurement of Consumers' Expenditure and Behavior in the United Kingdom, 1920-1938* (Vol. I, Cambridge U.P., New York, 1954), 257–60; and H. Wold, *op. cit.*, p. 94.

Section (ii)

A theory of preferences not using Axiom IV was presented by N. Georgescu-Roegen in the 1935–6 *QJE* paper already cited in A. See also H. Schultz: *The Theory and Measurement of Demand* (Chicago U.P., Chicago, Ill., 1938), 614–19 (these pages are due to Milton Friedman).

Section (iii)

The first person to use such a "lexical" counterexample in this context appears to have been G. Debreu ("Representation of a Preference Ordering by a Numerical Function," which is Chapter 11 of *Decision Processes* (ed. by Thrall, Coombs, and Davis, Wiley, New York, 1954)), although the example is standard in mathematics; some plausible examples of less extreme lexical orderings are contained in Georgescu-Roegen's 1954 *QJE* paper cited for C(ii). Actually this type of example is a little misleading in the context of Axiom V, for not only does it rule out the possibility of a *continuous* "real" representation, it rules out *any* real representation at all. With a continuously divisible commodity space, these two problems are necessarily intertwined; on this see Debreu's paper, and P. Newman and R. Read:

"Representation Problems for Preference Orderings," *Journal of Economic Behavior*, 1, 1961, 149–69, which contains a full bibliography.

The postulate here entitled "Wold's assumption" was first given in his 1943–4 papers cited for A, and may be found also in *Demand Analysis*, *op. cit.*, p. 82. A proof that it implies the existence of a continuous representation was given by T. Yokoyama: "Continuity Conditions of Preference Ordering," *Osaka Economic Papers*, 4, 1956, 39–45, while our incomplete demonstration is based on Wold, *op. cit.*, p. 83.

Theories of *demand* that essentially do not use representations have been developed by T. Yokoyama: "A Logical Foundation of the Theory of Consumer's Demand," *Osaka Economic Papers*, 2, 1953, 71–79; and by L. W. McKenzie: "Demand Theory Without a Utility Index," *Review of Economic Studies*, 24, 1957, 185–89; and, of course, in the work on revealed preference (basically due to Samuelson) which will be dealt with in Chapter 6.

Section (iv)

The redundancy of the word "marginal" has also been alluded to by J. M. Henderson and R. E. Quandt in *Microeconomic Theory* (McGraw, New York, 1958), p. 11, footnote 2. They propose the phrase "commodity rate of substitution," which seems less apposite than that in the text. The basic work by Savage on "personal probability" is presented in his *Foundations of Statistics*, *op. cit.* The phrase itself is due to T. C. Fry (Savage, *op. cit.*, p. 30), and occurs in much of the recent work of this "subjective" school of statisticians.

Yet another reason for using a different name for our concept is that it is a different concept from that given in most current textbooks. The confusion is caused by a change in terminology that was adopted by the inventor of the term "marginal rate of substitution," J. R. Hicks. In his original paper on the subject ("A Reconsideration of the Theory of Value," *Economica*, N.S.I., 1934, 52–76), Hicks defined the concept so that it was identical with our personal rate of substitution. This way of defining it of course makes the Axiom of Convexity (VI) correspond to *increasing* marginal rates of substitution. Unfortunately, however, Axiom VI plays a role in Hicks's (and our) theory similar to that of the older "law of diminishing marginal utility" in earlier theories. In order to harmonize with this earlier usage, therefore, Hicks in his later treatment (*Value and Capital*, 1st ed., Oxford U.P., New York, 1939, p. 20) redefined the marginal rate of substitution in such a way that the previous assumptions of "increasing marginal rate of substitution" became an assumption of "diminishing marginal rate of substitution"; and most textbook writers have adopted this definition.

But the word "marginal" has no business in either definition anyway, so the effort to adjust to earlier usage seems misplaced. Accordingly our treatment reverts to the 1934 definition, for which there is some precedent, e.g., G. J. Stigler: *The Theory of Price* (3rd ed., Macmillan, New York, 1952), p. 72. The rather tortuous 1939 version seems much less logical and for most students (at least in my experience) much harder to grasp.

Section (v)

An elementary mathematical treatment of convexity, with economic applications, is given in Kenneth Arrow: "An Extension of the Basic Theorems of Classical Welfare Economics," in *Proceedings of the Second Berkeley Symposium on Mathematical Statistics and Probability* (ed. by J. Neyman, California U.P., Berkeley, Cal., 1951), 507–32. See also the excellent expository essay by T. C. Koopmans: "Allocation of Resources and the Price System," which is the first of his *Three Essays on the State of Economic Science* (McGraw, New York, 1957).

Section (vi)

The "dimensional" analysis of this section is modeled on that given by P. H. Wicksteed: *The Common Sense of Political Economy* (Vol. II, Routledge, London, 1933), 755–59. This section, entitled "Dimensions of Economic Quantities," is a reprint of one of his contributions to Palgrave's *Dictionary of Political Economy* (1894). See also *The Common Sense*, 734–54, which is a reprint of an article by Wicksteed on Jevon's *Theory of Political Economy* (*QJE*, 1889).

Section (vii)

The device of using a food faddist to illustrate the pathology of substitution was suggested by Wicksell's early consideration of primitive least-cost diet problems in his review article on Pareto's *Manuel d'Economie Politique* (*Zeitschrift für Volkswirtschaft, Sozialpolitik und Verwaltung*, 1913). For an English translation see K. Wicksell: *Selected Papers on Economic Theory* (ed. by E. Lindahl, G. Allen, London, 1958) p. 164, note. The first use of indifference curve diagrams to illustrate extreme cases of substitution was by Irving Fisher (*op. cit.*, p. 71), as he was the first (p. 67) to draw indifference curves on the now familiar diagram (their inventor, F. Y. Edgeworth, gave a different illustration in his *Mathematical Psychics* (Kegan Paul, London, 1881, reprinted by Kelley and Milman, New York, 1954), p. 28.

E. *Section (i)*

See the references for Part A.

Section (ii)

For a history of preference theory, see the excellent articles by G. J. Stigler: "The Development of Utility Theory," *Journal of Political Economy* 58, 1950, 307–27 and 373–96, reprinted in *Landmarks of Political Economy* (ed. by E. J. Hamilton, A. Rees, and H. G. Johnson, Chicago U.P., Chicago, Ill., 1962), Vol. II, 380–452.

3

THE THEORY OF BILATERAL EXCHANGE

A. INTRODUCTION

In the next three chapters we shall analyze the classical problem of the exchange of commodities. A number of our model people come together in order to trade, and each of them is supposed to possess a commodity bundle which he (or she) wishes to exchange for a preferred bundle. Within each period the total stock of commodities available at the trading post is assumed to be *fixed*, a postulate which rules out trade with other markets and, more importantly, means that no person can alter his commodity endowment by means of *production* within the period. It follows that the goods concerned must be desired for final consumption, it being irrelevant—for our present purposes—that the goods might also be useful in production.

The next section discusses the conditions under which an exchange takes place at all, and then Section C proceeds with the analysis of *efficient trade*. We discuss carefully how bargaining processes may or may not lead to the attainment of such trades, which brings us by a short and natural step to a demonstration (in D) that equilibrium prices are not given exogenously in the exchange situation, from the outside so to say, but are intrinsic to the problem, *embedded* in the individuals' (axiomatized) preferences and initial endowments of goods. Chapter 4 then goes on to analyze the performance of adjustment mechanisms which are designed to search out these "efficient" price ratios, and Chapter 5 deals with some generalizations of bilateral exchange. Because there is some confusion still surrounding the subject of exchange, the closing Notes at the end of each of these chapters refer in some detail to its classical origins, especially to the brilliant contributions of Edgeworth, Marshall, and Walras.

This chapter is concerned only with the simplest possible version of the problem, in which there are only two commodities and two persons. The very simplicity of this case of *bilateral exchange* allows us actually to *prove* all the main results with simple geometrical tools. Generalization of these results to cover cases of more than two persons and/or commodities usually requires far more sophisticated mathematics, though not greatly different economics. But the complete treatment of the results for the simple case should lend considerable plausibility to the truth of their generalizations.

Although the present discussion is meant to be rigorous within its "geometrical" frame of reference, far fewer formal definitions are given than in Chapter 2, mainly because there are in fact fewer to be given, but also because we want to proceed faster than before.

B. CONDITIONS FOR EXCHANGE

(i) The Geometrical Approach

The analysis deals with two commodities, ale and bread, which we have already described, and with two persons, one of whom—Adam—is already on the scene. What could be more natural than that the other protagonist be Eve—particularly since it will help the exposition to be able to refer always separately to "he" and to "she"? Moreover the idyllic Eden conjured up by these *dramatis personae* serves to remind us of the idealistic nature of the whole model. If both persons obey Axioms I–VII, and all the definitions of Chapter 2 apply, then each of our characters will have a (different) preference structure, parts of which are depicted in Fig. 3.1(a) and 3.1(b), respectively. For reasons which will become apparent it is convenient to turn one of the diagrams through 180 degrees, and we unchivalrously choose to do this to Eve's diagram. This change implies that, in contrast to Adam, Eve gets *worse* off as she moves generally northeast, and better off as she goes southwest.

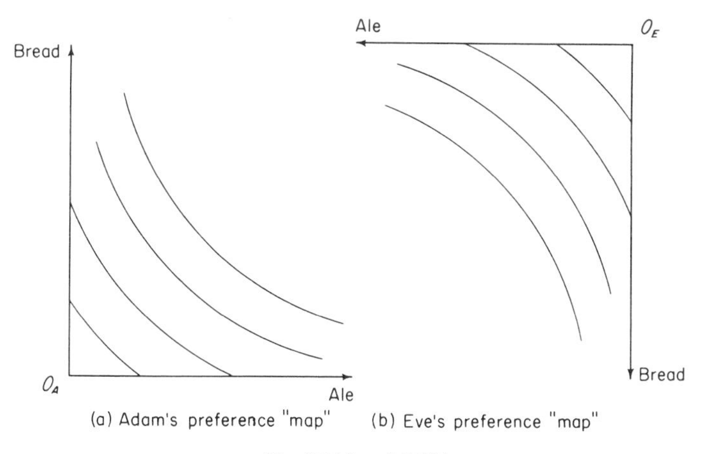

(a) Adam's preference "map" (b) Eve's preference "map"

Fig. 3.1(a) and 3.1(b)

Now we suppose that, in the given period, each person brings to the "market" a quantity of ale and a quantity of bread, either of which—but not both—may be zero; we shall denote Adam's initial quantities by a^{A0} and b^{A0}, and Eve's by a^{E0} and b^{E0}. Thus the total stocks of commodities held initially (and therefore, by assumption, held throughout) are $a^0(=a^{A0} + a^{E0})$ of ale, and $b^0(=b^{A0} + b^{E0})$ of bread. Any possible exchange is a *redistribution* of these fixed stocks among Adam and Eve. It is possible to give a very neat graphical depiction of this situation by means of a *box diagram*, which is shown below in Fig. 3.2. The "sides" of the box are of length a^0 and b^0, respectively, so that any point in the box (such as t) represents a *trade*, a reallocation of the initial stocks of the two commodities among the two persons; therefore giving us *four* pieces of information: (1) the amount of ale that Adam receives, a^A; (2) the amount of bread that Adam receives, b^A; (3) the amount of ale that Eve receives, a^E; and (4) the amount of bread that Eve receives, b^E. By assumption, $a^A + a^E = a^{A0} + a^{E0}$, and $b^A + b^E = b^{A0} + b^{E0}$, for any trade t.

A trade in the northeast part of the box (towards Eve's "corner") means that Adam has most of both commodities, and conversely for trades in Adam's "corner" in the southwest; while a trade in the northwest part means that Adam has most of the bread, Eve most of the ale (and conversely for the southeast). We could take our initial point t^0 to be *anywhere* in the box, but on balance it proves helpful to suppose that Adam brings only bread, and Eve only ale, to the market; the initial point t^0 is then the extreme northwest point. If we now superimpose Fig. 3.1(a) and 3.1(b), tailoring the length of the axes involved to the amounts a^0 and b^0, we can represent in one diagram (Fig. 3.3) the whole of the relevant commodity space X for both persons, plus their preference maps. However, it will be simplest if we draw just the indifference curves C^{A0} and C^{E0}, where C^{A0} is Adam's indifference curve corresponding to the initial allocation t^0, and similarly for Eve's C^{E0}.

Now the set of points which are no worse than t^0 for Adam is B^{A0}, the set of bundles (shaded by horizontal lines) lying on or above C^{A0}. Any trade in

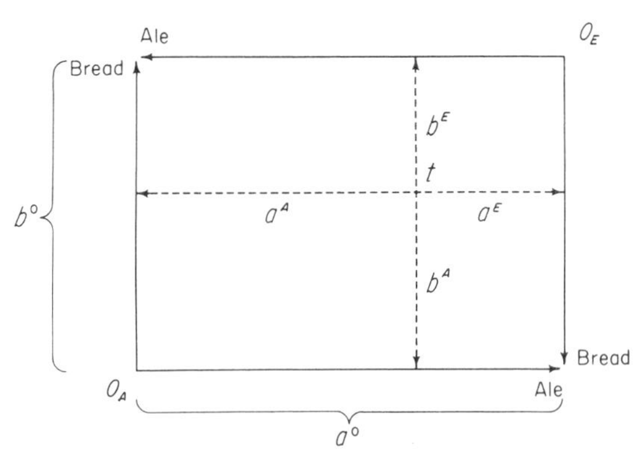

Fig. 3.2

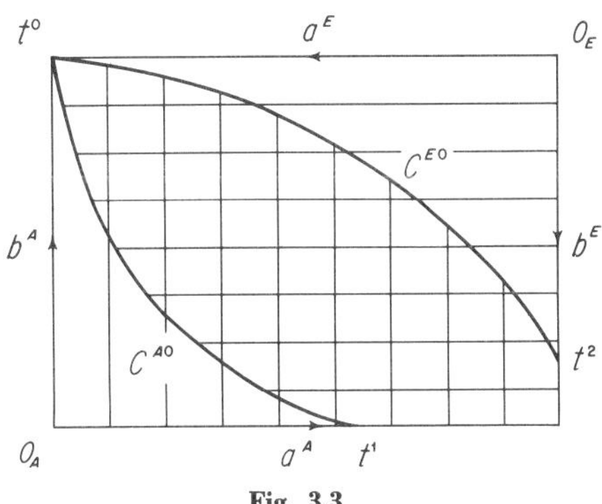

Fig. 3.3

the interior of B^{A0} is therefore better for Adam; and, by the same token, any trade lying inside B^{E0} (i.e., each of those "below" C^{E0} in the diagram, an area shaded in vertical lines) is better than t^0 for Eve. Since the diagram shows that these two sets overlap, it follows that there must—in this case—be trades which are both inside B^{A0} and B^{E0}, so that both Adam and Eve can be made actually better off by exchange. Let us call the set of points common to B^{A0} and B^{E0} the *trading set determined by* t^0 (in mathematical terms, it is the *intersection* of the sets B^{A0} and B^{E0}). It follows that mutually beneficial exchange can take place if (and only if) the trading set determined by t^0 does not contain just the point t^0 itself.

This result can be looked at another way. Although all trades inside B^{A0} are by definition better for Adam, he cannot *attain* every trade in that set, for some of them are worse for Eve than is t^0, so that without compulsion she would not consent to such proposed trades. Adam's attainable set is in fact Eve's better set B^{E0}, and clearly he will only be interested in trading from t^0 if there is overlap between his better set and his attainable set (i.e., between B^{A0} and B^{E0}); exactly the same condition holds for Eve, with the roles of attainable and better sets reversed.

It is easy to give a geometrical example where the trading set is t^0 alone (as in Fig. 3.4(a) so that trade cannot take place; but what does this mean in economic terms? Before discussing it let us draw some interesting geometrical implications from the result that we have just reached, which may be put in the obvious form: the necessary and sufficient condition that there be trade is that there should exist a nontrivial trading set. Suppose that t^0 were actually *inside* the box, and consider the possible relationships of the curves C^{A0} and C^{E0}. A little reflection shows that they can either cut (Fig. 3.4(a) or touch (Fig. 3.4(b)).

In the case where the curves cut (Fig. 3.4(b)), the diagram shows readily that a nontrivial trading set always exists. It follows that if t^0 is inside the box (i.e., each person bringing something of each commodity), the *only* case where trade is not possible is where C^{E0} is tangent to C^{A0} at t^0 (Fig. 3.4(c)).

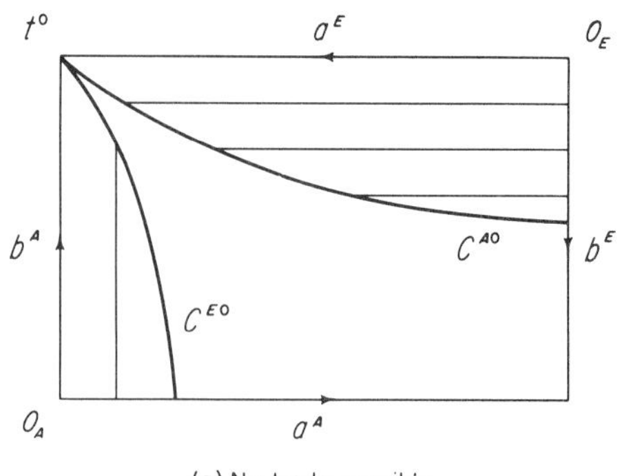

(a) No trade possible

Fig. 3.4(a)

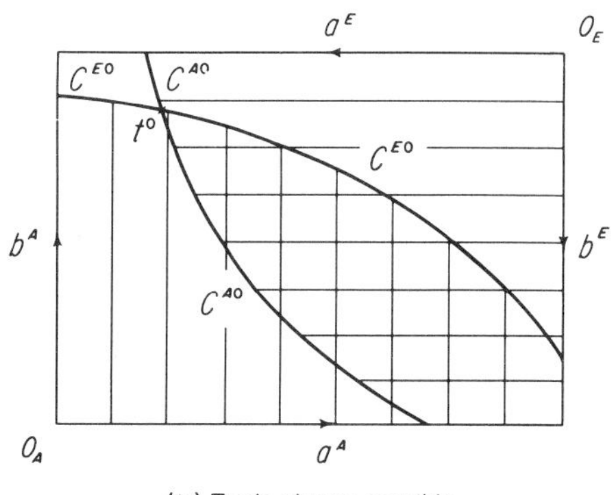

(b) Trade always possible

Fig. 3.4(b)

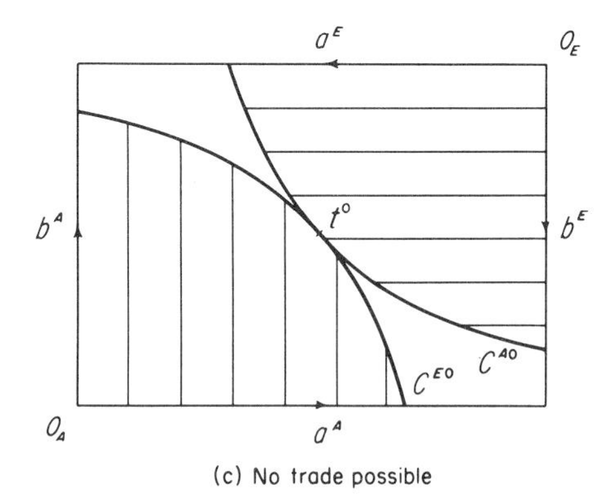

(c) No trade possible

Fig. 3.4(c)

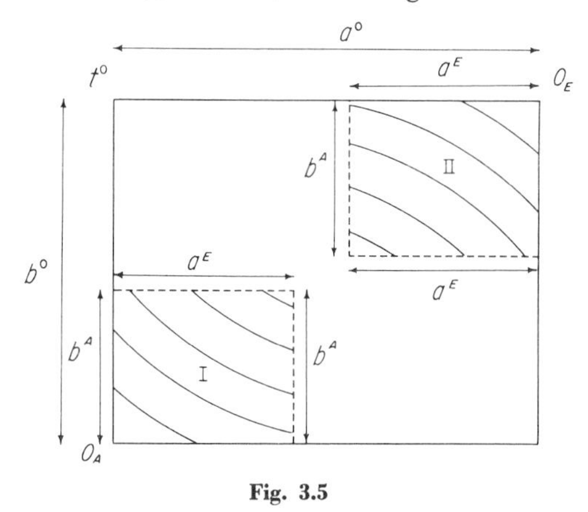

Fig. 3.5

The chances that the initial situation will conform to this condition are clearly remote, but the condition itself is of great importance, as we shall see.*

Finally we should notice that if the initial endowments are assumed to change, the *whole* box diagram will change. For not only will the length of each side alter, but the previously relevant parts of the preference structure will no longer be appropriate. Thus in Fig. 3.5, let the original initial endowment be, as usual, represented by t^0; and now consider a new initial position where Adam has only b^A of bread (and no ale), and Eve has only a^E of ale.

Then the new box diagram is formed, *not* by taking a subset of the original box but by taking Adam's indifference map in the sub-box I (of dimensions a^E, b^A) and superimposing on it Eve's indifference map from the sub-box II (also of dimensions (a^E, b^A), only this time referred to Eve's "origin"). Therefore the new initial position results in an entirely new trading set, and it is meaningless to say that it is a subset of the old, since the two sets do not refer to the same "containing" box.

(ii) The 'Common Sense' Approach

Let us now explore the conditions for trade in the "common sense" terms of the personal rates of substitution (*prs*) and without the use of geometry. Suppose that Adam were at some initial position t^0 and—contemplating the exchange of his bread for Eve's ale—wonders whether it is worthwhile to part with one unit of bread. He will wish to receive from Eve at least ${}_{ab}r^{A0}$ of ale for this amount of bread, for otherwise the exchange would lead him to a position less preferred than t^0. Now, how much bread would Eve demand in

* It follows from this analysis that we lose no generality by taking t^0 to be a "corner" point; for if t^0 *were* an interior point, we would restrict our attention to the trading set determined by t^0, of which t^0 is the extreme northwestern *or* southeastern point.

return for giving up ${}_{ab}r^{A0}$ units of ale? Unless this quantity of bread that she requires is no greater than one unit, a trade is not "on," as far as Adam is concerned; conversely, if it is less than one, the trade will be beneficial for Adam, leading him to a position that he would prefer to t^0.

If Eve's *prs* of bread for ale were constant over this range, she would demand at least $({}_{ab}r^{A0} \times {}_{ba}r^{E0})$ units of bread, for this quantity would just leave her indifferent to the whole transaction. But since, by Axiom VI, her *prs* of bread for ale always increases, she will demand *more* bread than ${}_{ab}r^{A0} \times {}_{ba}r^{E0}$ units, even in order to remain at the level of satisfaction equal to that she enjoys at t^0. This leads to the conclusion that the product ${}_{ab}r^{A0} \times {}_{ba}r^{E0}$ (which is a pure number) must certainly be less than 1, for otherwise Adam will not agree to trade. Since in the last chapter we found that ${}_{ab}r^{A0}$ is reciprocal with ${}_{ba}r^{A0}$ (and ${}_{ba}r^{E0}$ reciprocal with ${}_{ab}r^{E0}$), this condition can be written either as ${}_{ba}r^{E0} < {}_{ba}r^{A0}$, or as ${}_{ab}r^{A0} < {}_{ab}r^{E0}$.

Now how should these conditions be translated into ordinary words? Eve's *prs* of bread for ale at any point indicates the urgency of her thirst for *ale* at that point compared to her hunger for bread, since it states the amount of bread that is needed to compensate her for the loss of one unit of ale from that bundle; and similarly with Adam's *prs* of bread for ale. Thus we have shown that a necessary condition for trade of Adam's bread for Eve's ale is that, at the initial bundle, Eve's desire for ale must be less "urgent," relative to bread, than is Adam's; and this implies, conversely, that Adam's desire for bread in those same terms of ale must be less "urgent" at that point than is Eve's need for bread in those terms. When we ponder this a little, these conditions seem quite straightforward, indeed banally so. As stated, they are only necessary, not sufficient, conditions for exchange; but, given the continuity of all the relevant variables, it is easy to check that they are also sufficient.

A reference to Figs. 3.3, 3.4(a), and 3.4(b) demonstrates that the geometrical conditions conform to these "common sense" ideas. In Fig. 3.3, the "*a*-slope" of C^{A0} at t^0 is greater than the corresponding "*a*-slope" of C^{E0} (taken with respect to the upper *a*-axis), and there is a nontrivial trading set. In Fig. 3.4(a), the reverse is the case, and no trade is possible; while in Fig. 3.4(b) we must clearly have our conditions satisfied on one side or the other of t^0, so that trade is always possible, either of Adam's bread for Eve's ale, or of Adam's ale for Eve's bread. The consideration of the remaining case (Fig. 3.4(c)) leads naturally to the concept of efficient trade, which we now proceed to analyze.

C. EFFICIENT TRADE

(i) The Existence of Efficient Trades

Suppose that conditions are such that trade is possible. Are all trades equally "good" from the viewpoint of the total economic welfare of the two actors in our drama? If one could measure individual preferences in these situations as one measures height or length, *and* if these individual measures could be meaningfully added as lengths are so added—the problem of "interpersonal comparisons of utility"—then we could call efficient those trades which maximized total satisfaction. However no demonstrations of these two propositions have yet been offered that have carried general conviction, so that we have to fall back on a more modest definition of efficiency.

Consider any trade t^1 at which Adam is at a level of satisfaction represented by C^{A1}, and Eve at a level C^{E1}. Now suppose that a trade t^2 is possible such that C^{A2} is the *same* curve as C^{A1}, while C^{E2} represents a higher preference level for Eve than C^{E1}. Then t^2 is clearly a better trade, since Adam is no worse off with t^2 than with t^1, and Eve is actually better off. This leads to the following

Definition 23. A trade t^1, consisting of a commodity bundle x^{A1} for Adam, and x^{E1} for Eve, is said to be *dominated* by a trade t^2 if

(1) $$(x^{A2} R_A x^{A1} \text{ and } x^{E2} R_E x^{E1})$$

and

(2) $$\sim (x^{A2} I_A x^{A1} \text{ and } x^{E2} I_E x^{E1}).$$

If t^2 dominates t^1, we write $t^2 D t^1$.

Notice that we are here extending the idea of dominance from comparisons between *quantities* of commodities (as in Chapter 2) to comparisons between *preferences* for commodity bundles. One trade dominates another if at least one person is better off with the first trade, and *no one* is worse off. This enables us to define an efficient trade as follows:

Definition 24. A trade t^1 is said to be *efficient* if there is no trade which dominates it (i.e., no trade t^2 such that $t^2 D t^1$).

Two things should be noticed about this definition. First, efficiency is an all-or-none concept—a trade is either efficient or it is not; it is never "more efficient" or "less efficient." Secondly, and more important, the relation of dominance only provides what mathematicians call a *partial* ordering of the set of all possible trades, by which we mean that a postulate analogous to Axiom I is inapplicable to the relation D. It is *not* true that for every pair of trades in X, either $t^1 D t^2$ or $t^2 D t^1$. It might well be that t^1 does not dominate t^2, nor t^2 dominate t^1, which leads to the suspicion that there may exist a set consisting of *many* efficient trades in any exchange situation.

Let us now turn to the problem of distinguishing this set. In Fig. 3.6, suppose that the initial position is t^0, and consider whether the trade t^1 is efficient.

From the analysis of Fig. 3.4(b), we know that the diagonally shaded area of Fig. 3.6 is a trading set, inside which both Adam and Eve are better

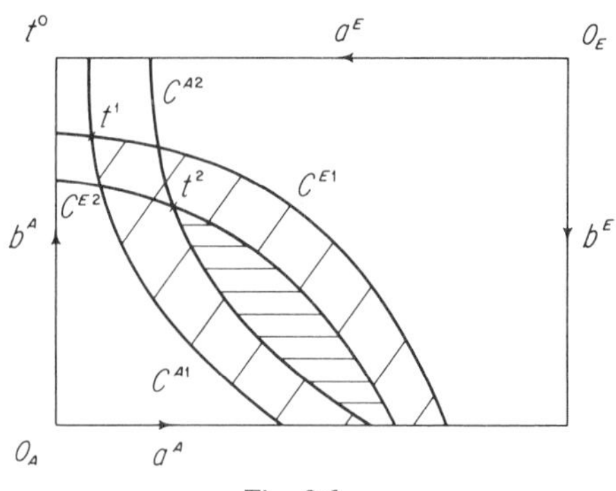

Fig. 3.6

off than at t^1, which is therefore not efficient. Suppose then that t^2, within t^1's trading set, is proposed as efficient. But then C^{A2} and C^{E2} are such that B^{A2} and B^{E2} overlap in the horizontally shaded area, signifying that both parties can be made better off; so t^2 is not efficient either. Obviously, as long as there is *any* nontrivial trading set determined by the proposed trade, it cannot be efficient. Hence a necessary condition for a trade t to be efficient is that the trading set determined by t must consist only of the point t itself. It is easy to see that, provided trade is possible at all, this condition is also sufficient. For if t's trading set consists only of t, then by definition the sets B^{At} and B^{Et} overlap only at t (as in Fig. 3.4(c), at t^0), and therefore one person's position cannot be improved without the other person's position worsening. Of course, if trade is not possible then initial and final positions are coincident and therefore in a sense "efficient"; but obviously in this case the concept of efficient trade loses relevance.

In Fig. 3.4(c), the point t^0 is efficient; and it is also a point of tangency between C^{A0} and C^{E0}, a statement which as we shall see (Fig. 3.9 below) carries the corollary that at t^0, ${}_{ba}r^{A0} = {}_{ba}r^{E0}$. This suggests that we could define efficient trades as those at which each personal rate of substitution of bread for ale (and, therefore, also of ale for bread) is the same. This version, although most of the story, is however not quite the whole truth. Consider Fig. 3.7.

Let the initial position be t^0, as shown, which is not efficient. Nor is t^1, lying inside t^0's trading set. But t^2 is efficient, since there is no trading set there except t^2 itself, and so is *any* other point along that edge of the box lying between C^{A0} and C^{E0}. Yet at no such point is there ordinary tangency of the indifference curves, and hence nowhere along the edge is there equality of the *prs*. Thus we can only frame the "efficiency condition" in terms of the equality of the individuals' *prs* as long as we are certain (heaven knows how) that none of the efficient trades is on the boundary of the box. On the boundary, the condition has to be stated in terms of the *inequality* of the *prs*; we will return to this point later.

Notice also that even if we knew that the efficient trades were all inside the

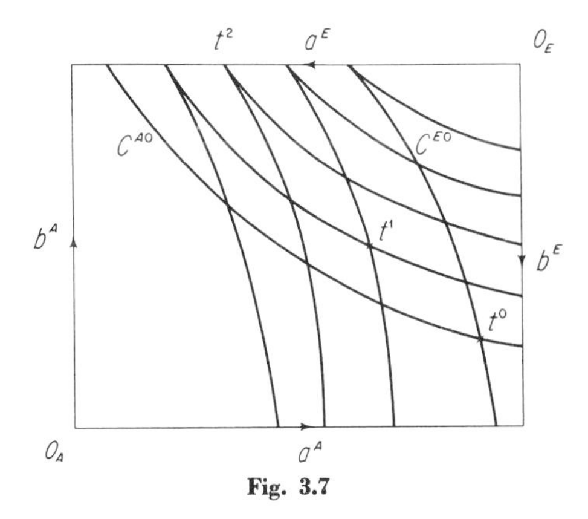

Fig. 3.7

box, if we did not have Axiom VII the efficiency condition could still not be given as the equality of the *prs*. For we might have the situation of Fig. 3.8.

If both C^{A1} and C^{E1} are "pointed" at t^1, then the *prs* of neither party is uniquely defined there, and hence talk about equality of those *prs* is meaningless. This remains true even if only one of the curves is "pointed" at t^1.

Bearing in mind the problems of "boundary" efficient points, and avoiding —by means of Axiom VII—the complications exposed by Fig. 3.8, let us concentrate attention on "interior" efficient points. These will consist, as we have said, of all points at which ${}_{ba}r^A$ is equal to ${}_{ba}r^E$, a condition which becomes intuitively reasonable in the light of the "common sense" approach of the last section. If the allocation of goods is such that Adam's hunger for bread, relative to his thirst for ale at that allocation, is the same as Eve's personal evaluation of those goods, then there is clearly no scope for further mutually beneficial trade; hence the allocation cannot be dominated by any other and is efficient. In geometrical terms, this shows up as tangency of the indifference curves of the individuals, as in Fig. 3.9.

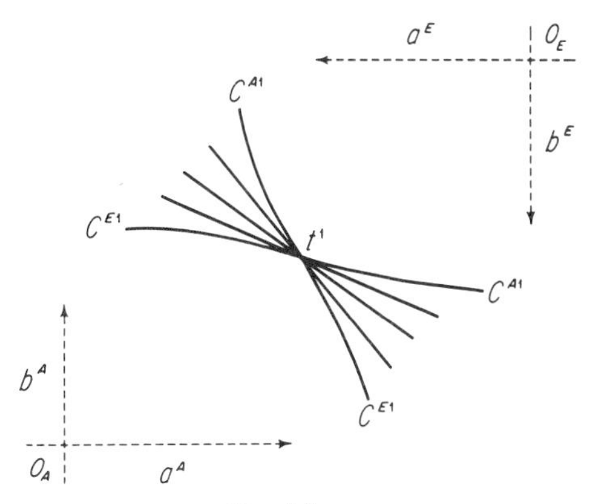

Fig. 3.8

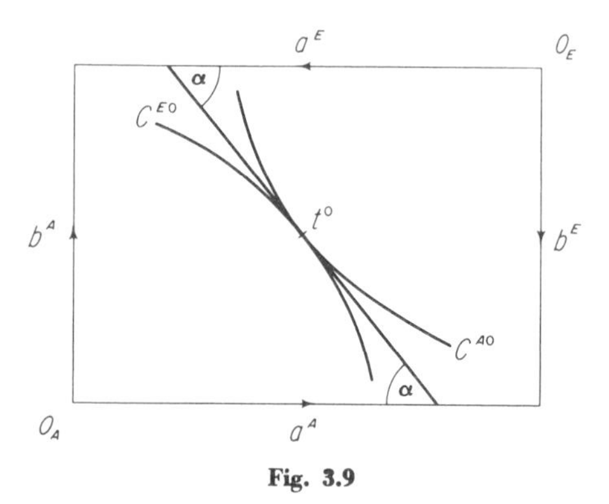

Fig. 3.9

The slope of C^{A0} at t^0 relative to the edge a^A—which is equal to ${}_{ba}r^{A0}$—is given by tan α; and the slope of C^{E0} at t^0 relative to the edge a^E, which is equal to ${}_{ba}r^{E0}$, is also tan α. Hence t^0 represents a point of common *prs* for Adam and Eve. It follows that the set of all efficient trades corresponds to the locus of all points of tangency between the indifference curves of each individual. This is shown in Fig. 3.10, where the curve PT is the locus of all such tangency points, and hence of all efficient trades; it will therefore be called the *efficiency locus*. But in fact this concept of the *complete* set of efficient trades is seldom used in the analysis of exchange, for in any exchange situation we start off from some definite initial position, and so need only be concerned with that part of the efficiency locus which lies *within* the trading set determined by that initial position. Thus if the initial point were t^0 in Fig. 3.10, only the segment QS of the efficiency locus would be relevant, since the section from P up to (but not including) Q consists of efficient trades which are worse for Adam than is the initial point t^0; similarly the segment from T up to but not including S contains undominated trades which are worse for Eve than is t^0. For initial points t^1 and t^2, the relevant segment of the efficiency locus would be QR and RS, respectively, while for t^3 it would be only the point t^3 itself.

Thus any initial allocation determines a section of the efficiency locus, a section which will be called the *contract curve* associated with that allocation.* Thus the contract curve consists of the set of all efficient trades which are acceptable to both protagonists in any exchange situation. For any trade t in the trading set but *not* on the contract curve, there are infinitely many trades on the curve which dominate t. One must be careful not to say that all points on the contract curve are better than all points in the trading set off it, since not all allocations on the curve can be related by the partial ordering D to all allocations off it. Thus in Fig. 3.10 the efficient trade R dominates

* This term was introduced by Edgeworth, who sometimes used it as synonymous with the efficiency locus and sometimes in the sense above; subsequent literature has continued the ambiguity.

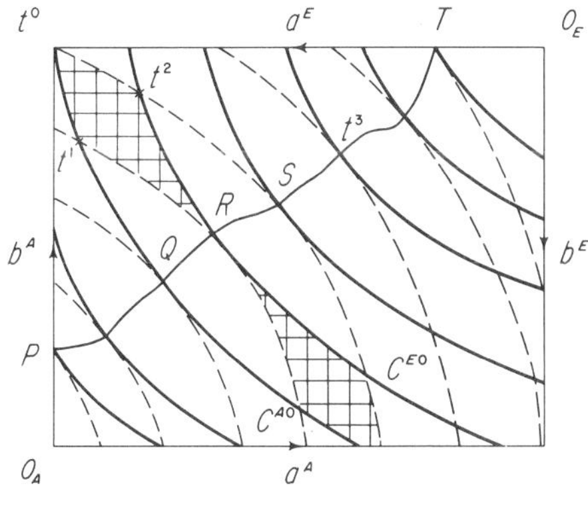

Fig. 3.10

only those trades in t^0's trading set which lie in the shaded areas; those in the unshaded part of that trading set are undominated by R, and themselves do not dominate R. The correct statement is that *the contract curve is the set of all undominated and attainable trades* in any exchange situation.

What does this concept mean in everyday terms? It implies that in any bargaining situation there will usually be a good deal of room for negotiations that will benefit both parties, for the probability that an arbitrary trade in a trading set will be off its contract curve is much higher than the probability that it will be on it. It follows that if and when the bargaining process leads the parties to the contract curve, there is then no further room for mutual accommodation between Adam and Eve, and the sex war assumes a Strindberg-like intensity. Indeed the contract curve has been renamed the "conflict curve," since whatever one person gains along that curve, the other loses. Assuming t^0 to be the initial position in Fig. 3.10, the closer Adam is to S, the more he scoops the (unmeasurable) "gains from trade," while the closer to Q, the more does Eve gain.

This remarkable Edgeworthian insight—that in the apparently hopelessly vague situation of bilateral trade, one can distinguish "efficient trades" from inefficient—has been applied also to the general theory of bargaining in social systems, in analyzing the concept of "areas of agreement." Parenthetically, one may remark that in such political and social systems a wise strategy would appear to call for continuous negotiations which do *not* proceed all the way to an efficient position, for there complete opposition of interest becomes manifest, tension rises, and the situation may explode, perhaps literally so.

(ii) The Attainment of Efficient Trades

By now the skeptical or attentive reader (the two are often the same) may have wondered just what relevance the contract curve has in our model of the exchange situation. It is true that if the parties were at an efficient trade, there is no nonauthoritarian way of dislodging them, since one person at least would be hurt by any proposed move that is attainable. But starting —as we usually do—from an initial point that is inefficient, how can we be sure that the process of bargaining will ever lead to an efficient trade? It seems paradoxical that we have blithely been deriving theorems about trading sets and contract curves without once discussing the bargaining process which may—or may not—lead the protagonists to an efficient trade; to this problem we must now turn.

To begin with, it is obvious that only in one case is there any reason at all why a single, isolated act of exchange would take place anywhere near the contract curve. Only if the people concerned had been in regular trading contact for some time, so that they knew each other's preferences rather well, would it be at all probable that a single exchange transaction would be close to "efficiency." But this case itself brings out the fact that the contract curve is normally only attained (if at all) as the *limit* of a sequence of inefficient trades, in the course of which each person acquires information about the preference structure of the other.

An important difficulty about this is that there is not just one but several "real life" interpretations of these bargaining sequences, depending on how we interpret the model of exchange. Let us first suppose that the analysis covers a span of many periods, over the whole of which preferences are assumed to remain constant. Within any one period, only one transaction can take place. This is not so severe a restriction as it sounds, for we can always chop up (if necessary) any period into a large number of sub-periods, within each of which our condition can reasonably be assumed to hold. But here we encounter a new difficulty of interpretation. In Chapter 2 all preference structures referred to a single period, so that no real problem arose of what it meant for the individual to "receive" a commodity bundle. Whether he wanted to *hold* the batch of commodities, or whether he wanted to *consume* them, in the literal sense, or whether he wanted some mixture of both operations, was irrelevant to that single-period analysis. But when we move on to multi-period analysis, the time dimension of every quantity must be carefully stated, and the problem is no longer trivial.

The tradition in economic theory is that we are not usually interested in how the individual organizes his domestic pattern of consumption of commodities, once he has obtained them by trade or production. We follow this usage by assuming that his preferences refer to what he wishes to *receive* each period (the length of which will itself affect those preferences), and that at the end of each period he decides what proportion (if any) of each commodity he wishes to consume. The balance of each commodity stock is then carried over into the next period and is available for trade as his initial holding. Following the usual custom, we do not analyze what determines the fraction of each commodity which he withholds from all further trade at the end of any period.

We can now postulate three main cases: (a) this fraction is zero, so that the total initial endowments persist over the whole span, simply being *redistributed* each period; (b) the fraction is unity, so that everything is consumed at the end of each period; but in order to give this case interest, we further assume that at the *beginning* of each period the *original* endowments are exactly replenished; (c) the fraction lies between zero and unity for each commodity, and no replenishment at all occurs. The first two cases both imply a fixed total stock of commodities applicable to the whole span, while the last interpretation is more difficult, since it involves a sequence of ever-diminishing box diagrams, each of them quite different from the predecessors (as we have seen in $B(i)$).

It follows from this discussion that we cannot say what role the contract curve will play until we have specified what interpretation of the model we have in mind. In case (a)—whose only near relatives in practice would seem to be such organizations as the world market for genuine Rembrandts—the process of reallocation would gradually increase information (except for exceptionally stupid or perverse traders) in such a way as to lead close to the contract curve after a suitable lapse of time. The second case is more realistic, provided that we are prepared to relax temporarily the assumption that no production takes place. If it does, then the replenishment each period need not fall like manna from heaven but can simply be regarded as the regular production, at a constant rate, of some perishable commodities. As in the first case, the bargaining process should lead the parties close to the contract curve as time goes on, assuming—as before—that the preference structures persist unchanged throughout.

Notice that in neither of these two cases can we say *where* on the contract curve the process will come to an end, for the terminal position will depend on the whole of the preceding sequence. This dependence of the final outcome on the previous path is sometimes expressed by saying that equilibrium is *indeterminate* in bilateral exchange, though other meanings of this term have been given in this context. This usage does *not* mean that a solution will fail to be reached, but simply that the assumptions of the theory determine only a *set* of outcomes—those on the contract curve—rather than a unique final allocation. The exact location of the ultimate point will depend on a host of noneconomic factors which determine relative "bargaining strengths." If Adam is susceptible to a woman's tears, he—poor man—will always end up near Q in Fig. 3.10, while a submissive Eve might find herself always near S. In trading with a used-car salesman, I always emerge at the "wrong" end of the curve, as I do with almost all traders in "underdeveloped" countries, whose bargaining skills are often very highly developed indeed.

A further point to observe in both cases (a) and (b) is that, once an efficient trade is attained, there is no reason—aside from outright coercion—why it should *ever* change as long as preferences and initial endowments persist. Suppose, for example, that we take the "production" version of (b) as a rough reflection of a static, feudal agricultural economy. Then the analysis implies that if, in some dim historical past, the earliest bargains had markedly favored one party to the exchange, thus leading the allocation to "its" end of the contract curve, then the bargains currently observed would also be at that end, unless tastes and techniques had changed considerably—or a revolution had supervened.

In any event, there is no serious reason to doubt that in both (a) and (b), the sequence of trades will emerge *somewhere* on the contract curve, even if the theory is not designed to tell us the exact place. The situation is quite otherwise with the apparently more realistic case (c); here it is not even clear what *meaning* can be attached to "emergence on the contract curve," since the original curve itself disappears from the analysis after the first trade in the sequence, as some of each person's holdings are withdrawn from all future trade. So we have to rephrase our inquiry concerning the efficiency of the ultimate position, and we do so as follows: Consider the total of all the ale which Eve gives up (i.e., trades *and* consumes) over the course of the whole trading sequence until exchange stops, and denote this by a^T. Let the quantity of bread similarly given up by Adam be b^T.

Now consider the allocation granting $(a^T, b^0 - b^T)$ to Adam and $(a^0 - a^T, b^T)$ to Eve. If this is on the original contract curve, then the total amount of bread surrendered by Adam, and of ale given up by Eve, over the course of the whole trading process would be equal to the deductions from t^0 obtained by a move direct to the contract curve in the first period. In this restricted sense, the trading sequence would be "efficient."

There is no particular reason to suppose that this "total" allocation would be on the original contract curve, but two important, simple, and quite independent postulates have been put forward, each of which practically ensures the result. The first (in terms of priority of original publication) is due to Edgeworth, whose characteristically oblique analysis consists in effect of pretending that case (c) is all a mistake, that its complicating features do not exist, and that it is essentially similar to (a) and (b) after all. Marshall invented the second approach, which is a typically Marshallian simplification that assumes the truth of the result and looks for a simple sufficient condition to guarantee it; it is convenient to deal with this first.

(iii) Marshall's Postulate

Suppose that the rate at which Adam is prepared to exchange ale for bread were always *independent* of the amount of ale that he has already acquired, while similarly for Eve, the rate at which she will substitute bread for ale is independent of the quantity of ale that she has already exchanged and consumed.* This means, in symbolic terms, that both ${}_{ab}r^A$ and ${}_{ab}r^E$ must be

* We are assuming here the usual "extreme northwest" initial position. If the exchange started instead from an "interior" allocation, then the Postulate takes the form that Adam's

independent of a at any feasible allocation; also since ${}_{ba}r^A$ is reciprocal with ${}_{ab}r^A$ (and ${}_{ba}r^E$ with ${}_{ab}r^E$) for any bundle, this assumption implies the same "a-invariance" of ${}_{ba}r^A$ and ${}_{ba}r^E$. Since the b-slope of any indifference curve measures the *prs* of ale for bread at the relevant point, Marshall's Postulate requires that, *within any trading set*, the slope of each curve depends only on the quantity of bread in the bundle concerned, and not at all on the amount of ale.

Therefore in the trading area all rates of substitution are functions solely of b, a fact illustrated in Fig. 3.11, which measures along the abscissa the amount of bread given up by Adam, and along the ordinate the ${}_{ab}r$ (we could equally well have drawn instead a diagram for the "reciprocal" ${}_{ba}r$). The zero point for b corresponds to the initial allocation t^0, and the assumption that trade is possible implies that ${}_{ab}r^{A0} < {}_{ab}r^{E0}$. Because of the Axiom of Convexity, ${}_{ab}r^A$ is an increasing function of b, and ${}_{ab}r^E$ a decreasing function. The two curves in the diagram will therefore tend toward each other, and Fig. 3.11 illustrates a case where they actually intersect *before* Adam has given up all his bread (i.e., the original endowment b^0).

Using Fig. 3.11 we can illustrate any trading process as a series of moves along the abscissa, as in the sequence 0 to b^1 to b^3 to b^5 (or—more briefly—0, b^1, b^3, b^5). At each trade in this series, the relation ${}_{ab}r^A < {}_{ab}r^E$ implies that Adam can improve his situation by further trade of bread for ale. This, together with the fact that he will consume some bread for his own use, means that he will move to the right at any trade to the left of b^T. If the periods involved are short, so that he is likely to give up small amounts of bread

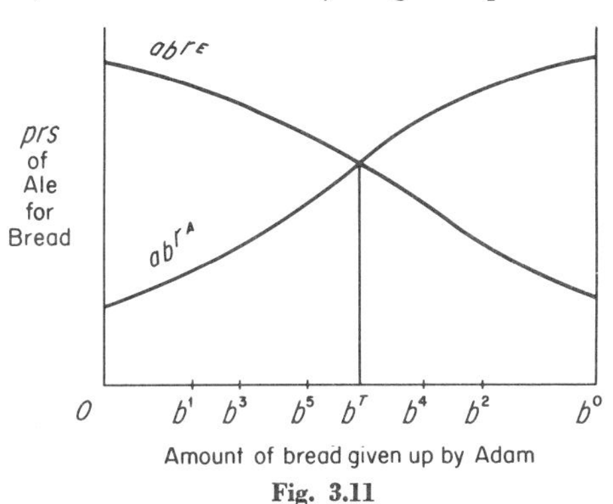

Fig. 3.11

rate of substitution of ale for bread must be independent of the ale *either* acquired *or* given up; and similarly for Eve.

Since Marshall's exchange theory was couched in terms of "measurable" utility functions (rather than representations), the actual form in which he presented the Postulate was that the marginal utility of ale be *constant*. But in representational language such a condition has no meaning, since a given preference structure may imply a constant marginal utility of ale with one of its representations, and a variable marginal utility with another. A discussion of the precise connection between the original version and ours is left to the Notes, since the matter, besides being a little technical, is mainly of historical interest.

each time, it is most probable that he will approach b^T entirely from the left. At b^T the equality ${}_{ab}r^{AT} = {}_{ab}r^{ET}$ means that there is no further incentive to trade, which therefore stops.

If the process were not so "continuous," it is possible that b^T might be "overshot," as in the sequence 0, b^1, b^2. At b^2 the inequality ${}_{ab}r^{A2} > {}_{ab}r^{E2}$ implies that Adam should engage in "reverse" trade, exchanging ale for bread.* Now if Eve has been consuming bread at the rate at which she has been acquiring it, she will have no bread available for this reverse trade, and the process will simply come to an end at b^2. This, however, is improbable, since in the move from b^1 to b^2 Eve would have gained a large quantity of bread, which she is unlikely to eat all at one gulp.

It is then likely that we would observe some such sequence as 0, b^1, b^2, b^3, b^4, b^5 . . . , in which b^T is approached by a series of oscillations of diminishing amplitude; or perhaps just one oscillation occurs, as in the series 0, b^1, b^2, b^3, b^5 . . . . But it is *possible* (though most unlikely) that the reactions of the people involved might be so perverse that we would witness a divergent series of oscillations, such as 0, b^3, b^4, b^1, b^2, . . . , which might result in b^T never being attained, although the limits imposed by the restricted initial endowments (plus Adam's consumption each period) would tend to drive such oscillations towards b^T, as the size of the "box" each period regularly diminishes.

Thus it is almost certain that b^T will be attained if the adjustments take place continuously, though even without this assumption it is most probable that b^T will eventually be reached. Since at b^T we know that ${}_{ab}r^{AT} = {}_{ab}r^{ET}$, it follows that each person's indifference curves are *tangent* at that point; since Fig. 3.11 refers to the *whole* of the initial endowment b^0, this in turn means that b^T is on the original contract curve. We have therefore shown that, provided adjustments take place "smoothly," Marshall's Postulate guarantees that the trading process will be "efficient" in the sense that we have described, the total amount of bread given up over the whole process being equal to that obtainable by an "efficient" first period contract.

Now suppose that the two curves in Fig. 3.11 did not cut. This may be due either to Adam's running out of bread before equality of the *prs* is reached, or to Eve's running out of ale. In the first case both curves will continue all the way to b^0, in the second the curve illustrating the behavior of ${}_{ab}r^E$ will terminate at some point before that, say b^E. In either case, whether adjustments are made "continuously" or not, trade will proceed from the left directly to the boundary, to b^0 or to b^E, as the case may be. At the boundary, the relation ${}_{ab}r^A < {}_{ab}r^E$ will, of course, imply boundary tangencies of the indifference curves, and hence a "boundary" contract curve; so our conclusions about "efficiency" of the trading process apply here also. As usually happens, analysis of boundary positions is actually simpler than that of interior allocations.

* This possibility of "reverse" trade implies that b^T must be interpreted as the *net* (not gross) amount of bread given up by Adam during the exchange process.

In addition to ensuring "efficiency" for all reasonably continuous trading sequences, Marshall's Postulate also has the side effect of reducing the amount of indeterminateness in bilateral exchange. This is best seen by examining the contract curve, which has a particular shape in this situation. Since within the trading set both *prs*'s of ale for bread are independent of a, if $_{ab}r^{AT} = {}_{ab}r^{ET}$ for some feasible allocation of ale, then the equality will hold for *all* feasible ale allocations that have the bread allocation b^T to Eve, $(b^0 - b^T)$ to Adam. This means that for every feasible allocation granting $(b^0 - b^T)$ to Adam in the original box diagram, his indifference curves must be tangent to Eve's indifference curves, so that—as shown in Fig. 3.12—the original contract curve becomes a straight line parallel to the a^A-axis, at a height $(b^0 - b^T)$; no such implication necessarily applies to the entire efficiency locus but only to the contract curve.

Therefore although the quantity of ale surrendered by Eve over any complete trading sequence is indeterminate within the limits t^0a^Q and t^0a^S, the total amount of bread given up by Adam is *fixed* at b^T, no matter what sequence is followed. But then the question arises: What is so special about bread? We can certainly obtain the reverse result by assuming that each $_{ab}r$ is independent, not of ale, but of the quantity of *bread* acquired or surrendered. In this case the contract curve becomes a vertical line at a distance $(a^0 - a^T)$ from the b^E axis, and while a^T is now fixed, b^T can vary between the limits imposed by the trading set.* As before, Marshall's Postulate applied this way still implies "efficiency" of the trading process; so why do we not make this assumption instead?

The answer, of course, is that no reason save that of convenience influenced the choice of independence of $_{ab}r$ with respect to ale rather than bread. But this brings out the need for an economic justification of Marshall's Postulate in either form, a problem we have so far sedulously ignored. The most

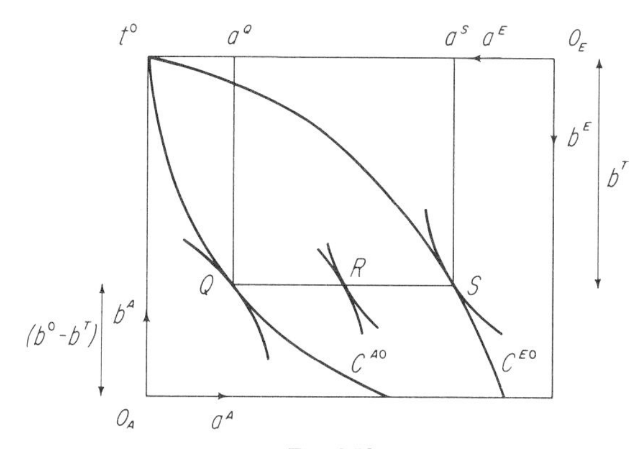

Fig. 3.12

* We cannot make the assumption *both* ways, since if each $_{ab}r$ is independent of a and of b, it is constant for *any* variation in the variables, and that would violate the Axiom of Convexity.

plausible reasoning is that given by Marshall himself, who pointed out in effect that if the protagonists each have large quantities of ale already in their possession (most of which, perhaps, they do not bring to the trading post), then variation in the quantity of ale they acquire or give up will make little difference to their already quite low *prs* of bread for ale; and so will hardly affect the "reciprocal" *prs* of ale for bread. Thus if the trade takes place in a district known chiefly for its barley and hops rather than its wheat, ale will probably be plentiful compared to bread, and the condition will tend to hold. Conversely, if the area is devoted mainly to wheat, each person's *prs* of ale for bread (measuring the urgency of his or her need for bread) is likely to be low, and so relatively unaffected by variations in quantity brought about by the transfer and moderate consumption of stocks of bread.

Marshall himself freely admitted that this argument was no more than plausible in the case of bilateral barter, applying as it does to a few special cases; but he firmly maintained that the Postulate was much more nearly justified in its application to a money economy, to which the study of barter is mainly an introduction.

(iv) Edgeworth's Approach

The approach taken by Edgeworth can be dealt with briefly, since (unlike that of Marshall) it does not place conditions on the behavior of individuals *within* the model of exchange but is a reinterpretation of the exchange model itself. He took the view that the bargaining sequences should be regarded not as series of actual trades but as series of *proposed* trades, as sequences of offers and counter-offers none of which except the last is finally binding on the parties concerned. In his words, each person is free to *recontract* at any time, provided the other agrees; and clearly, in bilateral exchange there is always scope for "recontract" as long as the trading position is off the contract curve. To quote the delightfully characteristic passage in which the word "recontract" first appears:

> "Is it peace or war?" asks the lover of "Maud," of economic competition, and answers hastily: It is both, *pax* or *pact* between contractors during contract, *war*, when some of the contractors *without the consent of others recontract*. Thus an auctioneer having been in contract with the last bidder (to sell at such a price *if* no higher bid) *recontracts* with a higher bidder. (*Mathematical Psychics*, p. 17; italics—and punctuation—in the original.)

With this interpretation, all three cases of the bargaining process that we have distinguished become essentially similar to case (a), in which, as we have seen, there is a very high probability that the information about each other's preferences garnered during the sequence will lead each person to the contract curve. Thus Edgeworth's approach "solves" the problem of how efficient trades are achieved by bartering sequences, but at the cost of putting the whole problem into a fanciful setting; whereas Marshall's Postulate, although admittedly placing highly restrictive conditions on the individual preference structures, at least operates within a realistic framework. If neither of these two special (and brilliantly conceived) assumptions is made, then there is little guarantee that the most normal type (c) of the barter process will imply an efficient final exchange. This leads up to the question: Is there any *mechanism* by which the two parties could be led to efficient trading positions without having to depend upon the possibly uncertain and probably long process of barter? The answer to this is "yes," and the elaboration of that answer constitutes one of the more important branches of the study of economic systems.

D. THE ROLE OF PRICES IN EXCHANGE

(i) The Existence of "Efficient" Exchange Ratios

Suppose that we introduce to the scene an individual whose job is to set up a game for the two participants, with certain rules, and to act as its referee or umpire. The rules are: The umpire announces a certain exchange ratio of ale for bread (and hence also of bread for ale), at which each party is free to exchange as much as he (or she) would wish. Each individual then takes ale (or bread, as the case may be) in any quantity to the umpire and receives the corresponding quantity of bread (or ale), as determined by the announced exchange ratio. This exchange ratio will thus be the amount of ale offered by the umpire in exchange for one unit of bread, and conversely for the ratio of bread for ale.*

If there exists at least one exchange ratio which would lead the parties to the contract curve, then this implies that the amount of ale actually offered to the umpire for exchange by one party will equal the amount of ale which the other receives from the umpire, and similarly for bread. It follows that in this event the umpire will have nothing of either commodity left on his hands—hands which are here only too visible, unlike the "Invisible Hand" of the free market. Indeed the "umpire" need not be human at all but could be a suitably programmed electronic computer, to whom Adam and Eve need simply turn over—independently of each other—a complete account of their preference structures (as given, e.g., by representations u_A and u_E), together with data on their initial stocks of both commodities. The umpire-computer, in this fully automated Eden, does the rest. It calculates and announces one of the appropriate "efficient" exchange ratios from the data handed to it, and tells each party to exchange as much as it likes at that ratio (subject to its initial stock limitations). The corresponding offers and demands

* Throughout this section we shall assume that no consumption (in the sense of B(ii)) takes place. The problems that it poses will be taken up again in Section C of Chapter 4.

by the participants will be in complete harmony and will in fact constitute an efficient trade.

The whole basis of this admirable procedure obviously turns on whether there does indeed exist at least one "equilibrium" exchange ratio of ale for bread, a ratio, moreover, which is determined entirely by the initial stocks and by individual preference structures. We now deal with this problem.

A good way to analyze the new situation is to regard it as *three* bilateral exchange situations, between Adam and the umpire, Eve and the umpire, and Adam and Eve. Let us consider the first case, between Adam and umpire, with Adam at the position t^0 as before. What is Adam's better set B^{A0}? Obviously, the same as before. But his attainable set has changed considerably from the Adam-Eve confrontation, for it is no longer bounded by Eve's "initial" indifference curve C^{E0}. If the umpire announces an exchange ratio of ale for bread, this can be represented diagrammatically by a straight line issuing from t^0, whose slope, relative to the bread axis, measures the amount of ale that the umpire is prepared to give Adam for every unit of bread that he turns in; thus Adam can *attain* any bundle of ale and bread lying on this exchange line. He can, of course, also attain any point lying *below* the exchange line, but because of the Axiom of Dominance, such bundles are of no relevance to his actual choice in this situation.

In Fig. 3.13, the umpire's exchange ratio (tan β) is represented by the line t^0t^z, and Adam's attainable set therefore by the triangle $t^0 0_A t^z$. In a sense, one can look at this set as composed of the umpire's "indifference curve," each of them being exchange lines of "b-slope" tan β; by hypothesis, the umpire is "indifferent" concerning which bundle on t^0t^z Adam actually selects.

What bundle *will* he select? What "trade" between Adam and the umpire is optimal for Adam? Clearly t^0 is not such a trade, for a move to F will lead Adam to a point *inside* B^{A0}. Indeed we can apply our earlier analysis contained in $B(i)$ and say that as long as there is overlap at each proposed trade between Adam's relevant better set and his attainable set, there is always

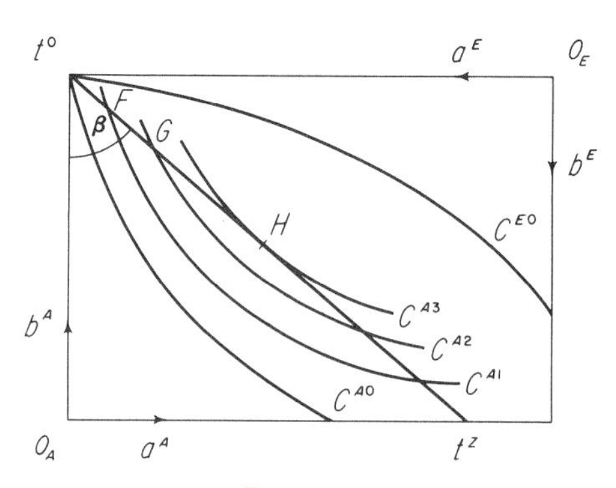

Fig. 3.13

scope for further trade; but since the umpire is a completely inert protagonist the trade will always be struck along t^0t^z. Hence, arguing as before, we conclude that Adam will reach an optimal position at a point of "no" overlap, i.e., at a bundle—in this case, H—where the exchange line t^0t^z is *tangential* to Adam's indifference curve through that point. Because of the Axiom of Convexity, the maximal set in the attainable set $t^0 0_A t^z$ consists of just the one point H; and because of Axiom VII, to each bundle such as H there corresponds a unique attainable "triangle," given the initial endowments.

Thus for any one of the umpire's exchange ratios, Adam will select a unique optimal bundle, depending on his initial stocks and his preferences. At the boundary the optimal bundle will consist only of one commodity (as at x^0 in Fig. 2.13), but it is still unique, and characterized by tangency of a sort. Moreover, since the b-slope of the exchange ratio line is the same as the b-slope of the indifference curve at the optimal (interior) point H, it follows that Adam's *prs* of ale for bread there is equal to the exchange ratio of ale for bread (and, conversely, that the exchange ratio of bread for ale is the same as his *prs* of bread for ale at H). At the boundary, the optimality conditions must be framed in terms of *in*equalities: thus the exchange ratio (*e.r.*) of ale for bread cannot be less than the *prs* of ale for bread at a boundary optimum, which in turn implies that the *e.r.* of bread for ale cannot be greater than the *prs* of bread for ale there.

A precisely similar analysis applies to the Eve-umpire exchange situation, and she will therefore also take up an optimal position at a point of tangency (or boundary tangency). Assuming an interior optimum, this means that for any given *e.r.* of ale for bread, both parties will take up optimum positions such that—since the *prs* of ale for bread of each person at those positions will be equal to the *e.r.*—both *prs*'s are *the same*. But this does *not* mean that the positions constitute an efficient trade, for they may simply not be a *trade*, the individual optima being incompatible, in the sense that total offers and demands of ale and of bread are not exactly matched. There may be a surplus of bread at the umpire's trading post, with a corresponding deficit of ale, or conversely. There is no guarantee that a given *e.r.* will result in an efficient single trade, although both individuals' *prs* will always be equalized; this is illustrated in Fig. 3.14.

Suppose that at the *e.r.* of ale for bread equal to tan β, Adam's optimal position is t^A, and Eve's optimal selection t^E. This will signify that Adam is prepared to give up t^0L of bread for Lt^A of ale, while Eve wishes to give up only Kt^E of ale, getting in return t^0K of bread. There will be an excess offer of bread of $t^EM(=KL)$ and an excess demand for ale of Mt^A, where *excess offer* is defined to mean actual quantity offered minus actual quantity demanded, and *excess demand* means the reverse.

Our question concerning the existence of "efficient" exchange ratios now becomes: Is there an *e.r.* such that no excess offer (and therefore no excess demand) will be present? A little reflection shows that in order to

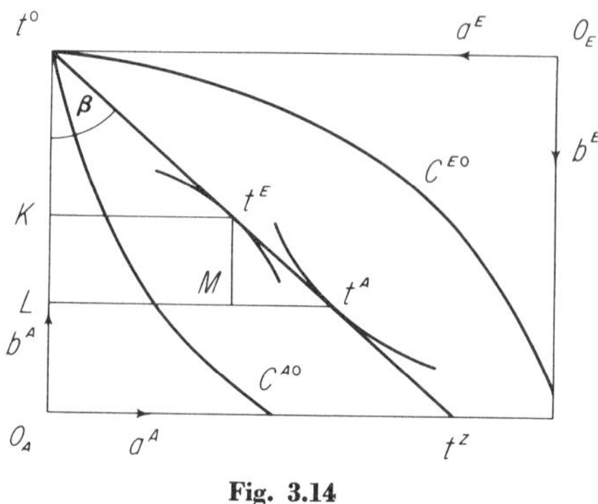

Fig. 3.14

achieve this, the optimal point for Adam on t^0t^z must coincide with the optimal point for Eve; only then will there be no excess offer. Moreover, since—at least for interior points—each *prs* will be equal to the *e.r.* and so to each other, the resulting allocation will be on the contract curve, by the very definition of that curve. So in geometrical terms, the question becomes: Is there a point P^* on the contract curve such that a line from P^* to t^0 will also be the (common) tangent to the two individual indifference curves at P^*? In this case Adam and Eve, by adjusting optimally to the announced *e.r.* represented by the slope of the line t^0P^*, will automatically be led to an efficient trade. Notice that, since to any point P on the contract curve there corresponds an exchange line, there will be a whole *set* of initial positions (all those on the exchange line) for which P is the efficient trade to which the corresponding exchange ratio would lead. But here we are looking at the problem the other way round. *Given* an initial position t^0, is there an exchange ratio which will lead the parties from t^0 to an efficient trade P^*?

Such a point P^* is shown in Fig. 3.15, but nothing in the analysis so far has demonstrated its existence. To assert without proof that it does indeed always exist would be an act of faith rather than of science, so a central

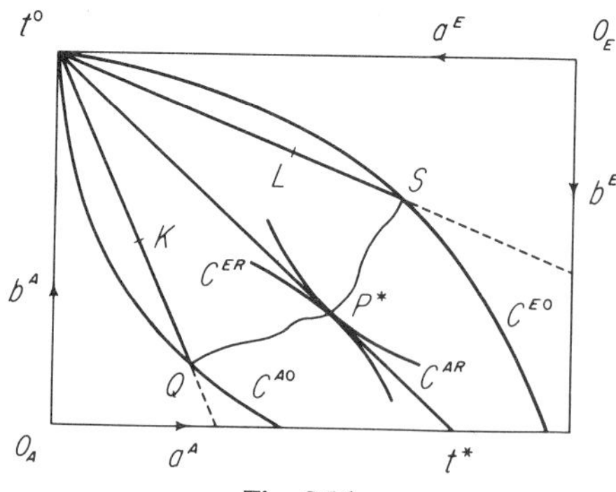

Fig. 3.15

feature of the theory must be a satisfactory demonstration of this fact. In order to accomplish this, let us first observe that to *every* point of the contract curve we can associate two slopes: (1) the common b-slope of the indifference curves through the point, which measures the personal rates of substitution of ale for bread; and (2) the b-slope of the line joining the point to t^0, which measures the exchange ratio of ale for bread. And these two slopes are independent of each other.

Notice further that at Q (the initial point of "Adam's end" of the contract curve) the b-slope of the exchange line will be *less* than the b-slope of C^{A0}. This is obvious geometrically, since t^0Q is the chord of a (strictly) convex curve, which must therefore lie everywhere to one side of the chord. Economically, it corresponds to the fact that at the *e.r.* represented by t^0Q, Adam would find an optimal point, such as K, somewhere in the *interior* of B^{A0}, and therefore the "umpire mechanism" could not lead to an efficient trade at Q. Exactly similar reasoning may be applied to Eve's end of the contract curve at S, where the b-slope of the exchange line t^0S will be *greater* than the b-slope of C^{E0} at S, and Eve will select a point, such as L, in the interior of B^{E0}.

If the *e.r.* of ale for bread is denoted by the symbol ${}_{ab}R$, then we can write a functional relation ${}_{ab}R = f(P)$, where P is *any* point on the contract curve, because we have noted that for each such P there is an exchange line joining P to t^0. It is clear that f is a continuous function of P, since the slope of Pt^0 changes continuously as we rotate the exchange line around t^0 through the "arc" QS. Similarly, if we denote the common *prs* of a for b at points on the contract curve by ${}_{ab}r$, then we may write ${}_{ab}r = g(P)$, where g is some other functional relation. Again it is clear from the diagram (and, as for the previous case, may be proved rigorously) that g is a continuous function of P.

Now the contract curve QS *is* simply a curve, and for any point P we can easily *represent* the "distance" of that point from Q by a number which corresponds to the distance, exactly as we mapped an indifference curve onto the abscissa in Figs. 2.10(a) and (b). This means that we can mark off along the horizontal axis a segment which corresponds to the "length" of the contract curve, and each point of this segment of the axis will correspond uniquely to a point P of the curve; indeed, we may denote the points of the segment by the symbol P also, since the segment is essentially a "stretching" of the contract curve into a straight line.

Thus to each point P of this segment there correspond two functional values $f(P)$ and $g(P)$; and the graphs of these continuous functions are plotted in Fig. 3.16. We have already demonstrated that at Q, $g(Q) > f(Q)$; while at S, which is Eve's end of the curve, $f(S) > g(S)$. Now since the two curves corresponding to the two functions are in a different relation at S to that obtaining at Q, and since the curves are *continuous*, it follows that they must *cut* for at least one point P^* lying between Q and S. Hence at such a point

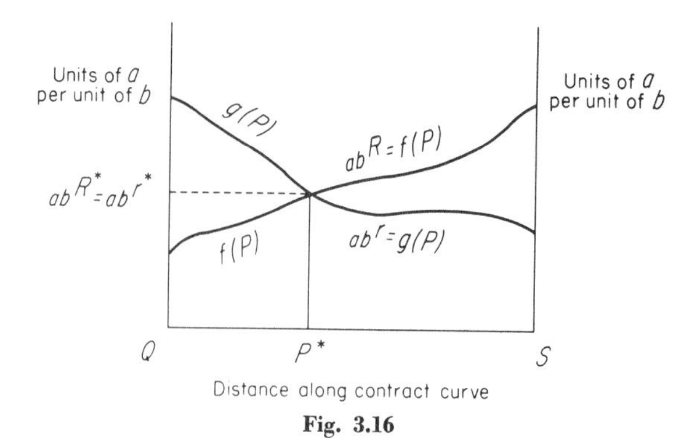

Fig. 3.16

P^*, the exchange ratio $_{ab}R^*$ equals the (common) *prs* of Adam and Eve $_{ab}r^*$, so that P^* is a point such as that illustrated in Fig. 3.15.

Notice carefully that this proof shows only that points such as P^* *exist*; it does *not* show that P^* is unique. The sole restrictions we have placed on the continuous curves are that $f(Q) < g(Q)$ and that $f(S) > g(S)$; the reader may amuse himself by drawing curves $f(P)$ and $g(P)$ which satisfy these restrictions yet yield many points of intersection which would correspond to many "efficient" exchange ratios. One simple sufficient condition for uniqueness is that $f(P)$ should rise steadily from Q to S, while $g(P)$ rises steadily from S to Q; as we shall see in the next chapter, this would be a severe restriction on the model, since it is certainly not implied by the axiom system.*

Let us review what we have proved. We have shown that *if* there is a trading set and *if* the contract curve is in the interior of the box, then—given the axiom system—there will always exist at least one exchange ratio between ale and bread such that, by each person's adjusting optimally (and independently) to it, each will be led to an allocation on the contract curve. Thus the mechanism we have described for obtaining efficient trades will always work, provided that the umpire (or computer) is able to calculate one of the "efficient" ratios. In the next chapter we shall deal with an umpire mechanism that is not assumed to be quite so clever, but which does almost as well by "searching out" an equilibrium exchange ratio by means of a systematic adjustment process.

Observe that the proof given requires the existence of a trading set, which is scarcely surprising, since if there is no possibility of trade, the concept of efficient trade is vacuous. Remembering a previous result—that if both parties bring something of both commodities to the exchange, there is always a trading set (apart from the special case of Fig. 3.4(c))—we can say that this

* If Marshall's Postulate holds, then the curve $_{ab}r = g(P)$ becomes a horizontal straight line, and the curve $_{ab}R = f(P)$ rises monotonically from left to right. It follows that $_{ab}R^*$ will be unique and, of course, equal to the constant $_{ab}r$.

latter condition on the initial stocks will guarantee the existence of "efficient" exchange ratios, given an "interior" contract curve; otherwise we are not sure, and have to postulate the existence of a trading set as a separate condition.

In order to complete the whole proof, we have to show that the result is true also for those cases where the contract curve lies wholly or in part along the boundary of the box, as in Fig. 3.7. It will be convenient to reproduce essentially the same diagram, shown below.

Because of the "generalized tangency" property of the points P belonging to the contract curve, it is no longer true that Adam's *prs* of a for b will be equal to Eve's *prs* of a for b at each point P. Thus in Fig. 3.17, ${}_{ab}r^A$ is always *greater* than the corresponding ${}_{ab}r^E$ along QS, so that to each point P of the contract curve there are now *three* slopes, rather than two as before.

Let us denote, as before, the b-slope of the exchange line from t^0 to any point P on the contract curve by ${}_{ab}R = f(P)$, the b-slope of the indifference curve for Adam by ${}_{ab}r^A = g_A(P)$, and the b-slope of Eve's indifference curve by ${}_{ab}r^E = g_E(P)$. Then it is again clear that each of these three functions is a continuous function of P, and that an "efficiency" exchange line (such as t^0P^* in Fig. 3.17) requires $f(P^*)$ to lie *between* the values $g_E(P^*)$ and $g_A(P^*)$. In symbolic terms, instead of requiring $f(P^*) = g(P^*)$ as for the "interior" case, we require a P^* either such that $g_E(P^*) \leqq f(P^*) \leqq g_A(P^*)$ or such that $g_A(P^*) \leqq f(P^*) \leqq g_E(P^*)$, depending on where the contract curve is located on the boundary of the box. For any given QS, *either* $g_E(P) < g_A(P)$, *or* $g_A(P) < g_E(P)$ for all points P; we shall deal only with the first case, since the analysis of the other is essentially similar.

Now observe that, as before, we can make definite assertions about the situation obtaining at Adam's end of the contract curve. The b-slope of t^0Q will be *greater* than Adam's *prs* of a for b at Q, since C^{A0} is a convex curve; thus, $g_E(Q) < g_A(Q) < f(Q)$. Similarly it is easy to show that $f(S) < g_E(S) < g_A(S)$; and we may therefore draw the following analogue (Fig. 3.18) of Fig. 3.16.

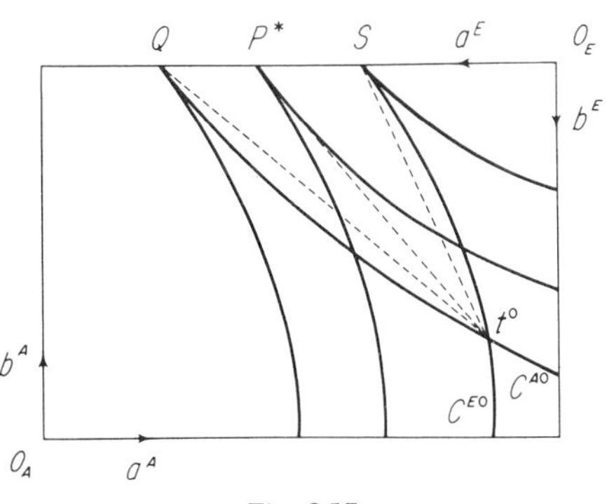

Fig. 3.17

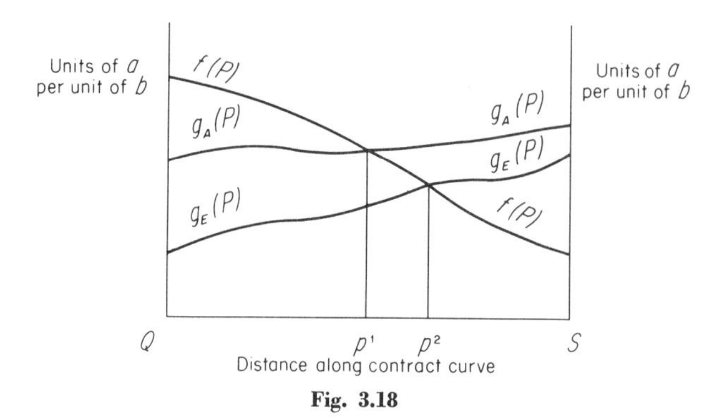

Fig. 3.18

Since the curves are continuous, it follows that $f(P)$ must cut both $g_A(P)$ and $g_E(P)$; and because $g_E(P) < g_A(P)$ for all P, it also follows that there will always exist a *range* of points P^* of the contract curve, here denoted by the segment P^1P^2, for all of which the required relations $g_E(P^*) \leqq f(P^*) \leqq g_A(P^*)$ hold. Hence there exists at least one whole *set* of "efficient" exchange ratios. This broadened result is not surprising, since the required efficiency ratios are required to satisfy inequalities, rather than equalities, so that there is much more "room" for the restrictions to be satisfied; once again conditions on the boundary are simpler than those in the interior. In the case illustrated in Fig. 3.17 and 3.18 there will be only one such connected set of efficient exchange ratios, since the f curve must be continuously downward sloping; but if the diagrams had shown the contract curve to be composed of separated pieces of the boundary of the box, joined by "interior" sections, then multiple sets of "efficient" ratios would have been possible.

(ii) Exchange Ratios and Prices

One way in which exchange ratios could be put into effect by the umpire would be for him to acquire a stock of counters from somewhere (as in many parlor games) and then to set *prices* on ale and bread in terms of those counters. Thus one unit of bread might be "worth" one counter, whereas one unit of ale might command two counters. These prices would imply that the exchange ratio of ale for bread would be $\frac{1}{2}$, since the counter obtained for one unit of bread could be used—and indeed in this model could only be used—to obtain $\frac{1}{2}$ unit of ale.

Having announced "counter-prices" p_a and p_b for ale and bread, respectively, the umpire could then issue to each contestant a number of counters equal to the counter-value of that contestant's initial stocks. Adam would receive $(p_a a^{A0} + p_b b^{A0})$ counters, and Eve $(p_a a^{E0} + p_b b^{E0})$. They would then be told to adjust optimally (i.e., in accordance with Axiom III) to the announced prices, by obtaining from the umpire that quantity of ale (bread) whose counter-value is equal to the value of the quantity of bread (ale) that they turned in. If we denote the new (optimal) positions taken by Adam and Eve by (a^{A1}, b^{A1}) and (a^{E1}, b^{E1}), respectively, it follows that

$$p_a a^{A1} + p_b b^{A1} = p_a a^{A0} + p_b b^{A0}$$

and

$$p_a a^{E1} + p_b b^{E1} = p_a a^{E0} + p_b b^{E0}$$

since, under the rules of the game, each person has to stay within the constraint of his limited initial counter-stocks. Adding these equations, we may write

$$\text{(W)}: \quad p_a(a^{A1} + a^{E1}) + p_b(b^{A1} + b^{E1}) = p_a(a^{A0} + a^{E0}) + p_b(b^{A0} + b^{E0}).$$

This simple equation is sometimes dignified with the name of *Walras' Law*, in honor of the man who first gave it prominence. Notice that it is *not* an identity, in the sense of following from our *definitions* of terms, but is derived instead from the Axioms of Selection and of Dominance, so that it is an implication of our *assumptions* about individual preferences. It is important to stress this, since the relation may be confused with another that looks very similar.

In assuming that Adam and Eve adjust optimally to the announced prices, there is—as we have seen—no presumption *whatever* that the bundles they select constitute a *feasible* trade; only if the announced exchange ratio is "efficient" will the individual optimal positions be compatible. Now consider *any* feasible trade, however brought about (i.e., consider *any* point in the box diagram, whether due to "optimal" adjustments or not). Because $a^{At} + a^{Et} = a^{A0} + a^{E0}$ for any trade t, and similarly for bread, it follows that for *any* counter-prices p'_a and p'_b, we have

$$p'_a(a^{At} + a^{Et}) = p'_a(a^{A0} + a^{E0})$$

and

$$p'_b(b^{At} + b^{Et}) = p'_b(b^{A0} + b^{E0})$$

from which, on adding, we get

$$\text{(T)}: \quad p'_a(a^{At} + a^{Et}) + p'_b(b^{At} + b^{Et}) = p'_a(a^{A0} + a^{E0}) + p'_b(b^{A0} + b^{E0})$$

which looks like (W) above. But clearly the resemblance is only superficial, for while (W) is deduced in an essential way from the axiom system and refers to optimal choices, (T) merely follows from the definition of a trade, and is therefore an identity, given that *t is* a feasible trade. One way of remembering (and reinforcing) the distinction is to realize that (W) is obtained by adding equations referring to *individuals*, while (T) results from adding equations dealing with *commodities*.

We have observed that an "efficient" exchange ratio has two quite separable characteristics: (1) it leads to optimal positions which constitute a feasible trade, since no excess demand for either commodity exists at such a ratio; (2) it leads to an *efficient* trade, so that neither party can improve upon the equilibrium allocation without hurting the other. Therefore, if the announced prices p_a^* and p_b^* are such that the ratio $p_b^*:p_a^*(\equiv {}_{ab}R^*)$ is "efficient," then characteristic (1) means that p_a^*, p_b^*, and the efficient allocation satisfy *both* (W) and (T). Characteristic (2) implies that for interior efficient allocations

$$ {}_{ab}r^{A*} = {}_{ab}r^{E*} = {}_{ab}r^* = {}_{ab}R^* = \frac{p_b^*}{p_a^*} $$

while for boundary positions either ${}_{ab}r^{A*} \leqq p_b^*/p_a^* \leqq {}_{ab}r^{E*}$, or ${}_{ab}r^{E*} \leqq p_b^*/p_a^* \leqq {}_{ab}r^{A*}$. Hence the personal rates of substitution will either be equal to, or will straddle, the inverse of the corresponding "counter-price" ratios (which, incidentally, will also be pure numbers). Thus a measure of the (common) relative urgency of the need for bread compared to that for ale at an interior equilibrium, a measure which is alternative to ${}_{ab}r$, is simply the ratio of the price of bread to that of ale. The higher this ratio is, the more "urgent" the need. To put it another way, equilibrium price ratios *are* simply "efficient" personal rates of substitution, a statement which is true for both interior and boundary positions (given a suitable interpretation for the latter).

Since the Axiom of Dominance implies that each commodity is always "positively" desired, one intuitively senses that the counter-prices can never be negative or zero but must always be positive. That this is indeed so is easily shown by reflecting that if any price, say p_b, were *not* positive, then each person could always increase his (or her) satisfaction by adding more bread (because of Axiom IV), without increasing his total expenditure of counters; if p_b were negative, this expenditure would actually decrease. Hence the "constraint" of the limited initial holdings of counters would be no constraint at all, and each person would proceed in the general direction of bliss by climbing swiftly (to use Pareto's phrase) "the hill of pleasure," the contours of which form the indifference map. But bliss would require —because of Axiom IV again—unlimited stocks of bread, and by hypothesis these are finite; so paradise cannot be regained this way after all. Given the axiom system, the effective working of this umpire's device *requires* each counter-price to be strictly positive; if the Axiom of Dominance did not hold, on the other hand, it is easily conceivable (and reasonable) that the price of a commodity, the desire for which is easily satiated, could be zero at an equilibrium position.

So far we have been rather vague about the exact status of the commodity called "counters" in the model, apart from the reasonable but implicit assumptions that no one wants the counters for their own sake, and that the "counter-price" of each counter is one counter. In a sense, counters have played the role of money in the system, since the assertion "the price of bread is one counter per unit" carries the quite definite implication that any person can go to where bread is sold (the umpire's trading post) and with one counter purchase one unit of bread, exactly as the statement "the price of bread is one dollar per unit" carries a similar implication about the "exchangeability" of bread and dollars. Since we want to avoid the complications inherent in models of an explicitly monetary economy, we shall now proceed to dispense with this device of "counters"; it has served its expository purpose.

To do so, we first introduce the idea of an abstract unit of account, to which we shall give the generic name of *guinea*. Like the actual British unit of that name, a *guinea* has no tangible existence but is merely a unit in terms of which prices are reckoned, as lawyers' fees are often so reckoned in England. In the same way that the pound sterling has the guinea price of 20/21 guineas, so our counters will have a *guinea*-price, say *c guineas* per counter. Then if the "counter-price" of a unit of bread is p_b counters, the *guinea* price is cp_b *guineas*. The ratio of the *guinea* price of bread to that of ale is then cp_b/cp_a, which is the same as the ratio of the counter-prices, and also equal to the ordinary exchange ratio.

Now in the assumed absence of any corporeal *guineas*, the bare statement that "the price of ale is one *guinea* per unit" carries no information that could conceivably influence anyone's behavior, and so—in a scientific theory—is mere noise. Only if the *guinea* prices of other commodities are available is information conveyed, and then only because people can then compare the relevant *guinea* price ratios. But since we have just demonstrated that these ratios are equal to the ordinary exchange ratios for any choice of *guinea*, it follows that we can choose a *guinea* (i.e., a unit of account) to suit our convenience. Sometimes it is useful to synthesize a *guinea* by the rule that the *sum* of all *guinea* prices of the commodities should be one accounting unit. But more often it proves useful to choose one of the ordinary commodities themselves to be a *guinea*. Thus from now on we will take the accounting price of ale always to be *one*, and reckon all prices in terms of this standard, or *numéraire* commodity, as Walras called it.

With this convention (for that is all it is), the "counter"-price ratio p_b/p_a can be written $\pi_b/1$, where π_b is to be interpreted as the "ale price" of bread. It is tempting to write this "relative price" ratio simply as π_b, but that would cause dimensional confusion, for $\pi_b/1$ is a pure number (both top and bottom having the dimension "units of ale"), while π_b is not. When we want to emphasize the pure magnitude of this "relative" price, we shall use a separate symbol p (with *no* subscript); but this is only for typographical convenience, since we already possess the symbol ${}_{ab}R$, which is always equal to p_b/p_a, and hence to $\pi_b/1$. From now on we shall use the word "price" *exclusively* in this relative sense, so that it is always identically equal to the relevant exchange ratio. The price ratio of ale is, of course, always 1, and the price of bread in terms of ale equal to π_b; hence the ratio is $\pi_b/1$, or p;

the reciprocal of this ratio, $1/p$, is equal to ${}_{ba}R$, the number of units of bread *per* unit of ale.

It must be emphasized strongly that all these various types of prices—"counter" prices, accounting prices, *numéraire* prices, even relative prices—are so much *superstructure*. What the theory determines is not the existence of these prices as such, but of *rates of exchange*, and particularly of equilibrium rates of exchange. As the reader has probably guessed, our omniscient umpire was merely a useful expository device by which to bring out most clearly the nature and existence of these equilibrium ratios, which are *embedded* in the exchange model, being the resultant of the interplay of the individuals' (axiomatized) preference structures and initial holdings of goods.

NOTES ON THE LITERATURE

A. A great deal of the analysis of the "statics" of exchange contained in this chapter is implicit, and much of it explicit, in F. Y. Edgeworth's endearing *Mathematical Psychics* (Kegan Paul, London, 1881). It was in that allusive and elusive book (in which a large slice of this purest of theory appeared in an appendix entitled "On the Present Crisis in Ireland"—Edgeworth was Anglo-Irish) that the contract curve first made its appearance, together with indifference curves. This work of Edgeworth on exchange is one of the few great insights into the nature of economic activity, in this regard standing on a par with such classical perceptions as the analysis of economic rent and the doctrine of comparative advantage; all of these are obvious once they have been grasped, but thousands of otherwise intelligent men seem never to understand them deeply enough to have their actions influenced thereby.

Apart from the work of Marshall and Walras, dealt with below, very little of the subsequent literature has until recently added significantly to the theory of bilateral exchange. W. E. Johnson ("The Pure Theory of Utility Curves," *Economic Journal*, 23, 1913, 483–513) systematized things a little, while A. L. Bowley (*Mathematical Groundwork of Economics*, Oxford, New York, 1924, Chapter 1) included a much more explicit treatment of the "box" construction, which is therefore often known as the Edgeworth-Bowley box. Several standard textbooks, such as those by Boulding (*Economic Analysis*, Harper, New York, 1941) and by Stigler (*The Theory of Price*, Macmillan, New York, 1946) have very brief treatments of bilateral exchange, while some of the more recent developments and generalizations are reported below.

B. No Comment.

C. (i) The term "conflict curve" for contract curve has been introduced by Boulding in connection with general conflict situations; see, for example, K. E. Boulding: *Conflict and Defense* (Harper, New York, 1962) Chapter 1.

Recent work by Thomas Schelling (*The Strategy of Conflict*, Harvard, Cambridge, Mass., 1960) has emphasized the role that economic-type reasoning can play in analyzing the nebulous concept of "bargaining strength."

C. (ii) Marshall's Postulate

Very little has been written on the dynamics of pure barter since the original work of Edgeworth (*op. cit.*) and of Marshall; the latter's analysis is contained chiefly in Appendix F of his *Principles of Economics* (see the Guillebaud variorum edition, published for the Royal Economic Society by Macmillan, New York, in 1961, Volume I, pp. 791–93).* In order to understand the role that Marshall's Postulate played in his theory, it is important to realize: (a) that as his editor tells us (Volume II, p. 790), the subject matter of the Appendix on Barter was in the first four editions placed at the end of the second chapter (entitled "Temporary Equilibrium of Demand and Supply") of Book V; and (b) that Book V was itself the original kernel of the *Principles* from which, in Marshall's own words, he extended "gradually backwards and forwards" until the entire volume was written (II, 7).

The recent publication of some very illuminating correspondence written in 1891 between Marshall, Edgeworth, and Berry (a Cambridge mathematician) (II, 791–98) shows that Marshall realized very clearly (as Edgeworth did not) that his Postulate meant that the barter process was determinate in everything but the quantity of the commodity whose marginal utility was constant. It is arguable that his analysis of barter processes was formulated at the same time as his subtle analysis of adjustment paths in foreign trade, and therefore it could be maintained that his adoption of the Postulate was *originally* meant as a self-conscious attempt to resolve the "problem of the path" of bartering processes, rather than as an assumption to validate his better-known constructions, such as consumer's surplus, in the static theory of demand (remember that Book III—on demand—was written after Book V). In any event, it is now very clear that the Postulate was not an afterthought, but a device deliberately adopted to secure determinacy in the barter process.†

We must now demonstrate the relation between Marshall's version of his Postulate and ours. For this purpose, a *little* knowledge of partial differentiation is required (the reader uninterested in technical details may skip this

* This edition supersedes the eighth, which appeared in 1920 (Marshall died in 1924), and it is therefore known as the "ninth." Just as Beethoven's Ninth has a chorus, so Marshall's ninth has a commentator, whose valuable comments and editorial additions form Volume II.

† Paul Samuelson's discussions of the Postulate in this connection (see footnote on p. 80 of his "Constancy of the Marginal Utility of Money" in *Studies in Mathematical Economics and Econometrics* (ed. by Lange, McIntyre, and Yntema, Chicago U.P., Chicago, Ill., 1942); and p. 190 of his *Foundations of Economic Analysis*, Harvard, Cambridge, Mass., 1947) do not give credit to Marshall for perceiving the difficulties of what Samuelson himself would call the analysis of true dynamic stability in the case of barter.

section without loss of continuity). For a given representation u of a preference structure, let u_a be the first-order partial derivative with respect to a, and u_b the corresponding symbol for b; we choose a representation u such that both partials are continuous functions of their arguments. Then in Marshall's (and almost everybody else's) terminology, u_a is the "marginal utility" of a, and u_b the "marginal utility" of b; it follows from Axiom IV that each of these is always positive. In terms of indifference curves, u_a is the rate of movement *up* the preference "surface" in the direction parallel to the ale axis from a given point, while u_b is the similar rate of movement parallel to the bread axis.

We can express personal rates of substitution in terms of these concepts. For let us reduce holdings of bread by one (arbitrarily small) unit; the loss in "utility" approximates closely to u_b units. Now how many units of *ale* are needed to compensate for this loss of utility? Clearly u_b/u_a units, for these will to a close approximation yield $u_a(u_b/u_a)$ units of utility, just balancing the previous loss of u_b units. Therefore u_b/u_a (which is a pure number) measures the amount of ale needed to compensate the individual for the loss of one unit of bread, i.e., it measures the magnitude of the personal rate of substitution of ale for bread. Notice that if we used another representation v (where, necessarily, dv/du is positive), then $v_b/v_a = v_u u_b/v_u u_a = u_b/u_a$, so that all statements involving *ratios* of marginal utilities are independent of the choice of representation (as we emphasized in the discussion of the *prs* in Chapter 2).

Let us first show that Marshall's version of the Postulate implies ours. His states that u_a is a constant, while ours states that u_b/u_a is independent of a, depending solely on b; this latter condition may be written $u_b/u_a = g(b)$, where the Axiom of Convexity implies that g is a *decreasing* function of b (since the *prs* always increases as ale is substituted for bread). Now if $u_a =$ constant, u itself can have only linear terms in a, which accordingly drop out on differentiation. Therefore u must be of the form $u(a, b) = f(b) + Ka + C$, where f is a function with a continuous positive first derivative f', K is a positive constant, and C is a constant of integration. Differentiating u, we get $u_b/u_a = f'(b)/K$, which may be written $g(b)$ since f' depends only on b. Because f' and K are positive, g is positive; and because Marshall assumes that b enjoys *diminishing* marginal utility, $f''(b)$—the second derivative—is negative. Hence $g'(b)$ is negative, and g a decreasing function of b, as required. *Q.E.D.*

Thus Marshall's version implies ours; but the converse is not true. The simplest way of proving this is actually to exhibit a function satisfying all our conditions and not Marshall's. Let $u(a, b) = be^a$, where e is the base of the natural logarithms. Then $u_a = be^a$, which is positive (for $b \neq 0$) and not constant, thus contradicting Marshall's version of the Postulate; but $u_b = e^a$, so that $u_b/u_a = 1/b$, which is a *decreasing* function of b alone. Thus the function shown is a valid representation of a preference structure satisfying the axiom system plus our version of Marshall's Postulate; but it does not satisfy his version.*

This is scarcely surprising, for his version—unlike ours—does not involve ratios of marginal utilities, so is *not* invariant with respect to choice of representation. This can be seen clearly if we consider the admissible representation $v = \log_e u$, where u is defined as above. Then $v(a, b) = \log b + a$, from which $v_a = 1$, a *constant*, while of course v_b/v_a equals $1/b$ as before. Hence by suitable choice of function we have produced a representation where *both* versions hold.

It follows that the original version of Marshall's Postulate is inadmissible in a theory based on preference orderings and not on measurable utility. But the use to which Marshall actually puts the assumption in his theory of barter does not depend on "cardinal utility," but only on the "independence" aspect which we have shown to be perfectly compatible with the axiom system, although of course it is a very stringent further assumption.†

D. (i) The device of the "umpire" is not in Edgeworth, but has been greatly used in modern work on the theory of allocation. To take it back no earlier, a similar device was employed (for the case of *production*) by Barone in Appendix A (written in 1908) to *Collectivist Economic Planning* (ed. by Hayek, Routledge, London, 1935). The line continues through Lange (*On the Economic Theory of Socialism*, Macmillan, 1938) and Lerner (*The Economics of Control*, Macmillan, 1944) to emerge full-blown (again for the case of production) in T. C. Koopmans' pioneering article: "Analysis of Production as an Efficient Combination of Activities," in *Activity Analysis of Production and Allocation* (ed. by Koopmans Wiley, New York, 1951) 33–97; see also the first of his *Three Essays on the State of Economic Science* (McGraw, New York, 1957).

In recent work on the theory of exchange, the umpire is often referred to as the "Secretary of the Market" (see, e.g., H. Uzawa: "Walras' Tâtonnement in the Theory of Exchange," *Review of Economic Studies*, 27, 1960, 182–94).

D. (ii) This treatment of the various kinds of prices is greatly influenced by that given by Don Patinkin (*Money, Interest and Prices*, Row, Evanston, Ill., 1956, 17–19), even to the use of his illuminating example of the British guinea. Although these problems are not of great importance for the main part of this book, which deals only with a "real" economy, it is very important to make the distinctions clear so that the transition to a study of monetary economies may get off to a good start.

* The representation is invalid only on the axis $b = 0$, where the *prs* is undefined; but from the analysis of Chapter 2, Section D(vi), we would expect minor trouble here, which can be overcome along the lines indicated in that subsection.

† It is only fair to point out that Marshall seemed to be under the impression (see e.g., I, 845, last paragraph of Note XII *bis*, and II, 797, last paragraph) that the way of writing the representation adopted by Edgeworth, viz.: $U(a, b)$ rather than $u_1(a) + u_2(b)$—where u_1 and u_2 are separate functions—meant that his Postulate could not be employed. This indicaets that he was probably not aware of the *exact* role played by the Postulate in his theory of barter; but he was very clear as to its consequences.

4

THE ATTAINMENT OF EQUILIBRIUM PRICES IN BILATERAL EXCHANGE

A. AN ADJUSTMENT MECHANISM AND ITS CONVERGENCE

The chief drawback of the umpire mechanism discussed in the last chapter, as a tool for actually obtaining the equilibrium positions, is its enormous appetite for information. In order to calculate what are probably at most just a few exchange ratios,* it has to engorge complete information on everybody's commodity endowments and preferences. This is bad enough in the case of ordinary bilateral exchange but becomes quite intolerable in very large exchange systems. It is therefore very desirable to invent a mechanism which would lead the protagonists to an equilibrium position, without having first to digest so much knowledge.

One such device would be analogous to what is known in engineering and physiology as an *adaptive control system*, a simple example of which is the usual household heating system controlled by a thermostat. Systems of this type contain a signal variable (or variables), a control mechanism and a controlled variable (or variables). The *signal variable* reflects the state of the system in such a way that a desirable level of performance of the system corresponds uniquely to a certain target level (or range) of the signal variable; if the system is not performing satisfactorily, then this is reflected by a value of the signal variable that diverges from the target value. The *control mechanism* registers this divergence, and by means of a built-in "feedback" device alters the value of the *controlled variable* in such a way as to bring the system to its desired level. Thus in our example the temperature reading (the signal variable) indicates, by a low value, that the inhabitants of the house are colder than they wish to be (the state of the system), and the thermostat (the control mechanism) increases the flow of fuel (the controlled variable) so as to bring the thermometer up to its preset level.

* It has been emphasized that more than one "efficient" price may exist, and it is in fact possible—though most unlikely—that there might be infinitely many, as we shall see.

In applying these ideas to the invention of a new umpire mechanism, we first have to select a signal variable. The exchange ratio seems an obvious candidate at first glance, but then we realize that we do not know what its target levels should be; indeed, it is one of the main purposes of the whole control system to find these out. So we have to think of something else which will infallibly indicate when the system is in equilibrium. Now the previous analysis has shown that, although in barter a feasible trade is seldom efficient, if a price mechanism is used, then an attainable trade is *necessarily* on the contract curve. So a characteristic of equilibrium in the latter case must be the absence of excess demand and excess offer of both commodities.

Since demand for one commodity can only be effectuated by an offer of the other, an excess demand for one commodity must correspond to an excess offer of the other, from which it follows that if the excess demand for just *one* of the two commodities vanishes, then the whole system is in equilibrium. Following the customary usage, we therefore take the *excess demand for bread* (denoted by b_e) as the signal variable; by convention, negative values of this signify an excess offer of bread. If the target value of zero is attained, then this implies harmony in the proposed demand and offer of both bread and ale, while a nonzero value corresponds to imbalance in both commodities.

The control mechanism *is* simply the new kind of umpire, who once more could be a suitably programmed computer. The controlled variable is the price of bread; by adjusting this, the umpire causes the system to react so as to change the value of the signal variable of excess demand. The main problem is to program the umpire-computer correctly, i.e., to determine a rule by which, when excess demand appears, price is adjusted in a direction that will tend to wipe it out.

Since everyday experience suggests that an increase in its price tends to reduce the quantity demanded of any commodity, it seems sensible to instruct the umpire to *increase* the price if the excess demand is positive, and to *lower* the price if the signal is negative. Thus a reasonable and complete computer program for this problem would run as follows: the umpire "calls" a price of bread, more or less at random but as close as he can to what he believes to be an equilibrium price (this guess might well be based on past experience). Each "player" then determines his optimal position and hands to the umpire a ticket on which is written his offer of either ale or bread, together with his corresponding demand (subject to the total amount available) for bread or ale. The umpire then compares these tickets. If the *net* demand for bread is zero, then the existing price is "correct"; if not, then he should raise the price if bread is in excess demand, and lower it if the reverse is true. The players then react to the new price and write new tickets, and the umpire again calculates b_e, once again adjusting p according to the rules. This process goes on until it *converges* to an equilibrium price $p^*(={}_{ab}R^*)$, at which the signal variable is zero and the system in "efficient" equilibrium.

Notice that this program does not require the control mechanism to learn directly *any* of the information that was necessary for the earlier umpire. What is reported to this new referee is simply the optimal position of each protagonist at each price, which means essentially that most of the required processing of information is *decentralized* to the individual parties to the exchange. It is they who have to digest the information provided by their preference structures and initial holdings in order to emerge with an equilibrium position at each price. All that the new umpire has to do is to add up the net demand for bread at each price and then to adjust that price in the direction indicated by the sign of the resulting total net (or excess) demand.

But what if the mechanism does *not* converge to an equilibrium position? Then either it would go on forever encircling an equilibrium, or it would send price either to zero or to plus infinity. In any event, the control system would have failed, and we would have to write a new computer program. We will now prove that these fears are almost entirely unjustified and that, under the conditions assumed in our analysis of bilateral exchange, the mechanism will almost always converge to an equilibrium.*

Let us first observe that the new mechanism employs the device that in barter we called *recontract*, since not one of the offers and demands made out of equilibrium is binding on the participants, each being simply a hypothetical statement written down on a ticket. We would therefore expect that the mechanism enjoys the property possessed by such bartering processes, *viz.*: that the free exchange of information permitted by the recontracting mechanism should normally lead the process to the contract curve.† Later on we shall discuss briefly a control mechanism that does allow actual trading at nonequilibrium or (to use Hicks' useful word) "false" prices.

We now turn to an examination of how each person's optimal position is traced out as the price of bread is varied. It is convenient to take first a general view, which indicates in a simple and symmetrical manner the optimal positions with respect to *both* commodities; later we shall concentrate on the excess demand for bread alone. In Fig. 4.1 we present a slightly embellished version of Fig. 3.15.

Taking the initial point to be the usual "corner" allocation t^0, it is clear that for low values of the price ratio p (measured by tan β, where β is defined as above), bread commands far too little ale per unit to induce Adam to part with any; he therefore sticks at t^0. On the other hand, Eve would find

* This result is one of the few that do *not* generalize directly to multilateral exchange systems, unless they also involve only two goods.

† The adjustment process we have described is often called a Walrasian mechanism, since Walras was the first to lay stress on the role of excess demand (he did not use this actual term) in bringing the system to equilibrium. However there is little evidence that the mechanism used in his theory of exchange permitted recontract, so we have refrained from using his name for the process. Similarly, to some writers the process is known by the Walrasian word *tâtonnement*, but in fact he meant something considerably different by this word.

These questions of interpretation of the literature are dealt with in the Notes.

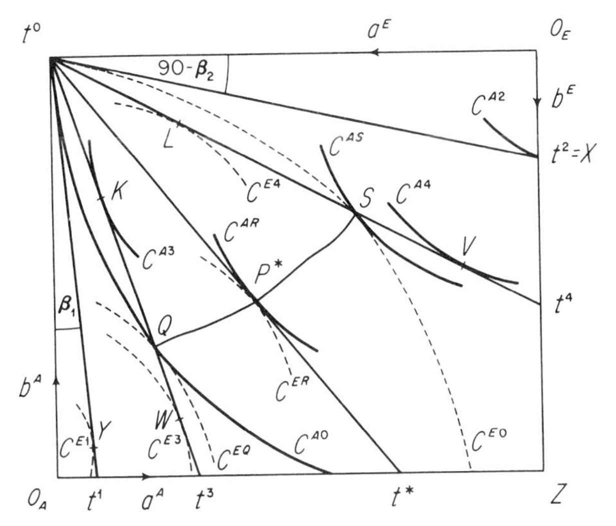

Fig. 4.1

$\beta_1 = \text{angle } O_A t^0 t^1$ $\quad \beta_* = \text{angle } O_A t^0 t^*$ $\quad \beta_2 = \text{angle } O_A t^0 t^2$

$\beta_3 = \text{angle } O_A t^0 t^3$ $\quad \beta_4 = \text{angle } O_A t^0 t^4$

$p^1 = \tan \beta_1$ $\quad p^* = \tan \beta^*$ $\quad p^2 = \tan \beta_2$

$p^3 = \tan \beta_3$ $\quad p^4 = \tan \beta_4$

bread very cheap and probably choose an optimal position (such as Y) which requires large quantities of it. Thus for all prices of bread up to p^1 (above which Adam will start to offer bread), there will be a positive excess demand for bread, and therefore the direction of price movement will always be upward.

Immediately beyond p^1 excess demand will shrink, and it is possible that it will fall so fast that it very soon becomes negative. But we do know that at p^3 it will be positive again, since at that price (as we have seen in Fig. 3.15) Adam will choose a point such as K, somewhere in the interior of B^{A0}, while Eve will make an optimal selection outside B^{A0}, at a bundle such as W. This latter decision takes place because at p^3 her attainable set is the quadrilateral $O_E t^0 t^3 Z$, and her indifference curve (C^{EQ}), which is tangent to C^{A0} at Q, actually cuts into the interior of this set; it follows by the Axiom of Convexity that Eve will select a point (W) on $t^0 t^3$ which is on the *other* side of Q from K. Hence W will be to the right of K and below it, and there will be a corresponding positive excess demand for bread. Therefore at p^3 price will be moving also in an upward direction.

A similar analysis may be applied for very high values of p (and therefore low ${}_{ba}R$'s), at which Eve will not think it worthwhile to trade at all, while Adam will probably want to buy large quantities of ale. In Fig. 4.1, at the price ratio p^2 he will enjoy a boundary tangency at $X(=t^2)$, at which he will therefore want to buy all of Eve's ale in return for $O_E X$ of bread. Thus there will be an excess offer of bread at p^2, and the price will therefore be lowered, following the rules of the adjustment mechanism. Again it is possible that the excess offer will be reduced so rapidly that it quickly becomes negative (and so b_e positive), but reasoning as before, we can show that in any event b_e will be negative at p^4, leading to a further fall in price.

Thus we have shown that the pair of prices p^1 and p^2 form "reflecting barriers" as it were, as do the prices p^3 and p^4. If, on its way down, the price ratio reaches either the level p^1 or the level p^3, it is promptly turned back up again; and conversely for the barriers p^2 and p^4. Moreover we have already shown that there is at least one price ratio, p^*, lying between p^1 and p^2, such that b_e is zero; so we have gone some way in proving the convergence of the mechanism.

Now let us look at another way of illustrating the same situation, which enables some of its aspects to be more readily understood. Figure 4.2 is obtained by rotating Fig. 4.1 by a 180° turn about the axis t^0O_E, so that Fig. 4.2 is an inverted mirror image of the former diagram.

Along the abscissa we measure both the amount of ale offered by Eve and that demanded by Adam, while the ordinate registers the bread offered by Adam and demanded by Eve (if t^0 had been an interior point, we would have had to include a southwest quadrant as well). The price ratios are still measured by the tangents of angles such as $O_At^0t^1$, but the orientation of these angles is different. The main novelty lies in the broken curves t^0KP^*VX and t^0LP^*WY; the first of these traces out the optimal positions assumed by Adam (i.e., regular and boundary tangencies) as the price of bread is increased from zero, while the second is the similar locus for Eve. Notice that

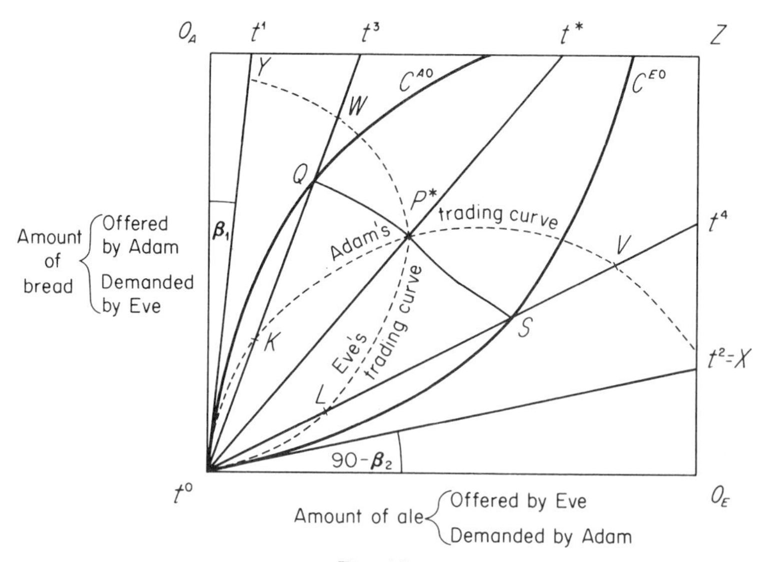

Fig. 4.2

these curves are determined by each person's preference structure *together with* his (or her) original holdings of goods; different initial endowments would imply different curves. It should also be noted that we need not investigate the behavior of these curves outside the "pencil" $t^1t^0t^2$, since only for points between these lines will *both* parties be prepared to trade.

Each of these curves indicates the trading position assumed by the relevant person at each price, from which it follows that, given the axiom system, neither party will ever be found in a position *off* his (or her) curve. It therefore seems appropriate to call these the *trading curves* of the parties concerned.* The information utilized by the new umpire mechanism is entirely contained in these two curves, which summarize all the knowledge of the individuals' behavior needed for its operation.

At a price ratio which corresponds to a point of intersection of the two trading curves (as at p^*), the trading positions taken up by each person are in harmony, and the proposed trade is feasible and therefore "efficient." If the two curves do not intersect each other for a given exchange line, then the corresponding price is not at the equilibrium level. This leads us to observe that, because of the Axiom of Convexity, no ray (or exchange line) through the origin t^0 can cut a given trading curve more than once; for the contrary would imply (from Fig. 3.13, for example) that the indifference curves are not convex. This restriction implies that Adam's trading curve will tend to be concave to the ale axis, and Eve's concave to the bread axis. It also enables us to use them to provide rules about the direction of price movement.

Thus for any price, such as p^3, let us suppose that the corresponding ray (t^0t^3) cuts Adam's trading curve (at K) *before* it cuts Eve's curve (at W). It follows that W lies above and to the right of K, so that there is positive excess demand for bread (and so an excess offer of ale) leading to a *rise* in the price ratio from p^3. Similarly, if Eve's curve cuts an exchange line nearer to t^0 than does Adam's (as with t^0t^4), then b_e is negative and the price of bread should fall. These rules are very simple to apply, and show that in the case illustrated in Fig. 4.2 the adjustment mechanism always converges (provided, as we shall see, that it works "smoothly") to the equilibrium point p^*. Moreover we can see that, if an "efficient" equilibrium is unique, then the mechanism must necessarily converge to that equilibrium, in view of the various reflecting boundaries.

We will defer until Section B a proof that the axiom system does *not* imply that equilibrium is unique, and for now simply take it as a provisional assumption that the trading curves can "legally" cut more than once. It is not in fact difficult to draw trading curves that intersect many times between t^0t^3

* A term more usually employed is *offer curve*, but this has little historical justification and, more importantly, has the serious defect of arbitrarily singling out one side of the proposed trade, the offer, rather than of keeping in view the essential symmetry of the whole analysis. On this question of terminology see the Notes.

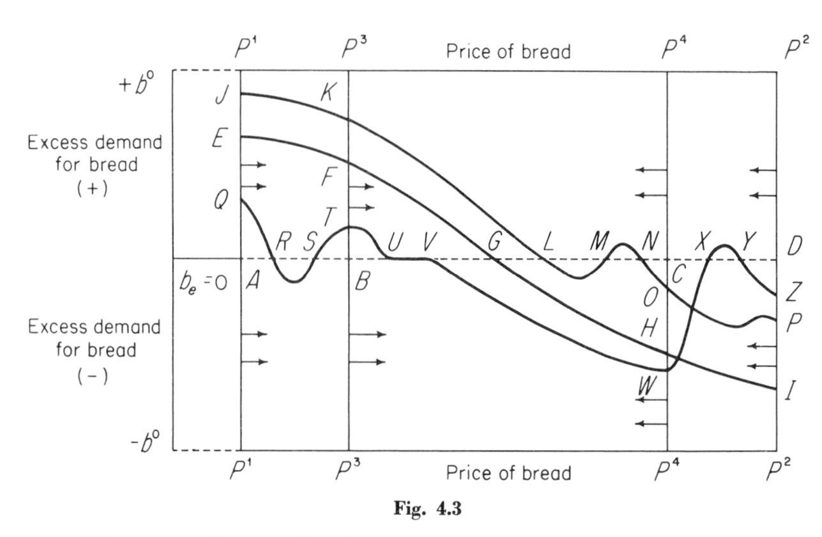

Fig. 4.3

The arrows show the direction of price movement at the prices indicated.

and t^0t^4, although much less likely (but still possible) to have the same thing happen between t^0t^1 and t^0t^3 (and/or between t^0t^2 and t^0t^4). All such points of intersection naturally belong to the contract curve, however, and the resulting diagram is far too cluttered to make it a useful analytical tool.

In order to continue the analysis of convergence, therefore, we turn our attention to the signal variable, which is the excess demand for bread. We obtain a convenient diagram by reading off from the trading curves the amounts of bread that are demanded and/or offered at each price, and so obtain the excess demand at each price. Because of Axioms V and VII, each quantity is a well-behaved, continuous function of the price of bread, and therefore so is the excess demand curve, examples of which are shown in Fig. 4.3.

This diagram illustrates three possible excess demand curves, one of which (*EFGHI*) is "normal," while the others are distinctly odd, though not inconsistent with the axioms. In each case the reader should check carefully that the curve obeys the two sets of restrictions that the theory has implicitly placed on them: (1) Since to each price there corresponds a unique demand and a unique offer (given the initial holdings), then the excess demand must also be unique; therefore no excess demand curve can cut a vertical line more than once. (2) At p^1 and at p^3 the excess demand must be positive, and at p^2 and p^4 it must be negative.

Using Fig. 4.3, we find it a simple matter to demonstrate several important propositions. First let us note that we can immediately prove the existence of an equilibrium price ratio between the limits p^3 and p^4. Because the excess demand curve must lie above the abscissa at p^3 and below it at p^4, it follows that it must cut the line $b_e = 0$ for at least one price between those limits. This proof, though even easier than the proof of existence given in Section D(i) of Chapter 3, neither contains nor is contained within that earlier result. On the one hand, the present treatment assumes the applicability of the selected control mechanism, while the earlier proof was entirely independent of any assumptions about the nature of the adjustment processes; on the other hand, the analysis in 3, D(i) only proved that an equilibrium existed *somewhere* on the contract curve (i.e., between p^1 and p^2),* while this proof demonstrates that an "efficient" price must lie between the narrower limits of p^3 and p^4.

Turning now to the problem of the uniqueness of equilibrium, let us simply describe the characteristics of the three cases shown, leaving their analysis for a little later. The "normal" case (*EFGHI*) is straightforward, giving just one crossing of $b_e = 0$ at G, and therefore just one equilibrium. The curve *JKLMNOP* is more complicated, with three crossings between p^3 and p^4, giving three equilibrium points. The last case (the curve *QRSTUVWXYZ*) is the most curious of all, giving four isolated equilibrium points (outside the limits p^3 to p^4) at R, S, X, and Y, and an infinity of equilibrium points in the range UV. Notice that (apart from ranges of this latter type) because of the restrictions at the "barrier" prices, there can only be an even number of points of intersection between p^1 and p^3, and between p^2 and p^4; and an odd number of crossing points between p^3 and p^4; and therefore only an *odd* number of equilibria altogether.

Now let us look at the reasons for these varying types of behavior of the curves. In the "normal" case, the excess demand curve slopes downward throughout, which implies that excess demand is a strictly *decreasing* function of price. This leads to the suspicion that multiple points of equilibrium can only occur if, over one or more ranges, excess demand does not fall as price increases. This suspicion is confirmed by an examination of the other two cases, where multiple equilibria only occur either where excess demand increases with price or where it is constant (the segment UV in the third case). Notice that the condition is only *necessary*, not sufficient, as a glance at the section OP will show.

It follows that a necessary condition for multiple equilibria (at least in simple bilateral exchange) is that *either* Adam's offer of bread must not increase steadily as the price of bread increases or Eve's demand for bread must fail to decrease as its price rises; if both phenomena occur, of course, the probability of multiple intersections is increased. In the next section we will show that these alternative necessary conditions *can* occur within the model, though they are perhaps not very likely to do so.

* For those readers who doubt the truth of this, observe first that any equilibrium must lie in the trading set, i.e., within the "pencil" $t^1t^0t^2$. Now turn to Fig. 3.16 and, noting that $f(Q)$ equals p^3, let the function f turn downward immediately to the right of Q. Then g and f can intersect at a point below $f(Q)$ and need intersect nowhere else, which proves the above assertion.

Before dealing with this, let us complete our discussion of the convergence properties of the adjustment mechanism. First note that if the umpire adjusts price in a very jerky way, with big jumps from one announced price to another, there is a possibility that an approach will not be made to an equilibrium, but that oscillations of perhaps increasing amplitude may set in. Since we have already dealt with a similar phenomenon in the case of barter (see the discussion following Fig. 3.11), we will not stop to examine this, except to note that the analogy with a sluggish thermostat (as in the office where this is being written) is complete.*

We shall therefore assume that the umpire is reasonably efficient and moves price in a "smooth" and sensitive manner. In the first case, such a continuous mechanism would necessarily approach the unique equilibrium point G; as a corollary, if equilibrium *were* established at G and somehow disturbed, the control mechanism would necessarily return it from whence it came. This "attractiveness" of G is usually expressed by saying that G is a point of *stable equilibrium.* We will adopt this terminology, with the strong warning that it is *not* the point itself that is stable, but *the point considered in relation to the adjustment mechanism concerned.* If we had adopted a (foolish) mechanism which lowers price with a positive excess demand and raises it with an excess offer, then G would have been an *unstable* equilibrium point (i.e., all sequences would have diverged from it, and if it had by chance been established, subsequent slight deviations would send the system rushing away from it).

It follows from this terminology and our previous analysis that if there are a finite number of equilibrium points then: (1) in the range p^3 to p^4, the first point from the left is stable, the second unstable, and so on, with the last point in the range being stable; (2) in the range p^1 to p^3, the first point from the left is stable, the second unstable, and so on, with the last point unstable; (3) in the range p^4 to p^2, the first point from the right is stable, the second unstable, with the last again unstable. Thus stable equilibria alternate with unstable equilibria, and the two "outermost" equilibria are always stable. Points inside such ranges as UV are usually described as possessing *neutral stability*, since slight disturbances in the range simply roll one equilibrium point to another nearby. The end points of such ranges will either be *one-sidedly* stable (U and V) or unstable (if the curve had cut $b_e = 0$ the other way).

But this discussion of stable and unstable *points* really obscures the main problem at issue, which is the convergence of the whole control system. In this essential aspect, it is clear from the preceding analysis that—barring very

* An interesting situation occurs if we assume that one of the "players," say Eve, reacts not to the current price called by the umpire, but to the price called before that (ignore, for the sake of argument, how such a mechanism could get started). Suppose then that the umpire is also sluggish and moves a price that was substantially above an equilibrium to one somewhat below it. It is then possible with this dilatory Eve that, even with "normal" curves, there might be excess "offer" at the low price, resulting in a *fall* in price rather than the required increase. Many such odd patterns can be devised by assuming differing lags in response, and an even more complicated (but realistic) model by supposing that these lags obey some probability law.

odd cases of extreme jerkiness in the umpire-mechanism—the adjustment process will *always* converge toward some equilibrium position or other, no matter from where it starts; the presence of the most bizarre types of multiple equilibria makes no difference to this important conclusion.

B. THE POSSIBILITY OF MULTIPLE EQUILIBRIA

We have just proved, among other things, that isolated multiple equilibria can exist only if (i) the amount offered is sometimes a *de*creasing function of price, and/or (ii) the quantity demanded is sometimes an *in*creasing function of price. It follows that, given the adjustment mechanism, unstable equilibria can occur only if at least one of these conditions is fulfilled. But it is clear that it is the existence of multiple equilibria, rather than of "local" instability, which those conditions primarily make possible. For with a different adjustment mechanism (as we have seen), equilibrium positions which were unstable under the old mechanism may be "stabilized"; but the same set of equilibria will persist in each case, for this set is determined by the "statical" properties of the trading curves and have nothing to do directly with the adjustment process assumed.

In this section we shall demonstrate: (1) that the axiom system allows conditions (i) and (ii) to occur, (2) the exact circumstances under which they do occur, and therefore (3) that multiple equilibria in bilateral exchange are rather unlikely to exist. The proof that we shall give simultaneously exhibits the possibility of both (i) and (ii).

In Fig. 4.4, let us suppose that a price $p^1 (\equiv \tan \beta_1)$ is called to begin with, and that Adam moves to his optimal position K, at which he trades t^0L bread for t^0M ale. Now let the umpire raise the price of bread to $p^2 (\equiv \tan \beta_2)$, and consider Adam's new optimal position along t^0t^2. Since his old attainable

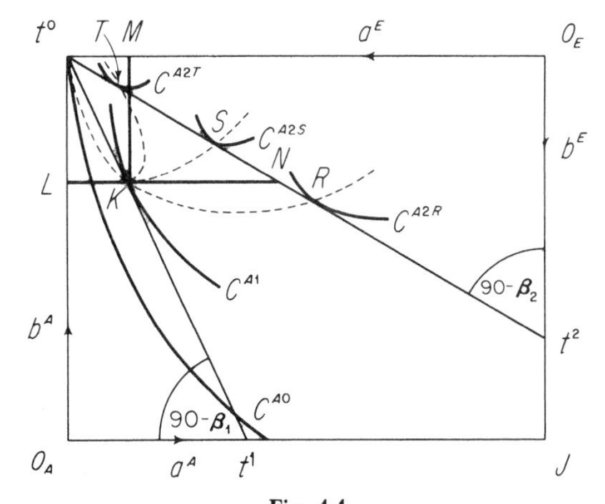

Fig. 4.4

set $O_A t^0 t^1$ is a small *subset* of the new one $(O_A t^0 t^2 J)$, he is *unambiguously* better off with the new price, which corresponds to the obvious economic fact that he has only one food to sell and the price that it can command has risen. If t^0 had been an interior allocation, at which he necessarily holds ale as well, the rise in price of bread would have lowered the relative price of ale, so that—depending on his preferences—the net result might not have been an improvement in his economic position.

Where on $t^0 t^2$ can his new optimal choice lie? Let us list the possibilities: (1) the rise from p^1 to p^2 means that, with the same offer of bread as before (KM) he could obtain far more ale (LN compared to LK); alternatively (2) he could move along some such trading curve as $t^0 KS$ to the point S. In a perhaps more "normal" case (3)—the move along $t^0 KR$—the relative fall in the price he has to pay for ale (i.e., the rise in the "terms of trade" open to him) will lead him to offer more bread in order to obtain yet more ale. In the really abnormal case (4)—the trading curve $t^0 KT$—not only does Adam offer less bread, but he also demands less ale, which means that he obeys condition (i) for bread and condition (ii) for ale.

We can now see that there are two aspects to this rise in the price of bread. On the one hand, Adam's original endowment of bread can now command a greater quantity of both ale and bread; this *endowment effect*, as it may be called,* is indicated by an enlargement of the original attainable set. On the other hand, the improvement in his economic position has not taken place in a symmetrical fashion, as it would have if price had not risen but instead an increase had occurred in his holdings of either ale or bread (or both). The improvement has been "biased" because ale is now relatively (to bread) much cheaper than it was; this is shown by the twisting of the boundary of the attainable set in the ale "direction."

These ideas can be made more precise in demonstrating the exact conditions under which multiple equilibria can (but not necessarily will) occur. In Fig. 4.5, we illustrate a method which allows us to do this.

We have already pointed out that the rise from p^1 to p^2 makes Adam definitely better off. Now let us perform the conceptual experiment of simultaneously raising the price of bread and reducing Adam's initial holdings of bread in such a way as to keep him just as satisfied—no more and no less—as he was at K. Geometrically, this corresponds to rolling him around the indifference curve C^{A1} as the exchange lines get flatter and flatter (with respect to the ale axis). Eventually we fetch up at the new higher price p^2, at which his optimal selection is G. The amount of bread that we have removed from Adam in this process—the "compensating variation"—is $t^0 F$, so that his initial endowment is now $O_A F$.

* In the theory of consumer's choice, essentially the same phenomenon is known as the *income effect* (and the trading curve as the *price-consumption curve*); but income is a flow concept, and here we are dealing with—and heavily emphasizing—the *stock* aspect of exchange. So it seems appropriate to mark this with a different name, although of course in strictly one-period analysis the distinction between stock and flow vanishes.

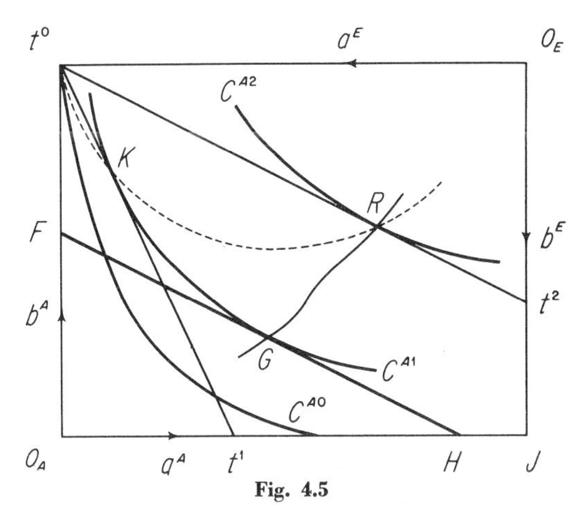

Fig. 4.5

By construction, Adam ranks position G equally with K, so that they belong to the same level of his preference structure, although in both of the other relevant aspects—initial holding and price ratio—they are quite different situations. Thus the conceptual experiment in a sense isolates the element in Adam's behavior which reflects the pure *change* in the terms on which the umpire offers alternatives to him; the experiment has removed any trace of the endowment effect. It is customary to describe this "pure" effect of a price change by the name *substitution effect*, a term which is very apposite, since it refers solely to the consequences of changes in the personal rate of substitution as Adam moves around his indifference curve through K.

This device of a "compensated" (by *minus* t^0F) price change also shows that the substitution effect always goes in a definite direction. Since the b-slope of t^0t^1 is less than the b-slope of t^0t^2, the optimum position on t^0t^2 must be to the right of and below that on t^0t^1 because of the Axiom of Convexity. This means that the substitution effect alone always leads to an increase in the quantity demanded of the commodity (ale) whose relative price has fallen and to an increase in the amount offered of the commodity (bread) whose price has risen.

The conceptual experiment which isolated the substitution effect can be continued to isolate the pure endowment effect; for having moved Adam from K to G with a compensated price change, we can now increase Adam's holdings of bread back up to t^0, *keeping the price of bread at* p^2. This procedure will sweep out a locus of optimum positions as the attainable set advances in a "symmetrical" way from O_AFH to $O_At^0t^2J$; a segment of this locus is shown in Fig. 4.5 as GR. Such curves are commonly called *Engel curves*,* and are

* This name is in memory of the father of modern budget studies (and not, as students often appear to believe, in honor of Marx's collaborator and disciple, Engels). In the theory of consumer's choice, the term *income-consumption curve* is perhaps more often used; for the same reason as that given in the last footnote, this usage is not entirely appropriate in the present context.

defined as the loci of optimum positions traced out by increasing attainable sets, corresponding to increasing endowments at a *given* exchange ratio. Each such ratio uniquely determines an Engel curve.

This new curve illustrates the endowment effect alone, uncontaminated by any "biases" introduced by changes in the price *ratio*. Fig. 4.6 illustrates the possible behavior of the Engel curve from the point G.

The "usual" case is for the endowment effect to be *positive* for both commodities; i.e., as total available endowments increase, the individual wishes to increase his holdings of both commodities. Geometrically, this corresponds to a movement from G along any Engel curve which is confined to the quadrant YGW. In examining the various possibilities in this case, let us look first at GR; this locus shows that at all stages both commodities enjoy a positive endowment effect, and that at the terminal position R, the amount of both bread and ale demanded has increased, compared with the position at G. The same is true for any terminal position between Z and W on t^0t^2, although it is quite possible that the Engel curve may "twist" on the way, as with GR'' and GR'''. In the first case, beyond the point V, increasing endowments reduce the quantity of ale demanded, while in the second the same conditions lead to a reduced demand for bread.

Thus although on balance the endowment effect on ale is positive from G to R'', on the way it is *negative* over at least one segment of the Engel curve; and similarly on at least one part of the curve GR''' the endowment effect on bread is negative, although over the whole stretch it is positive. Sometimes this phenomenon of a negative endowment effect is expressed by saying that the good involved is *inferior* over the relevant range. But this terminology is a little dangerous, for it is easy to slip into the habit of thinking a good to be inferior for *all* possible attainable sets, while—more importantly—this

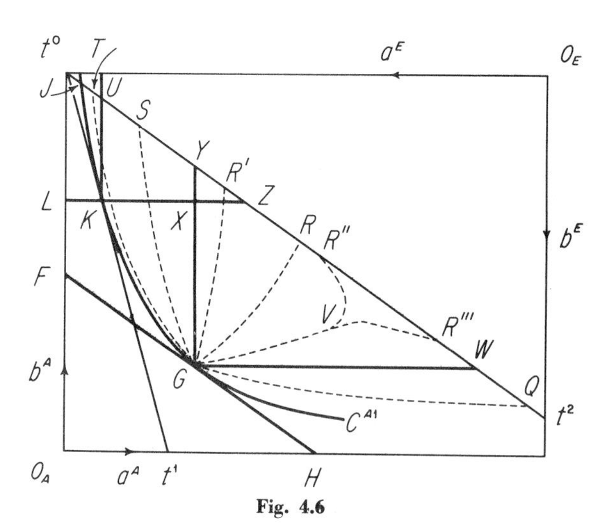

Fig. 4.6

usage directs attention away from the fact that the "inferiority" resides in Adam's preference structure and does not inhere in the commodity itself; one man's meat is another man's *poisson.**

As long as the terminal position of the Engel curve lies between Z and W, the *total* effects of the price change are "normal." The substitution effect and the endowment effect, being additive, both increase the quantity of ale demanded (e.g., in Fig. 4.5, R lies to the right of G, and G to the right of K). It is true that the positive endowment effect increases the quantity of bread demanded compared to G, but this is not strong enough to outweigh the substitution effect from K to G, which increases the amount offered; so, on balance, the rise in price of bread leads to an increase in the amount of bread offered (and an increase in the ale demanded).

A further case which produces the "normal" result is one in which the Engel curve from G to t^0t^2 on balance shows a *negative* endowment effect on bread (as with the curve GQ), and a positive endowment effect on ale (which follows from the obvious consideration that both endowment effects cannot be negative). In this case, the endowment effect *adds* directly to the increase in bread offered, and the total effect of the price change, from K to Q, is of "normal" type.†

So far no case has been such as to give rise to the possibility of multiple equilibria; let us now examine those that do. Even keeping to the "usual" case of endowment effects where both are positive, we can see from Fig. 4.6 that there is a range (between Y and Z) of terminal positions for the Engel curve which would lead Adam to offer *less* bread as a result of an increase in the price of bread, although demanding more ale. Thus in this range his behavior might be said to be "seminormal," since his "demand behavior" is not of the "abnormal" type (ii), while his "offer behavior" does conform to (i); but clearly there is really nothing odd about his actions, for both endowment effects *are* positive. We therefore conclude that the phenomenon of the amount offered *falling* with increase in price is quite possible, and simply follows from a preference structure assigning rather more urgency to his need for the commodity which he holds initially, and whose price has risen, than to his need for the commodity he does not hold; there is nothing at all "irrational" about it.

If we now consider the range of terminal points UY, within which the Engel curve from G on balance shows a *negative* endowment effect for ale, then we again obtain the seminormal case, with a fall in the relative price of

* Similar considerations apply in the theory of consumer's choice, although they are much less relevant for *market* demand functions than for individual demand functions.

† Let us note that, if Marshall's Postulate for ale holds, so that the indifference curve at W is parallel to the indifference curve at G, then the endowment effect on bread is always *zero*, and the Engel curve from G becomes the line GW. Alternatively, if the Postulate is adopted for bread, the Engel curve from G becomes GY. In the first case the total behavior is "normal," in the second, just on the boundary between "normal" and "seminormal" (for which see the following paragraphs).

ale still leading to an increase in its quantity demanded, since the negative endowment effect is swamped by the "positive" substitution effect (i.e., S is to the left of G, but G is so much to the right of K that S is also to the right of K). The amount of bread offered, however, again falls as the price of bread is increased.

Only in the extreme case, where the negative endowment effect on ale is so strong that the terminal position of the Engel curve on t^0t^2 lies in the range JU, will the amount of ale that Adam demands fall with a drop in the relative price of ale. In this really "abnormal" (though still possible) case, both conditions (i) and (ii) are satisfied, although of course (i) refers to the offer of *bread* and (ii) to the demand for ale.

Let us summarize these investigations and their implications for the probable shape of the trading curves, assuming that Eve's preference structure is of the same general type as Adam's. With a rise in the price of bread, Adam may or may not offer more bread (since his offer can fall even with a positive endowment effect), but it is extremely *un*likely that he will want to demand less ale (since this would require an extremely large and negative endowment effect).* Similarly, with the same rise in the price of bread (and hence fall in the relative price of ale), Eve may or may not offer less ale, but she is extremely unlikely to increase her demand for bread; she is very much more likely to decrease it.

Thus considering the influence of a rise in the price of bread on its excess demand, we see that Eve's "demand" share of the reaction will almost certainly be to *reduce* b_e, while Adam's "offer" share will probably be to reduce it also, although the presumption is not nearly so strong in his case. Even if his reaction is "perverse," i.e., his reducing his offer, the counterweight of Eve's reduced demand will probably cause a net fall in the excess demand. Therefore we would expect a rise in price to lead usually to a *fall* in excess demand: but if Adam holds large quantities of bread, and the price rise is substantial, and his need for bread is more "urgent" than his need for ale, then we might get the opposite reaction.

In Fig. 4.7, we examine the implications that these conclusions have for the shape of the trading curves (shown as solid curves). As the price of bread (tan β) rises, Adam will tend to increase his offer of bread and his demand for ale; beyond some point (such as C), he will probably lower his offer of bread as tan β increases. But it is extremely unlikely that he would also lower his demand for ale; if he did, then this would make his trading curve bend back toward the bread axis. Similarly Eve's curve will probably rise with positive slope to begin with, but her offer of ale might begin to contract beyond some point (such as D), and it is certainly possible that the trading

* In the language of the theory of consumer's choice, case (ii) can only occur if ale is a very strongly inferior good over the relevant range. Goods falling in this case (ii) are called *Giffen* goods, after the man who, it has been alleged (by Marshall), called attention to their existence. Giffen goods are necessarily inferior goods; and it is a common mistake to assert the converse proposition, that inferior goods are Giffen goods.

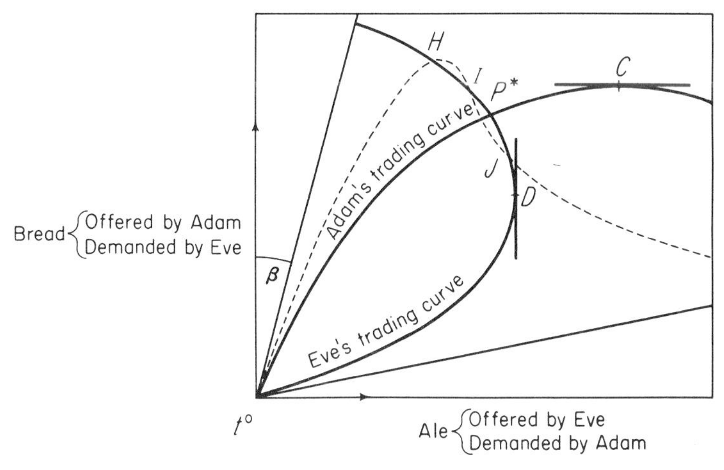

Fig. 4.7

curves will intersect in a range where one or more curves are exhibiting "seminormal" behavior. But, as with Adam, it is most unlikely that her trading curve will bend back towards the ale axis, which would indicate that her demand for bread falls with tan β.

This extreme unlikelihood of the curves "turning back on themselves" reduces the possibility of multiple intersections, but the latter are still certainly possible even with the more probable shapes, as with the broken curve (representing an alternative trading curve for Adam), which intersects Eve's curve in three places, at H, I, and J. Thus our conclusion must be that systems with unique equilibria are by far the most likely possibility, that it is by no means impossible that systems with a few equilibria might occur, but that a large finite number of equilibria is most unlikely, since this would probably imply "abnormal" behavior over some ranges; the chances of infinitely many equilibrium points, where the trading curves *coincide* over a range, seem even more remote.

C. AN ALTERNATIVE ADJUSTMENT MECHANISM

Earlier we noted that the control mechanism which we have been analyzing is highly analogous to Edgeworth's assumption of a recontracting barter process, in that at no point are any actual transactions made between the parties until the umpire-computer has announced an equilibrium price. If we are to use the theory of bilateral exchange as a help toward understanding real exchange systems, we must clearly relax this fanciful assumption, which has great pedagogic value, but which is otherwise very undesirable.

The most natural assumption to make is that if a "false" price is called such that positive excess demand for bread occurs, then *all* the available offer of bread is exchanged, and the price of bread is then raised, either by the umpire being informed of the existing "frustrated" demand, or by the frustrated Eve herself raising the price; a reverse procedure is followed if the "false" price leads to negative excess demand for bread.

We now have to investigate the convergence properties of this alternative adjustment mechanism, and for this purpose it is necessary to recall to mind the distinctions made in Chapter 3 C(ii), between three types of barter processes: (a) where the fraction of each commodity consumed at the end of each period is zero; (b) where the fraction is unity, but the *original* endowments are exactly replenished each period; (c) where the fraction of each commodity consumed lies between zero and unity, and no replenishment occurs. These distinctions are just as relevant to this "nonrecontracting" price adjustment mechanism and, as for barter, we shall take each case in turn; indeed we shall discover that much of the previous reasoning about barter is highly applicable to this adjustment mechanism.

In case (a), any transaction which takes place at a false price simply changes the allocation of fixed total quantities of both commodities. Therefore, reasoning as in the similar case with barter, we can argue that the process of reallocation brought about by varying prices will increase information over time (again, except for stupid traders), so that an equilibrium will eventually be obtained.

This is true also for case (b), if we are prepared to make sensible assumptions about behavior. Thus, suppose a price is called at which a noticeable excess demand occurs. Then in the next period, in which the parties again start out from t^0 (having wiped the slate clean, as it were), it seems only sensible to suppose that a price higher than before would be called by either the umpire or Eve herself. Summing up, we can say that—as in barter—cases (a) and (b) give no trouble.

But again—as in barter—it is quite otherwise with case (c). Here we cannot apply the usual analysis, and of course the problem of appropriate definition of efficiency occurs exactly as before. Because of this, the question of attainment of equilibrium diverges from the question of the attainment of "efficient" equilibrium, if we define efficiency as in case (c) for barter. It seems sensible to suppose that, even with actual consumption taking place at the end of each period, if excess demand still persists after the consumption has occurred, then price should rise. This will normally cut down excess demand, and so the process will go on in the usual way, with of course a much richer variety of oscillatory and other behavior possible in this more complicated case which admits consumption. A close approach to an equilibrium will usually be made by the system, although this equilibrium will itself be upset as further consumption takes place. The whole picture becomes blurred as this consumption continues, and also becomes less realistic, for to allow extensive withdrawals by actual consumption without permitting additions from production is a rather odd way for economic analysis to proceed.

The question of the attainment of "*efficient*" trades in case (c) is a much more doubtful matter, although of course the definition of "efficiency" in this case is somewhat less compelling than in the others. Obviously, the satisfaction of Marshall's Postulate will imply that the mechanism always leads to such a trade, as an examination of the detailed argument in C(ii) will show; but this assumption, which implies that the corresponding endowment effect is always zero (at least in the trading set), is very stringent. The Marshallian justification we gave earlier is certainly applicable in some situations, and approximately so in far more, so that we would sometimes expect "approximate efficiency"; but this is a vague and unsatisfactory way to leave matters, especially since there seem to be no other reasonably simple conditions to guarantee "efficiency" in this case.

One way to ease our theoretical consciences about case (c) is to ask just how important it really is. How many cases of actual exchange are likely to conform to this situation? In spite of its apparent realism, the answer would appear to be "not many." On the one hand, we have just pointed out that to assume a long process of consumption, without also bringing in production, is not very realistic; on the other hand, if there is only a small amount of consumption relative to initial stocks, then the situation is like case (a), which we have analyzed satisfactorily. In this connection it must be realized that actual situations always have a past history; the price that is initially called in the period under analysis—by umpire or protagonist—is not really called *au hasard*, to use a term of Walras, but is heavily influenced by the prices that have recently been ruling, which were probably not too far from an equilibrium. Thus deviations from equilibrium are not likely to be very great, save in quite exceptional situations, and the quantity of trading that occurs at significantly "false" prices is likely to be relatively small in comparison with the total volume of transactions that take place.

In the next chapter we will explore in greater detail this transition from the simple theory of bilateral exchange to the theory of markets.

NOTES ON THE LITERATURE

Walras' Discussion of Adjustment Mechanisms

A good deal of the modern literature on adjustment mechanisms, especially that written by the more mathematical economists, appears to misinterpret the nature of the adjustment mechanisms treated by Léon Walras in his

*Eléments d'Économie Politique Pure.** This note therefore attempts to clarify some of the issues involved.

It has often been assumed that Walras, in formulating the "excess demand" control mechanism, explicitly supposed that no actual transactions took place at false prices. But as Patinkin has convincingly demonstrated (*Money, Interest and Prices*, Row, Evanston, Ill., 1956, 377–85) in a brilliant analysis of the problem, this was true only for Walras' treatment of *production*; there is no evidence that Walras considered the problem of "false trading" to be at all serious for *exchange*. This is shown by his detailed discussion (*Elements*, 84–86) of his original example of exchange, where he explicitly states that trading does take place at "false" prices. Since he did not assume Marshall's Postulate (although he wrote the utility function in the "separable" form), logically he therefore should have dealt with the problem of the effect of such false trading on the convergence of the mechanism. That he did not do so—in spite of being a very logical man—seems to reflect his belief (p. 106) that exchange mechanisms converge very rapidly, so that "the current equilibrium price is determined within a few minutes," and the vast bulk of transactions therefore occurs at "true" prices.

This interpretation of Walras' analysis of exchange conflicts with the usual view that he employed the device of *tâtonnement* (the nearest English equivalent, as Jaffé says, is "groping") in order to deal with the problem of false trading. The standard view of the *tâtonnement*, held even by such acute scholars as Jaffé and Patinkin, is that it is essentially our first adaptive control mechanism without (as Patinkin has emphasized) an explicit incorporation of recontracting.

But this Walrasian device was in fact *not* meant to deal with false trading which, as we have seen, he explicitly allowed for and considered minor. What the device was meant to cope with—and it did so very inadequately in the light of modern "stability" analysis—was the problem of convergence of the "excess demand" mechanism in *multiple market* situations, where interrelations of substitutability and complementarity make the analysis of convergence in simple two-commodity markets just too simple to apply without considerable change.

There is strong evidence for this interpretation of Walras. The concept of *tâtonnement* is not used at all in the analysis of the exchange of *two* commodities, where it logically should be if it were designed to deal primarily with the false trading problem. Its arrival is delayed until Lesson 12,

* This work first appeared in 1874, and the last edition (*édition définitive*) in 1926. An excellent translation, with very helpful notes, was published by William Jaffé in 1954 as *Elements of Pure Economics* (for the American Economic Association and Royal Economic Society, by Allen and Unwin, London). All references will be to this English version. Let us note, incidentally, that our treatment of exchange follows Jaffé's excellent usage in always employing the word "offer" rather than "supply," the latter being used exclusively to refer to situations where *production* is going on. This terminology allows us to remove much unnecessary ambiguity about exactly what problem is under discussion.

which discusses the exchange of n (> 2) commodities and where the problem of the adjustment of interrelated markets first appears. Even stronger evidence is in Appendix I ("Geometrical Theory of the Determination of Prices") where, after a discussion of the "statics" of price determination in multiple markets, he turns to an analysis of how the adjustments are carried out in this complicated situation:

> It is quite true that in determining the price of (C), we may destroy the equilibrium with respect to (B), that in determining the price of (D), we may destroy the equilibrium both with respect to (B) and with respect to (C), and so forth. But since the determination of the prices (C), (D), . . . will, on the whole, entail certain compensating effects on the relationship between the demand and offer of (B), in all probability equilibrium will be approximated more and more closely at each successive step in the groping process. *We enter here on the theory of groping* [tâtonnement] which I have developed in my book . . . . (p. 470, italics mine.)

Thus it seems clear that *tâtonnement* applies to a multimarket situation, and refers to a device where we perform a "conceptual experiment" by which the price in one market is brought to an equilibrium, without paying attention to what happens elsewhere; and then one moves on to the next price, and does the same; and so on (see pp. 170–72). Of course few prices will lie quiet at equilibrium while others are brought to heel, and the whole thing may turn out to be like the labor of Sisyphus; Walras' treatment of convergence here is distinctly weak. But no other economist seems to have recognised explicitly the problem of convergence in multiple markets until Samuelson wrote in 1941, and—especially important for our purposes—the device Walras used for the multimarket situation was tailored just for that, since it is meaningless in a single market.

Trading Curves

Curves having a similar appearance to our trading curves were introduced by Marshall in his privately printed paper on *The Pure Theory of Foreign Trade* (1879; reprinted by the London School of Economics, 1949). But these were *not* trading curves, for they involved production as well as exchange. This important point is easily grasped if we realize that it was an essential part of Marshall's analysis to deal with what happens if the two countries concerned are *off* their curves. But, as we have stressed, the axiom system in exchange—especially Axiom III, the "maximizing of utility"—prevents any individual from being off his trading curve in a recontracting process. The essential difference is that pure exchange theory usually assumes that the individual can (and does) move to his optimum position *immediately*, while production theory sometimes assumes that the producer takes a significant period of time before attaining his optimum position, so that, while we cannot observe *both* "traders" to be in nonoptimum positions, we can observe both producers to be so.

The invention of trading curves in the strict sense was by Edgeworth in *Mathematical Psychics*, though again without name; throughout his life he continued to draw close and wholly misleading analogies of these with the Marshallian curves. They were first christened "offer curves" by W. E. Johnson ("The Pure Theory of Utility Curves," *Economic Journal*, 23, 1913, p. 487), a term which was repeated by Bowley (*Mathematical Groundwork of Economics*, Oxford, New York, 1924, p. 7). It is one of the minor ironies of doctrinal history that most economists (in my experience, at least) believe that Edgeworth invented the term "offer curve," while the fact is that in his review of Bowley's book (*Economic Journal*, 34, 1924, 432) he explicitly condemned the term on the grounds of its asymmetric emphasis on offer in a symmetrical situation.* Wicksell expressed similar disapproval in his review of Bowley's work (*Selected Papers on Economic Theory*, G. Allen and Unwin, London, 1958, p. 210) and suggested names which translate (from Swedish) into English as "exchange curve" or "bargaining curve."

Confusion was further compounded by A. P. Lerner in his important articles on international trade theory in the August 1934 and August 1936 issues of *Economica* (reprinted in *Essays in Economic Analysis*, Macmillan, New York, 1953). These ascribed trading curves in *both* the exchange and production senses to Marshall; he called the "exchange" trading curve the "familiar Marshallian willingness-to-trade curve" (*Essays*, p. 107), and the "production" trading curve, "Marshall's 'offer curve' apparatus" (*ibid.*, p. 123).

With this checkered early history,† it is not surprising that current international trade theory often displays some inconsistency in the matter. We should emphasize that the actual terms we use do not really matter very much; what does matter is that a consistent terminology should be adopted which allows for the maintenance of a clear distinction between "exchange curves" and "production curves."

Lagged Adjustment Mechanisms

The phenomenon discussed in the footnote on p. 92 is closely analogous to that of the "cobweb theorem" in the theory of production; a good discussion is given in Kaldor's early article in the *Review of Economic Studies* (1934) on "The Determinateness of Static Equilibrium" (reprinted in *Essays on Value and Distribution*, Free Press, New York, 1960, 13–33). This paper is a useful and stimulating nonmathematical survey of several of

* It is curious that in his extended review of Johnson's article (see *Papers Relating to Political Economy*, Vol. II, reprinted by Franklin, New York, 1962, 450–78), Edgeworth does not take Johnson to task for his introduction of the terminology; after all, Bowley was only echoing Johnson's innovation.

† Another often-used term, which can be traced back in its essentials to Mill, is "reciprocal demand curves;" this is also a little asymmetrical and needlessly complicated.

the problems discussed in this chapter, although there are naturally some important points of disagreement. In an unpublished Ph.D. thesis at the University of Michigan (1962), F. T. Sparrow has presented a remarkable analysis of market adjustment mechanisms with random "arrival times," employing the tools of the theory of queues.

Stable and Unstable Equilibrium

The history of these terms is rather curious, and can only be explained satisfactorily on the basis of a brilliant hypothesis advanced by Patinkin (*op. cit.*, p. 384, footnote 23). As he says, neither Marshall nor Walras discussed stable and unstable positions out of the context of multiple equilibria although, logically speaking, the question of stability (convergence) of the adjustment process does not in general depend on the presence of such multiple points of intersection. By the words "stable" and "unstable" they both seem to have had in mind primarily the way the relevant curves cut each other, rather than the adjustment process at hand;* only in this way can we explain why the normally very punctilious Marshall claimed to have anticipated Walras in this regard, since his theory (published in *Proceedings of the Cambridge Philosophical Society*, Part XV, 1873, 318–9) refers to *production*, and Walras' theory to exchange; and the relevant adjustment mechanisms are quite different.

This "static" attitude to the stability of equilibrium positions gained the upper hand of the question of the convergence of the adjustment mechanisms, and dominated discussion in this area for many years, as may be seen in its apotheosis in Hicks's *Value and Capital* (Oxford U.P., New York, 1939). Even today, so able a theorist as Mrs. Robinson can say that an equilibrium is stable in a formal sense "when the relevant curves cut each other the right way. It is stable in a real-life sense, *once it has been reached*, when minor chance departures from it quickly reverse themselves" (Joan Robinson: *Essays in the Theory of Economic Growth*, Macmillan, New York, 1962, p. 6—italics hers).

It was Samuelson in a 1941 article in *Econometrica*, substantially reprinted as Chapter 9 of his *Foundations of Economic Analysis*, who made it clear that there was an almost exact correspondence between the "stability" of an equilibrium position and the convergence of the adjustment mechanism which did or did not lead to that position. This opened up a major new field of exploration, whose most recent emphasis—which this chapter has continued—has been on the importance of the convergence properties of the *whole* system under discussion, rather than of individual equilibria. For this reason, it would seem desirable gradually to cease using the terms

* It follows from what was said above that I do not agree with Patinkin that this might be an explanation for Walras' late introduction of the *tâtonnement*; but I would agree that Walras did divorce the question of the convergence of the adjustment mechanism from questions of the "stability" of points of equilibrium.

"stability" and "instability"—and perhaps even the word "dynamic"—in this context, thus freeing these overworked words for less ambiguous duty in the full dynamic setting of economic growth; for such "second-order" dynamic problems as those of exchange adjustment mechanisms, the word "convergence" seems quite adequate for most purposes.

The theory of consumer's choice to which reference is made in the footnotes has its classical expressions in H. Schultz: *The Theory and Measurement of Demand* (Chicago U.P., Chicago, Ill., 1938), and J. R. Hicks, *op. cit.*; a good elementary textbook treatment is in A. W. Stonier and D. C. Hague: *A Textbook of Economic Theory* (Longmans, London, 1953). The alternative approach taken by the theory of revealed preference is discussed in Chapter 6.

For an account of why we say that Giffen is *alleged* to have discovered the phenomenon that bears his name, see G. J. Stigler: "Notes on the History of the Giffen Paradox," *Journal of Political Economy*, 55, 1947, 152–56.

There is very little subsequent to Walras and Marshall on the problem of nonrecontracting adjustment processes; the main source until recently was Hicks's very sensible but brief treatment on pp. 127–29 of *Value and Capital*. More recent work has formulated much more definite mechanisms, but in a highly mathematical context; the work of Hahn is particularly relevant (see F. H. Hahn: "On the Stability of a Pure Exchange Equilibrium," *International Economic Review*, 3, 1962, 206–13; and F. H. Hahn and T. Negishi: "A Theorem on Non-Tâtonnement Stability," *Econometrica*, 30, 1962, 463–69). Along with all the other mathematical economists, these writers regard a *tâtonnement* as a "recontracting" adaptive control mechanism.

Marshallian and Walrasian Processes

Before leaving this episodic survey of the literature, it is necessary to clear up some confusion about what are often known as the Marshallian and Walrasian "stability conditions." The literature is very confused and so, as a consequence, are many students. The difficulty arises because, in the adjustment process postulated in Marshall's theory of *production*, we obtain "stability conditions" different (in terms of the implications of the supply and demand curves cutting a certain way) from those that we obtain in Walras' theory of *exchange*. That this is so is surely not remarkable, for the adjustment mechanisms are completely different, as one would expect in the two quite different situations.

Yet much confusion has sprung up. It is difficult to know where it started, but already in 1939 we find Hicks recording with puzzlement (*op. cit.*, p. 62, footnote) that Marshall's stability conditions *in exchange*, as he called them (see his index), are more appropriate to conditions of monopoly in exchange than of pure competition, which is scarcely surprising, since Marshall designed them explicitly for *production*. Samuelson's treatment in *Foundations of Economic Analysis*, 263–69, is much clearer, though even here there is some ambiguity about the Marshallian stability analysis in the *Pure Theory of Foreign Trade*. But, somehow, textbooks have taken up the apparent divergence between the two analyses, partly because the incubus of the sole consideration of "stability" in terms of equilibria, rather than in terms of the adjustment mechanism involved, still lingers on in economic analysis. Thus we can find Henderson and Quandt (to take just one example) seriously arguing as to which of the two adjustment mechanisms—Walras' "excess demand" or Marshall's "excess demand price"—is more appropriate for an *exchange* market (*Microeconomic Theory*, McGraw, New York, 1958,109–17).

The fact of the matter is that both Marshall and Walras had theories of pure exchange which were very similar; they also each had a theory of production in which there were some similarities. In particular, the implicit adjustment mechanism in Marshall's theory of "temporary equilibrium" is certainly excess demand (I, p. 333), as it is in Walras' theory of exchange. In Marshall's theory of *production*, the adjustment mechanism is based on entrepreneurs' moving resources in such a way as to equalize the rate of profit; *and so it is in Walras' theory of production* (*Elements*, pp. 41–2). In other words, in their theories of exchange, the two authors employ the *same* adjustment mechanism, though Walras—except in the analysis of barter—is much more explicit; in their theories of production, they also employ a common adjustment mechanism, though Marshall pursues its ramifications much further than does Walras. To oppose their theories in this regard is simply wrong from a historical point of view and brings in its train the serious substantive error of muddling up exchange with production. In this, as in many other respects, Marshall and Walras were considerably clearer and more sophisticated than their intellectual descendants.

One reason why the confusion may have arisen is that Marshall quite deliberately *never* drew diagrams in his analysis of exchange, while Walras did not draw any in the relevant part of his theory of production; this made it easier to identify each man's diagrams as covering the same basic situation, which they did not. In Marshall's case, as he made plain several times (II, p. 65 and p. 365, also *Memorials of Alfred Marshall*, ed. by Pigou, Macmillan, New York, 1925, p. 435) he was reluctant to use curves to describe a situation where the holdings of *stocks* of commodities was at issue, as in the case of pure exchange; he reserved curves for *flow* situations, involving production. This is seen clearly in the following quotation from his 1898 article in "Distribution and Exchange," substantial parts of which are reprinted in the Ninth Edition:

> I found also that curves hindered rather than helped in such discussions as those towards the end of my *Principles*, V, II [Temporary Equilibrium of Demand and Supply]. The contrast between "stocks" of goods dealt with for market problems; flows of goods produced by "stocks" of plant for short normal problems; and secular movements where all is flow is emphasized on p. 450 (II, p. 65, footnote 2).

Walras' reluctance to draw curves for production probably stemmed from his comparative lack of interest in production compared to utility analysis, and—more importantly—from his emphasis on the more general equilibrium aspects of production.

In any event, the confusion which has often been attributed to one or other (or both) of these great men on this issue is present, not in the older analysis, but in the failure of the present generation of theorists to comprehend the full nature of the earlier analytical systems.

5

GENERALIZATIONS OF BILATERAL EXCHANGE THEORY

A. "STRAIGHTFORWARD" GENERALIZATIONS

In this chapter we will discuss some generalizations of bilateral exchange theory. Extension of the results of Chapters 3 and 4 is for the most part straightforward, economically speaking, but requires of the reader a level of mathematical expertise higher than that which we have assumed here. We can deal more easily with another, and very stimulating, type of generalization concerned with the *viability* of allocations in the m-person case; and that will be investigated in Section B. But first, we shall glance very briefly at the ways in which the preceding analysis can be "straightforwardly" generalized.

(i) To More than Two Commodities

As in Chapter 2, it would be an excellent exercise for the reader to carry through (if only in his "mind's eye") the main part of the analysis of Sections B, C(i), and D(i) of Chapter 3 for the case where each individual is endowed with *three* commodities, say (again) ale, bread, and cheese. The "box" would now be a cube, and the loci of indifferent bundles would be bowl-shaped surfaces. The contract curve would have the same definition as before, and still be a *curve*—in three-space rather than in two-space. The "exchange lines," however, would now be *planes*, depicting the positive counter-prices p_a, p_b, p_c, or the equivalent *numéraire* prices $1:\pi_b:\pi_c$. The existence of a "list" of efficiency exchange ratios would then imply the existence of a plane which contained the initial point t^0 as well as the point P^* on the (interior) contract curve, and whose "slopes" (i.e., the direction cosines of the normals to the plane) would be equal to the common "slopes" of the individuals' indifference curves at the point P^*.

As before, such a plane would exist, provided a trading set existed, and this would be guaranteed if t^0 corresponded to each of the participants bringing some positive quantity of each commodity to the exchange. A similar analysis could be carried through for "boundary" contract curves.

For the general case of $n \geqq 4$ commodities, these graphical techniques fail us, and much more advanced methods have to be used. But similar results emerge, viz.: the existence of a (not necessarily unique) list of positive efficient exchange ratios, if each person brings something of each commodity to the exchange. This condition becomes less and less realistic as more commodities are "added" to the analysis, but it should be observed that it is a sufficient condition only. The simple and natural condition is that, if trade is possible, then there will always exist—given our axioms—at least one list of positive equilibrium exchange ratios.

(ii) To More than Two Individuals

Reasonably comprehensible geometrical techniques immediately fail us once we have three people in the exchange, even for the case of only two commodities, as the reader may verify. But the same tools which prove the results for two people and n commodities may very easily be extended to cover the case of $m > 2$ people and $n > 2$ commodities. There is now no contract *curve*, but there is a set of efficient trades. A trade is now an allocation of commodity bundles $x^A, x^B, x^C \ldots$, among the m people $A, B, C \ldots$, such that the total quantity of each commodity, $x_1, x_2, x_3, \ldots$, remains constant. Then a trade t is efficient if it is not dominated by any other trade t^1, where we say that t^1 *dominates* t if the bundles $x^{A1}, x^{B1}, x^{C1}, \ldots$, are such that $x^{A1} R_A x^A$, $x^{B1} R_B x^B$, $c^{C1} R_C x^C$, $\ldots$, with actual preference holding for at least one individual, e.g., $x^{A1} P_A x^A$. These are natural generalizations of the corresponding definitions for the case of two persons.

The proof of the existence of equilibrium prices for the general case again demonstrates that, if each person brings something of each commodity to the exchange, at least one list of positive equilibrium prices exists; but this sufficient condition is even less realistic this time. However, less stringent conditions might suffice for the basic result. An interesting possibility is that trading *subgroups*, each with its own price system, might appear if the various trading sets do not all overlap.

Just as the analysis of the existence of efficient trades requires much more advanced tools in the m-person, n-commodity situation, so does the problem of the convergence of adjustment mechanisms in the same situation.* Unlike the existence theorems, however, the convergence theorems do not generalize quite so readily. Although convergence has been proved for our first control mechanism in several special situations, it has been shown by Scarf that this convergence need not occur if $m \geqq 3$ and $n \geqq 3$. Since his examples of this failure depend upon rather odd endowment effects due to lack of substitutability in the individuals' preference structures, we are perhaps justified in assuming that *normally* the control mechanism will be convergent, as will the mechanism of Section C, Chapter 4. There are many unresolved

* Some aspects of multilateral *barter* processes are discussed in the next section.

mathematical puzzles in this area, but they do not appear to be of great economic interest or importance.

B. THE THEORY OF VIABLE ALLOCATIONS

The addition of more *persons* to the analysis of the bilateral exchange of two commodities, however, opens up a whole new realm of ideas which was originally explored in 1881 by Edgeworth (on pp. 35–39 of *Mathematical Psychics*), was then almost completely neglected for three-quarters of a century, and has only very recently become a topic of renewed theoretical interest. Because of this, there has not yet been time enough for the terminology of the problem to have become standard, and that used here—including the title—is partly new; the analysis itself, however, is in its essentials almost wholly due to Edgeworth.

(i) Quadrilateral Exchange

The new ideas arise because, with more than two people, we can now envisage the formation of *coalitions* among the various parties to the exchange; and, as Edgeworth himself said in a slightly different connection, "at those heights ... [of analysis] ... are observed some curiosities of theory, like Alpine flowers, found only at great altitudes". Accordingly, let us now introduce into the analysis of bilateral exchange two new protagonists, say Adam-two and Eve-two, who convert the scene to one of "quadrilateral" barter. These new actors are such that Adam-two has exactly the same preference structure as the old Adam (Adam-one) and exactly the same original holdings of ale and of bread; and similarly for Eve-two with respect to Eve-one. These outrageous assumptions enable us to use some of our previous geometrical tools in the new situation, and the reader is asked to be patient and withhold his contempt until the results of the analysis have been obtained, when they will not appear to be so odd.

The box diagram can still be used in this new analysis, but we have to reinterpret it rather carefully. In bilateral exchange an *allocation* among the participants corresponded uniquely with a point in the box; in the new situation this is not true in general. A full description of an allocation, as we shall see, might involve using two, or even three, separate points in the box. Only if both Adams receive *identical* bundles, and both Eves similarly so, will a single point in the box correspond completely to an allocation.

Now if we assume the possibility of recontract—which we shall do throughout this analysis*—then there cannot *in equilibrium* be two different exchanges

* Alternatively, as in the discussion in Chapter 3 concerning the attainment of equilibrium in barter, we could assume case (a) of Section C(ii) there, namely, that the total initial endowments persist over the whole span, simply being redistributed each period. In this way the opportunity for improvement in trading positions would become manifest as time passed, and "recontracting" movements would be made over the long run; a similar argument holds for case (b) of 3, C(ii).

t^1 (at which, say, Adam-one trades with Eve-one); and t^2 (where Adam-two deals with Eve-two). This is illustrated in Fig. 5.1.

Let the points t^1 and t^2 in the diagram be two such separate "bilateral" deals. Then obviously Adam-one (at t^1) could profitably recontract with Eve-two (at t^2), both moving to the point t, or a similar point close by, at which both are better off. For *any* pair of bilateral trades, the possibility of recontract means that a suitable regrouping could be made which would result in a more advantageous position for at least one out of each pair of individuals; and so, given the enlightened self-interest postulated by Axiom III, the regrouping would come about.

Suppose that the pair of trades did merge to a single point, such as t. Even this will not be a final contract for all four participants, because—arguing as in the last chapter—it will be apparent that all of them could be made better off by a move to an appropriate point on the contract curve; and therefore, given recontract, this move also will take place.

But would the contract curve in this case of four people be the *same* as that for bilateral exchange? The answer is a definite NO, for the "new" contract curve will be a segment of the old. To be quite specific, the ends of the original curve, at Q and at S, will drop off, and the curve shrink to a part of its former self. Edgeworth's discovery of this "contracting" contract curve resulted from the line of reasoning set out below, which is subtle even for his deft mind.

In Fig. 5.2, t^0J' is the line which joins the initial position t^0 to the contract curve at Q; although it shares all the *geometrical* properties of the corresponding exchange line, it will not receive that interpretation in this setting, except for a certain class of exchange ratios to be discussed later. Notice that both C^{A0} and C^{EQ} are convex, so that the latter curve cannot cut or touch t^0J' between t^0 and Q. It follows that if we consider the Eves' indifference curve

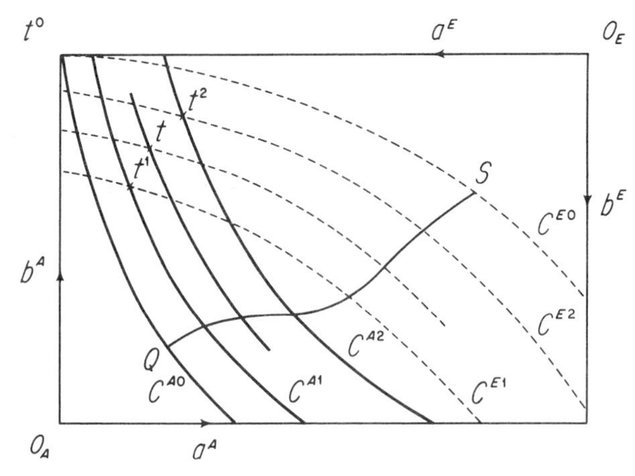

Fig. 5.1

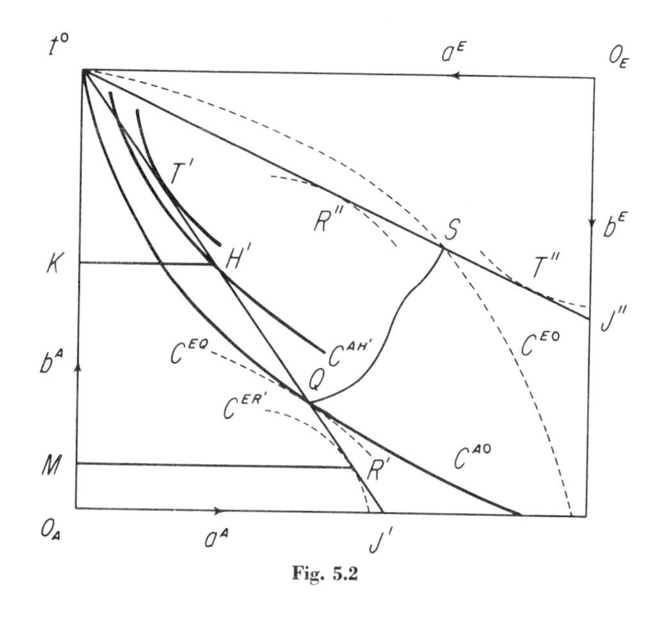

Fig. 5.2

$C^{ER'}$ to which t^0J' is tangent (at R'), this curve cannot touch the line at a point to the left of Q either, for otherwise $C^{ER'}$ would have to intersect C^{EQ}, contrary to the axiom system. By the same argument, C^{EQ} cannot intersect t^0J' between Q and R', so that $C^{ER'}$ necessarily represents a higher level of satisfaction for each Eve than does C^{EQ}. Moreover, as we showed in the discussion concerning Fig. 3.15, the point T', at which t^0J' is tangent to an Adams' indifference curve, must lie to the left of Q.

For exactly similar reasons it can be demonstrated that, if a line t^0J'' is drawn from t^0 to the other end-point S of the contract curve, then the point T'' at which t^0J'' is tangent to the Adams' indifference curve must lie to the right of S, and the corresponding point R'', at which one of the indifference curves belonging to both Eves touches t^0J'', must lie between t^0 and S.

It follows that as we swing a line in a continuous arc from t^0J' to t^0J'', the points at which this line (which we shall call t^0J) touches the "Eve" indifference curves will swing from the right side of the contract curve (R' on t^0J') to the left (R'' on t^0J''), while the corresponding points for the Adams' curves swing from left (T' on t^0J') to right (T'' on t^0J'').* Since the change in the slope of t^0J' to t^0J'' is continuous, it must be the case that at least one of these points, say P^*, will be on the contract curve itself; and because of the definition of this latter curve, P^* will be a tangent point both between the relevant t^0J (say t^0J^*) and an Eve indifference curve, and between t^0J^* and an Adam indifference curve. In fact, as the reader has probably guessed, at such a crossing point the line t^0J^* becomes geometrically identical to an

* This switch may occur several times, but must occur at least once.

"efficient" exchange line, and the point P^* coincides with an "equilibrium" barter position like that shown in Fig. 3.15.

Let us now return to the main task, which is to show that, under conditions of "quadrilateral exchange," neither of the two end-points Q and S of the contract curve which was applicable in the bilateral case can be *sustained* by the self-interest of the four participants, and will therefore fail to be a part of the new curve.

We shall first take the allocation Q. Because $C^{ER'}$ is "higher" than C^{EQ}, it will "pay" either one of the two Eves (let us say Eve-one) *to enter into a coalition with both Adams*, in the following manner: she offers to exchange with both Adams together an amount MR' of ale, in return for t^0M of bread, which is to be provided in equal shares (t^0K) by each Adam, so that KH' equals one-half of MR'. Since the Adams' preferences are identical and "convex," the point H' which is common to both is better for each than is Q, since $C^{AH'}$ represents a higher level of satisfaction than C^{A0}; they will, therefore, accept this proposed allocation, in preference to what they would receive under the allocation Q.

The new allocation enforceable by the coalition cannot be represented by a single point in the box but needs three points. The point H' indicates the position of each Adam, the point R′ the position of Eve-one, and the point t^0 the position of Eve-two, since she will not have traded at all; the whole allocation needs the three points H', R', and t^0 for its full description, together with a statement of the person (or persons) to whom each point is applicable. Notice that there is no reason why the point H' should in general be a position where t^0J' is *tangent* to an Adam indifference curve (i.e., no reason why H' should coincide with T''), which is partly why the reader has been warned against giving an "exchange-line" interpretation to any line such as t^0J'.

So if recontract is permitted, the coalition of the two Adams with Eve-one can enforce this allocation, under which each of them is better off than at Q; and so they will vote to break up or *block* the allocation Q on the old contract curve, and to move to the one that we have just described (or to one very similar). Now this arrangement, as we have seen, leaves the resentful Eve-two out in the cold, so that in her own interest she will make a counter-proposal to the two Adams which will contain slightly better terms for them than they were planning to get from Eve-one. While this proposition will not be as advantageous for Eve-two as was the previous scheme for Eve-one, at least it will be considerably better for her than was t^0—or even Q.

But, on the other hand, neither will Eve-one permit this new deal to go through, and she will strike in again with a yet improved offer for the Adams. There will then ensue a sequence of coalition forming, breaking, and reforming, which, it is intuitively clear (given the axioms and conditions of the problem, including recontract), will eventually lead to a single point on the contract curve. It is not to our present purpose to analyze these convergence problems in detail, however, for the main point has been to show that

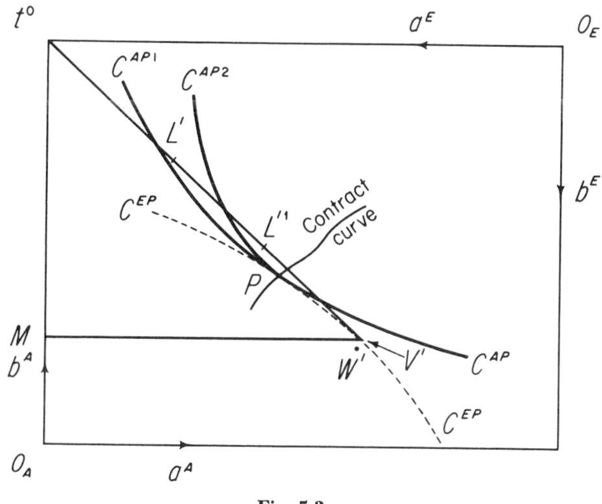

Fig. 5.3

the allocation Q on the old contract curve is no longer *viable* in the new situation, since it can be blocked by suitable coalitions among the parties to the exchange. By similar arguments we can show that a coalition of one Adam conspiring with two Eves can block the allocation S at the other end of the contract curve; it is a good exercise to work through the relevant line of reasoning.*

Let us now investigate further the conditions which must be satisfied if points on the old contract curve are to remain viable in the new situation; the reasoning involved is illustrated in Fig. 5.3.

Suppose that P is *any* point on the old contract curve QS, and let C^{EP} be the Eves' indifference curve through P, tangential to C^{AP} at that point (and only at that point). Then since C^{EP} is convex, we can always draw a tangent line t^0V' from t^0 to C^{EP}, meeting the curve at a unique point V'. We shall assume, *pro tempore*, that V' always lies to the *right* of P, so that it is never coincident with the line joining t^0 to P, a line (t^0J) which is not shown in the diagram.

Now suppose that the Adams' indifference curve through P had the shape of the curve C^{AP1} so that L'—the mid-point of the segment t^0V'—always lay inside the "better set" of P for both men. Then, obviously, they would prefer the position at L' to that at P, and so be prepared to bribe one of the Eves to move to a point in the upper wedge† of V', such as W', which would

* If we had introduced only *one* additional person, say Eve-two, then we could still have analyzed the situation in the same way, only then we would have had to pretend that Adam divides himself into two identical halves. The proof of the nonviability of Q that we have given would have gone through just as before, but in this "triangular" case the other end of the contract curve (at S) cannot be shown to be "blockable" by this type of argument.

† Remember that this upper wedge of V' is with respect to the origin O_E.

be better for the Eve concerned than would P. The Adams could not in fact each attain the point L', because some of their "surplus" would have to be used to bribe Eve; but—given Axioms IV and V—they could each secure a position very close to it and certainly inside their better set of P. Thus a coalition could—and would—be formed that would block the allocation P.

Therefore a *necessary* condition that P be viable is that L' should not lie to the right of C^{AP}; but this is not a sufficient condition. It is true that if C^{AP} lay to the right of L' (as in the case of C^{AP2}), then the latter point would lie in the worse set of P for the Adams, and no allocation *of the type that we have described* can be brought about by a coalition. But the possibility exists that a *different* type of allocation might be better than P for a group of people that could enforce it.

Such a possibility is shown in Fig. 5.4; here C^{AP} is to the right of L' and t^0T is *twice* the distance t^0K, so that t^0Z is twice t^0N. The important characteristic of this example, however, is that the distance ZX' (from Z to C^{EP}) is *less* than twice the distance NM (from N to C^{AP}). It follows that each Adam could offer to trade an amount t^0K of bread in return for KM of ale, and still be as well off as he would be at P. On the other hand, the Eve involved in the coalition would then be at W' (determined by the relation $TW' = 2KM$), and therefore better off than at P. Given the continuity of everyone's preferences that is postulated by Axiom V, a slight alteration in these terms in favor of the Adams would produce an allocation that would make all three people better off than at P; and so they would move to block

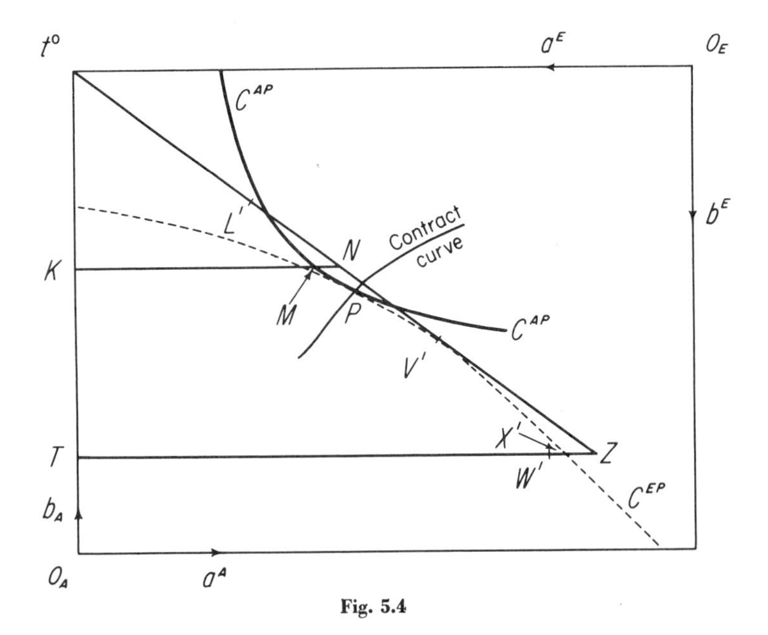

Fig. 5.4

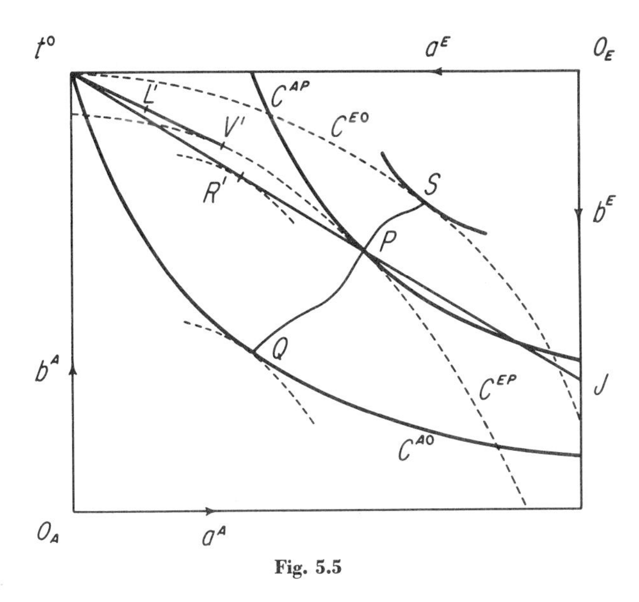

Fig. 5.5

P. But this again would leave one of the ladies without any trade at all, so that she would canvass another proposal for the Adams' consideration, and so on, as before.

It does not seem useful to search for a general set of sufficient conditions for the viability of P in the new situation, since it would probably not be a very elegant set and, in any case, is of no great relevance for the present analysis. However one very important statement that we can make is that one particular type of allocation on the contract curve will *always* be viable. If the allocation P^* were such that the line t^0J^* through P^* corresponded to an "efficient" exchange line, then C^{AP^*} would lie entirely above the line, except where it was tangent at P^*; and C^{EP^*} would lie entirely below, again apart from the tangency point.[1] The whole of t^0J^*, except P^*, would lie in the worse sets of P^* both for the Adams and the Eves, so that no coalition of *any* kind could be found—and enforced—that would block P^*. A careful reading of this argument shows that its validity does not depend on there being only four participants, so that we have in fact shown P^* to be viable *no matter how large the number of persons on each side*, provided that each "side" has identical preferences and endowments.

To complete this discussion of quadrilateral barter, we have finally to deal with the case, illustrated in Fig. 5.5, where V' can lie to the *left* of P.

Because both C^{EP} and C^{AP} are convex, it follows that C^{AP} cannot cut t^0V', since otherwise C^{AP} would have actually to cut C^{EP}, contrary to the hypothesis that P lies on the contract curve. Therefore the whole of t^0V', including

[1] In this case the point V' is identical with P^*, and therefore the line t^0V' coincident with the corresponding segment of t^0J^*.

L', lies to the left of C^{AP}, and no coalition of the two Adams with one Eve can be arranged. But if V' is to the left of P on C^{EP}, then, as the diagram shows, R' will lie between t^0 and P. Given a fairly regular pattern of the indifference curve "map," this probably means that P will be close to the other end of the original contract curve at S; and in this event, P is very possibly blockable by a coalition of one Adam with two Eves.

(ii) The General Case

Suppose now that we introduced two more protagonists, a third Adam identical in all respects with the other two, and a similarly identical third Eve. Obviously we now multiply considerably the number of possible coalition patterns and the number of possible bargaining sequences. Our interest, however, is still focused on the question: What, in this new situation, happens to the contract curve that was applicable in the previous case?

The easiest way to analyze the problem is by means of Fig. 5.3. Instead of the possibility of one Eve's plotting with two Adams, we now have the possibility of *two* Eves' dealing with *three* Adams. A feasible arrangement would be that each of the two Eves gives up the amount MV' of ale, each receiving t^0M bread in return; while the three Adams would each contribute *two-thirds* of the amount t^0M of bread and receive *two-thirds* of the amount MV' of ale. Thus the allocation would again be represented by three points: (a) the point L'^1, *two-thirds* of the way down t^0V' from t^0, which applies to each of the Adams; (b) the point V', representing the position of two of the Eves; and (c) the point t^0, which is where the other Eve would be.

It follows that any point P on the "quadrilateral" contract curve can only possibly survive unblocked in the new situation (and perhaps not even then), if the tangent to C^{EP} from t^0 does *not* have its "two-thirds" point L'^1 lying to the right of C^{AP}. Now if P were very close to the end of the "quadrilateral" curve, then it is certain that L'^1 would lie in the better set of P for each of the three Adams, so that a coalition of the type that we have just described would find it profitable to block P in this "hexagonal" situation. Similar conclusions apply to the other end of the curve.

So in this new case of "three-a-side" the contract curve again contracts with the addition of more participants, although again we can be sure that the "competitive" allocations (i.e., those corresponding to "efficient" exchange ratio lines) will lie on the new contract curve, for the same reasons as before.

The analysis can be continued with four Adams and four Eves, and so for any equal number (say m) of persons on each side. We have shown that there always exists a point L' which must *not* lie to the right of C^{AP} if the allocation P is to be viable; and further that with four persons, L' lies on t^0V' at exactly one-half the distance from t^0 to V', while with six people it is two-thirds the way down t^0V' from t^0. By similar reasoning, we may show that it must lie three-fourths the way down with eight participants, four-fifths with ten, and so on; the general formula is that with $2m$ persons (m on each side), the point L' must lie on t^0V' at exactly $(m - 1)/m$ times the distance from t^0 to V'.

Now in Fig. 5.3 we drew the tangent line t^0V' from t^0 to C^{EP}; but we could equally well have drawn a tangent line, say t^0V'', from, from t^0 to C^{AP}, the point of tangency being V''. Using the same line of argument, we could then have demonstrated that, in the case of "two-a-side," there always exists a point L'' on t^0V'' which must not lie to the *left* of C^{EP} if the allocation P is to be sustainable. In the general case of $2m$ participants, the same pattern of reasoning as before shows that the ratio of the distance t^0L'' to t^0V'' is again determined by the fraction $(m - 1)/m$, where each side has m "equal-natured" people; again it is a good exercise to work through the appropriate argument, together with the relevant diagram.

These results mean that L' (or L'') moves steadily to the right on t^0V (or t^0V'') as m increases, and although we cannot be sure that the contract curve actually shrinks with *each* increase in m (because the conditions we are dealing with are only necessary for viability, not sufficient), we do know that the set of viable allocations will tend to decrease as the relentless advance of L' (or L'') toward V' (or V'') cuts down all those allocations that can be blocked by coalitions.

What happens in the limit as the number of persons on each side becomes infinitely large (i.e., as m tends to infinity)? Since $(m - 1)/m$ then moves arbitrarily close to unity, it is obvious that L' tends to coincidence with V', and L'' with V'', but not so clear that they all tend to coincide at the point P. Let us suppose that this is not, in fact, the case, so that—in the limit—P, V', and V'' are all *distinct* points; this means in turn that t^0J, t^0V', and t^0V'' are all different.

There are two possibilities to examine, the first being that t^0V'' lies "north" of t^0V', and the second the reverse case. The first situation is easily disposed of, since C^{AP} lies entirely to the "north" of t^0V'' (except for V'' itself), and C^{EP} entirely to the "south" of t^0V' (except for V'). These facts, together with the hypothesis that t^0V'' lies north of t^0V', means that C^{AP} and C^{EP} have no points in common, contrary to the definition of P as a point on the original contract curve.

The second case, illustrated in Figs. 5.6(a) and (b) is more interesting. In both subcases t^0V' lies north of t^0V'', but in the first, V' lies west of V'', while in the second, V' lies east of V''. In both diagrams, the point P (on the contract curve) whose viability is being questioned cannot lie above t^0V' or below t^0V'', for reasons similar to those of the last paragraph. Nor, because of the (strict) convexity of C^{AP} and C^{EP}, can it lie to the right of V'' or to the left of V' in Fig. 5.6(a); nor to the right of V' or to the left of V'' in Fig. 5.6(b).

Therefore in both diagrams the point P must lie between t^0V' and t^0V'', and actually between V' and V''. But again because of the convexity of the

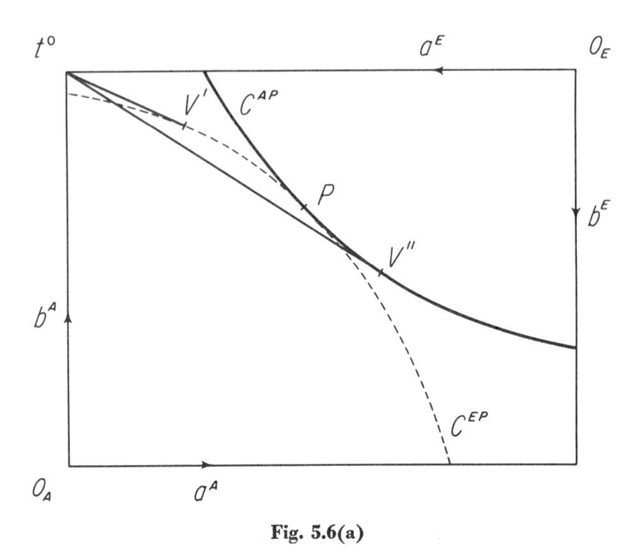

Fig. 5.6(a)

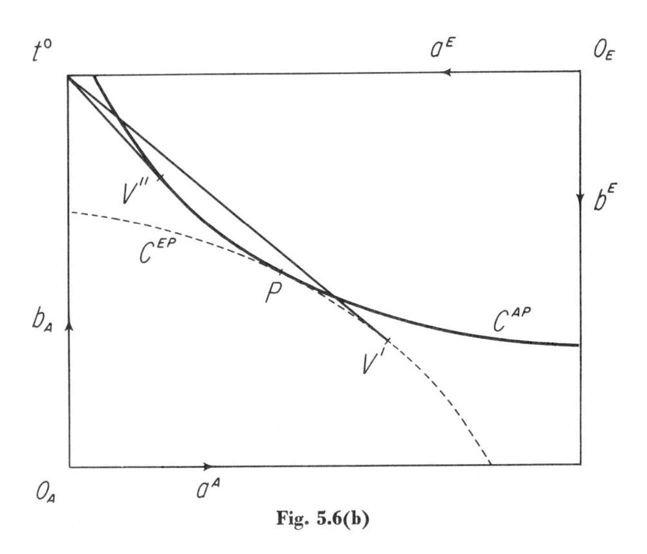

Fig. 5.6(b)

indifference curves, this must mean that one of the necessary conditions for viability is bound to be violated. Either C^{EP} must cut t^0V'' (Fig. 5.6(a)), or C^{AP} must cut t^0V' (Fig. 5.6(b)). Since in each case L' coincides with V', and L'' with V'', this means that there is bound to exist *some* coalition which can enforce an allocation more preferable to it than P.

It follows that if P is to be viable when $(m - 1)/m$ is arbitrarily close to one, then t^0V' and t^0V'' must coincide, which means that at V', where t^0V' has the same slope as C^{EP}, the curve C^{AP} must also have that slope, so that

V'' coincides with V'. But because C^{AP} and C^{EP} are of equal slope there, P must also coincide with V' and V'', by the definition of P. And, obviously, P must therefore be a "competitive" allocation P^*, since t^0V' (and t^0V'') in this case simply coincide with t^0J^*.

We showed some time ago that the "competitive" allocations are always viable, no matter how large the number of participants on each side; now these new results show that they are the *only* allocations to remain viable as the number of "players" on each side increases without limit. Modern studies have therefore termed such allocations the *core* of the exchange economy concerned, since—once established—they can never be upset, even by the most complicated coalition arrangements.

Before going on to report some recent generalizations of Edgeworth's analysis, let us note some minor qualifications and extensions of the argument. First, as we saw in Chapter 3, it is by no means true that in any exchange situation the competitive allocation is unique. If not, and if the various competitive equilibria are "isolated" points, then as the number of participants is increased, the shrinking contract curve will tend to break up into isolated segments around each such equilibrium ratio, until in the limit it consists of just those isolated points.

Secondly, the proof given above requires that the number of persons on *each* side increases without limit. It is not enough for one side alone to become infinitely numerous in order that the contract curve should always be reduced to the core; in general both sides must do so.

Finally, we have assumed that the contract curve lies entirely in the *interior* of the box diagram. But it is not difficult (and provides valuable practice) to show that conclusions very similar to those above apply to the viability of allocations on *boundary* segments of the contract curve.

It may be objected that these remarkable results obtained by Edgeworth are very special, leaning as they do on geometrical arguments that cannot be extended to more general cases and, even more serious, depending on the absurd assumption that each Adam and each Eve is identical, both as to preferences and as to initial stocks. But some recent work of Scarf and others has lessened the force of these objections. By using rather advanced mathematical techniques, it has been shown that we may consider not two but *any* finite number of different kinds of participants, and any finite number of commodities. It is still possible to prove that, as the number of "players" *of each kind* increases without limit, the "competitive" allocations are the only ones which remain in the core, i.e., unblockable by *any* coalition.

In these generalizations, the assumptions on each person's preference structure are basically the same as in Chapter 2, while in order to ensure that the core is not empty, it is assumed that each individual has positive holdings of each commodity, which as we have seen is a sufficient—but not necessary—condition for at least one equilibrium exchange-ratio (and therefore at least one "competitive" allocation) to exist. These generalizations have also extended the analysis to cover a system involving production as well as exchange.

(iii) The Interpretation of the Theory

This whole Edgeworthian analysis of viable allocations throws quite a new light on the nature of equilibrium price systems. We have seen in Chapters 3 and 4 that, for any given initial commodity holdings and preference structures, equilibrium prices: (a) "clear the market," so that at equilibrium all offers and demands are harmonized, and no excess demand persists; and (b) lead to "efficient trades" in which no individual can be made better off without harming at least one other person. We can now see that these equilibrium exchange ratios have a third role: (c) they result in a set of allocations which are *viable*, by which we mean that no coalition exists that could *enforce* some other allocation outside the set, under which each of its members would be better off than under an allocation in the set.

Seen in this light, equilibrium prices appear not merely as a means for attaining economic efficiency in commodity utilization but also as devices for reducing social instability in the acceptance of commodity allocations. But this interpretation must be taken very much *cum grano salis*. Everything that has been said in this chapter and the last about the useful properties of equilibrium prices is *relative* to the initial commodity distribution. If that is unfair, no amount of economic and social "efficiency" in the exchange mechanism will do more than make the best of a bad job—and even that cautious assertion about the merits of the "Hidden Hand" may not really be valid. In any actual situation it might well be that, by any reasonable ethical standards, a coalition of those less well endowed with this world's goods *should* block an allocation on the contract curve. And a competitive "core" allocation, with everyone playing the market mechanism game according to the rules, would frustrate this desirable change. If "equilibrium is just equilibrium," then the *status quo* is most certainly just the *status quo*.

Moreover, even if the analysis of viability reveals yet another "virtue" of equilibrium prices, it also reveals one more difficulty in the task of actually arriving at those prices in a market situation. In the analysis of the convergence of the adjustment mechanism in bilateral exchange, we saw that we had to be careful: (a) to specify whether the process was continuous or discontinuous in time; and (b) to state whether the process was one of recontract or not. In generalizing this analysis to more people and more goods, the "straightforward" (but mathematical) theories have in addition to indicate: (c) whether there are "few" or "many" traders on the market; and (d) whether they are dealing with a single market for two commodities or a network of interrelated markets for several goods. And we now see that we also have to stipulate: (e) whether coalitions are permitted.

The number of combinations of variants of these five types of assumption is obviously very great, and it would not be appropriate to explore here the convergence problems of each, or indeed any, of the many possible submodels. Our main concern is to point out that if coalitions are allowed (which can certainly happen without recontract, though Edgeworth's analysis would then need modification), then the path of adjustment to equilibrium might find itself blocked, particularly if on one "side" or the other there are relatively few protagonists, so that coalitions can easily be formed.

Thus suppose that on a two-commodity market a price is called that is some way from an equilibrium ratio, and that the usual "excess demand" adjustment mechanism gets to work, pushing the price towards an equilibrium whose location is *unknown* to the traders in the market. One of the more enterprising of these traders might perceive that a profitable coalition could be formed successfully and then proceed to do so, thus taking a probably large group of people out of the market. This will not only block the path of the previous adjustment process but will also result in a new set of equilibrium prices for the rump of the market, since the original set of initial endowments and preference structures will have been considerably reduced.

Then either a new adjustment path will start up (with the possibility that it in turn might be blocked by another coalition), or attempts will be made to break the original coalition with a new one. The number of possible outcomes is quite large and certainly includes the possibility that the whole process might come to a kind of "equilibrium" which has little to do with the allocations associated with an equilibrium price ratio; this is especially true if the individuals involved are not very numerous.

It may be objected that this example contradicts the usual assumption of market analysis, that in a free exchange market only one price can rule at a time. But this assumption applies only to a market which is in equilibrium and which has no barriers to entry. If either of these two conditions fails to hold, then there is certainly no reason why only one price should prevail at any instant. Indeed, unless one makes the unrealistic supposition of a price-cutting umpire, it is difficult to see how price *could* get to equilibrium without there being momentary differences in price on a single market.*

So we can see that, although there are strong mechanisms which could drive "false" prices toward equilibrium, there are also many difficulties on the way. For this reason it is very important for the analyst to find out, in any particular case, just what is the precise nature of the adjustment process in the market and what are the obstacles to it. A mere description of the pleasant properties of an equilibrium position is not a convincing argument for a price system, unless care is also taken to indicate how the equilibrium is to be attained.

* Most of the mathematical discussions of convergence do reason as though there were only one price at a time on a market, but do not always say whose behavior is thereby represented. Since these discussions usually assume recontract, it seems that some kind of umpire mechanism is envisaged; this is sometimes stated explicitly.

Even if it were attained, this does not mean that an equilibrium position is necessarily "better" (or "worse") than nonequilibrium, except possibly for the economic theorist, for whom statics is easier than dynamics. What we can say, speaking very roughly, is that a price system that does not have too fragile an adjustment mechanism will serve the interests of the original distribution of economic power (as represented by the initial endowments) probably better than would most other allocation systems in exchange. What is false is to attribute to prices redistributive functions that they do not possess and to suppose that the free working of an untrammeled price system would necessarily turn out to the advantage of everybody, regardless of the initial commodity distribution. The price system makes a good servant but a bad master, a sentiment which is perhaps better expressed by reversing Francis Bacon's aphorism about Nature: "Those who wish to obey the price mechanism, must first command her."

NOTES ON THE LITERATURE

A. (*i*) There is surprisingly little on existence theorems for general *exchange* systems alone. The main reference is H. Nikaido: "On the Classical Multilateral Exchange System," *Metroeconomica*, 8, 1956, 135–45, and the same author's "Supplementary Note . . . ," *ibid.*, 9, 1957, 209–10. There are many such models involving production as well as exchange. The most famous is Wald's version of the Walrasian system, which first appeared in 1938 and was translated as "On Some Systems of Equations of Mathematical Economics," *Econometrica*, 19, 1951, 368–403. (Wald also wrote on exchange in this article.) Important subsequent treatments are K. J. Arrow and G. Debreu: "Existence of an Equilibrium for a Competitive Economy," *Econometrica*, 22, 1934, 265–90; and G. Debreu: *Theory of Value* (Wiley, New York, 1959). The latter has a full bibliography up to 1959; for subsequent work see G. Debreu: "New Concepts and Techniques for Equilibrium Analysis," *International Economic Review*, 3, 1962, 257–73. More elementary treatments are in Koopmans' first of his *Three Essays on the State of Economic Science* (McGraw, New York, 1957) and in Chapter 13 of R. Dorfman, P. Samuelson, and R. Solow: *Linear Programming and Economic Analysis* (McGraw, New York, 1958).

Some very specialized linear models of exchange are treated in Chapter 8 of D. Gale: *The Theory of Linear Economic Models* (McGraw, New York, 1960): this analysis includes an interesting analysis of "sub-groups" in trading problems.

(*ii*) The counterexamples of Scarf on lack of convergence are in H. Scarf: "Some Examples of Global Instability of the Competitive Equilibrium," *International Economic Review*, 1, 1960, 157–72. A clear discussion of the mathematics of convergence, together with an account of Scarf's examples, is in Chapter 4 of J. G. Kemeny and J. L. Snell: *Mathematical Models in the*

Social Sciences (Ginn, Boston, 1962), while an interesting account of the whole convergence problem is the survey article by T. Negishi: "The Stability of a Competitive Economy," *Econometrica*, 30, 1962, 635–69.

B. As we have stated, almost the whole of this theory is contained on pp. 35–39 of Edgeworth's *Mathematical Psychics*, while a further development is to be found in the last ten pages of his book (pp. 139–48). His controversy with Marshall and Berry, which took place in the *Giornale degli Economisti*, 1891, also contained an account of his theory, and this Italian version is rather poorly summarized in English on pp. 313–19 of Volume II of his *Papers Relating to Political Economy* (reprinted by Franklin, New York, 1962).

His work was almost completely neglected until recently; the only references known to me are: J. R. Hicks: "Edgeworth, Marshall, and the Indeterminateness of Wages," *Economic Journal*, 40, 1930, 215–31, especially 216–22; J. R. Hicks: *The Theory of Wages* (Macmillan, New York, 1932, reprinted by Peter Smith, New York, 1948, p. 26); G. J. Stigler: *The Theory of Price* (Macmillan, New York, 1946, p. 81). The last two of these were mere passing mentions, while the first is concerned with wages only and does not carry the general argument any further.

The modern period in the study of the problem was initiated by a stimulating paper by Martin Shubik: "Edgeworth Market Games," in *Contributions to the Theory of Games*, IV, ed. by R. D. Luce and A. W. Tucker, (Princeton U.P., Princeton, N.J., 1958), 267–78. The most important advances have occurred in H. Scarf: "An Analysis of Markets with a Large Number of Participants," *The Princeton University Conference*, Ivy Curtis Press, Philadelphia, 1962; and H. Scarf and G. Debreu: "A Limit Theorem on the Core of an Economy," *International Economic Review*, 4, 1963, 235–47. The last paper shows that Edgeworth's results constitute a third way of looking at equilibrium price systems.

The quotation from Edgeworth about Alpine flowers is from p. 430 of his review of A. L. Bowley's "Mathematical Groundwork of Economics," in *Economic Journal*, 34, 1924, 430–34, while the well-known remark that "equilibrium is just equilibrium" is due to Lionel Robbins: *An Essay on the Nature and Significance of Economic Science* (2nd ed., Macmillan, London, 1935, p. 143).

Koopmans has stressed the difficulty of interpreting most mathematical models of "stability" analysis (*Three Essays on the State of Economic Science*, Essay III, p. 179), while Kenneth Arrow has explored the problems of disequilibrium adjustments that involve imperfections of the market ("The Allocation of Economic Resources" in *Essays in Honor of B. F. Haley*, Stanford U.P., Stanford, Calif., 1959, Chapter 3). His analysis, however, suffers a little by not distinguishing clearly between exchange and production.

6

THE THEORY OF DEMAND

A. INTRODUCTION

The most common use of preference theory in the economic analysis of the last fifty years has not been in the theory of exchange at all but in a rather different context, which goes variously by the names of the theory of consumer's choice, or consumer's behavior, or—simply—demand. In the theory of pure exchange we assume that each individual has a preference structure established on the relevant field of choice and that each has an endowment of definite quantities of the commodities involved. We then study the interplay of these different patterns and endowments as the exchange proceeds, and in particular we are concerned to bring out the role of certain equilibrium or "efficient" rates of exchange, to which we give the name of equilibrium prices.

In the theory of consumer's choice, some of these basic features are changed. We retain the postulate that each individual obeys the axiom set contained in Chapter 2, and so assume that he establishes a preference structure over the field of choice appropriate to the commodities concerned.* But we do not, as we did in exchange theory, assume that he has an endowment of physical stocks of commodities, for we are not now primarily interested in understanding how prices arise "naturally" in the exchange situation. Instead, we proceed as in the discussion of "counter" prices in Section (Dii) of Chapter 3, and assume that each commodity has a positive market price expressed in terms of "money," and that the rationale of these prices has been accounted for by the theory of exchange.†

Moreover, we assume that in any one period each individual has a limited stock of "money," and that he is free to allocate this stock among the

* As with exchange theory, we can certainly think of other axiom systems for the theory of choice; but—as before—we shall keep to the pedagogically simplest set, in order to ease the task of exposition.

† The *positiveness* of each commodity price is assured mainly by the Axiom of Dominance, as we have seen.

various commodities available (compare the discussion of "counter" stocks in 3, D(ii)). Purely in order to make matters simple, and because it is the most realistic case, it is usually assumed that the individual's stock of money (or *income*, to use the conventional term) is such a small fraction of the total amount of buying power on each of the commodity markets involved that he cannot, by his own actions, influence any one of the prices; in the usual phrase, the consumer is assumed to be buying under conditions of "perfect competition."

The main concern of the theory of demand is essentially econometric. It is to deduce properties of *market* demand functions from certain reasonable postulates about individuals' preference or behavior, so that economic analysis of the available data may bring to light important relationships that would otherwise remain hidden. The theory proceeds by way of deducing properties of individual choice functions from the restrictions on individual preferences or behavior, and then aggregating the individual functions suitably in order to form the market demand functions. Clearly it is the first step which is much the most important, the aggregation being relatively simple—though by no means trivial.*

So the chief task before us in this chapter is, given the existence of a preference structure for the individual, to discern what (if any) regularities of pattern there are in the changes that he makes in his selection of a commodity bundle, as one or more prices are changed or as "income" is varied. A typical problem is to explore the validity of the "Law of Demand" which asserts that as the money price of any commodity is increased, and other prices and income remain constant, then the quantity of that good demanded by any individual (and hence by the market) will decrease, provided that the person concerned was buying it in the first place.

If we restrict ourselves to the analysis of just two commodities, then the theory of demand is easy to develop along lines similar to—and indeed a little simpler than—the discussion in Chapter 4, Section B. Thus let the consumer's "income" be denoted (conventionally) by M, and the unit prices of the two commodities be p_a units of money for ale, and p_b units of money for bread. Then in Fig. 6.1 we may represent the attainable set for the consumer (whom we shall still occasionally call Adam) in the following way.

The distance OA corresponds to Adam spending all of his income on ale, and thus obtaining M/p_a $(=OA)$ units, while the distance OB $(=M/p_b$ units of bread) similarly refers to a situation where the consumer spends the whole of his income on bread. At the halfway point H on AB, Adam will be buying $M/2p_a$ units of ale and $M/2p_b$ units of bread, as can be checked easily by the geometry of similar triangles; hence he will be spending his total income M at this point. Similarly, if we take *any* point on AB (say K) at a distance

* Some of the problems that it raises will be discussed in the next chapter.
Throughout we will use "choice function" synonymously with "demand function," but will reserve the former term mainly for individual behavior, the latter for market behavior.

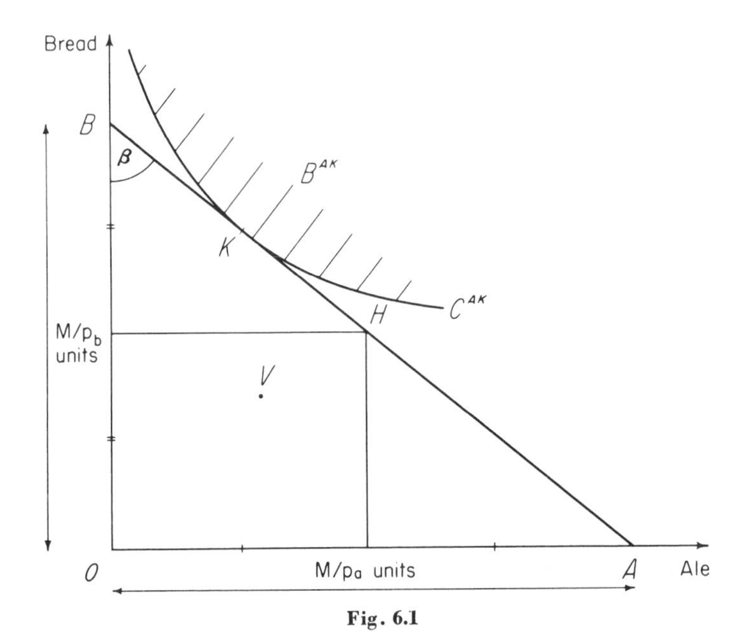

Fig. 6.1

$(k \times AB)$ from A, where $0 \leqq k \leqq 1$, then Adam will be buying $(1-k)M/p_a$ units of ale, and kM/p_b units of bread, so that his total expenditure will be given by

$$\left(\frac{(1-k)M}{p_a} \times p_a\right) + \left(\frac{kM}{p_b} \times p_b\right) = M$$

units of money; and again he spends all his income.

It is easy to see that at any interior point of the triangle OAB, such as V, Adam will be spending actually *less* than his income, while any bundle outside the triangle will—at the prevailing market prices—involve the expenditure of more than M. Along AB, Adam will be spending exactly his income M, and the "b-slope" of AB, given by tan β, will be equal to $(M/p_a) \div (M/p_b)$, which is the price ratio p_b/p_a.

Therefore the triangle OAB is the attainable set for the consumer, as the reader has probably already guessed from the resemblance of Fig. 6.1 to such diagrams as Figs. 2.13 and 4.4. But notice that there is an important difference; in those diagrams we envisaged Adam being initially at the point t^0 and moving *via* exchange to an optimal position on the exchange line. In the theory of demand we make no assumption about such an initial position but simply endow Adam with an attainable set, any point of which he may select as his optimal choice; there is no initial *position*. For this reason it is preferable to call AB the "budget line," rather than the "exchange line."

Having identified the attainable set in Fig. 6.1, we could now go on to determine the optimal selection, by the condition that Adam should choose that commodity bundle whose better set has only one point (the bundle itself) in common with the attainable set; in Fig. 6.1 this is the point K on C^{AK}, whose better set is B^{AK}. A similar method could be used to handle the effects of *changes* in prices and income, and we could then arrive at conclusions similar to those of Chapter 4, B, e.g., that the "Law of Demand" is false as a general proposition, since very strong negative "income" effects (analogous to the endowment effects of the last three chapters) could, in extremely rare cases, offset the always positive substitution effect, resulting in a rise in the quantity demanded with a rise in price.

We can in fact extend the range of this geometrical treatment considerably, by means of a simple but ingenious argument due to Hicks. As we have already pointed out in Chapter 3, economic theory is not usually interested in the actual *consumption* of a commodity but only in the purchase or exchange of it; we do not care—as economists—what disposition of the good among its various possible final uses the individual decides upon in any market situation but only in the fact of so much being bought at a certain price. Now suppose that we consider a group of commodities which are such that the price ratios among them remain *fixed*. Then we can construct from these a "composite" commodity using these price ratios as weights, and the "price" of this composite commodity will remain in the same proportion with all the other prices of the group, as they vary in proportion with each other.

Thus suppose that we have a group of three commodities x_1, x_2, and x_3 (the numbering is arbitrary), with price ratios $1, p_2/p_1$, and p_3/p_1; the total expenditure on this group will be $(p_1x_1 + p_2x_2 + p_3x_3)$ units of money. We now form the composite commodity $\bar{x}$ by taking the mixture given by the formula $x_1 + p_2x_2/p_1 + p_3x_3/p_1$ (where the price ratios are pure numbers), exactly as if we were compounding some chemical mixture using fixed proportions of the basic constituents; the units in which $\bar{x}$ is measured will have to be stated with care in any particular case, since they are not "natural" units of a single commodity.

In order to find the corresponding price $\bar{p}$ of $\bar{x}$, we utilize the condition that the expenditure on the "composite" commodity, i.e., $\overline{px}$, must be equal to total expenditure on the group. This gives the equation

$$\bar{p}\left(x_1 + \frac{p_2x_2}{p_1} + \frac{p_3x_3}{p_1}\right) = p_1x_1 + p_2x_2 + p_3x_3$$

which has the unique solution $\bar{p} = p_1$. Then the ratios of the other prices to $\bar{p}$ will be equal to 1, p_2/p_1, and p_3/p_1; the first of these is "identically" constant, and the other two are also constant, by the assumption that all the prices in the group vary in *proportion*.

Now if we are primarily interested in examining the choice functions for a commodity *outside* this group, we can apply the previous reasoning and say that for our purposes we may regard $\bar{x}$ simply as an ordinary commodity, with an ordinary price $\bar{p}$, and that we need not concern ourselves with how the consumer arranges his expenditure *within* the group. In fact it can be shown that this composite commodity obeys all the restrictions that the assumption of a preference structure places on the choice functions, so that it does indeed play the role of a single, ordinary commodity.

It follows from this that if we want only to analyze the consequences of a change in the price of ale, or of income, on the amount of ale purchased, then we can lump all the other goods into a composite commodity in the way that has been described, and so summarize their behavior by a single variable $\bar{x}$. This remains true even if the money prices within the group change as well, provided that they all change in the same proportion. Therefore we may now reinterpret the word "bread" to be shorthand for that composite commodity drawn from all other goods in the field of choice besides ale.

The range of the elementary geometrical approach is greatly widened by this construction, but it still does not allow us to deal with the important class of cases where several prices are changed simultaneously and not proportionately. These problems can be handled by fairly straightforward extensions of the geometrical arguments, but the methods that are normally used are based on rather advanced mathematics, particularly on some fairly sophisticated tools from the differential calculus. Since we are not assuming such mathematical knowledge in the main sections of this book, we must find another way of coping with the general "n-dimensional" problem.

B. THE THEORY OF CHOICE BEHAVIOR

(i) Preliminary Axioms

An alternative to making assumptions about Adam's preferences and then deducing restrictions on his choice functions is to place "reasonable" conditions directly on his choice behavior, and then to deduce those more complicated restrictions on choice functions that form the bulk of the theorems in demand theory. In doing this, however, we have to be careful not to place *stronger* conditions on choice behavior than are implied by the postulate that the individual chooses on the basis of a preference structure and an attainable set, for otherwise we could be constructing what is essentially a different theory. So an important aspect of this approach *via* choice behavior —which is due mainly to Samuelson—is to check that the assumptions placed on it are indeed implied by a preference structure.

But it is important to note that there is absolutely no antagonism between the two approaches. Although the choice behavior method—or "revealed preference," as it is often called—is a swifter and easier route for most of demand theory, it does take as a basic assumption that the (positive) market prices are given and does not attempt to explain their existence. This latter task is accomplished by the theory of pure exchange, which is in turn based on preference structures. The only question of relevance concerning the choice between "ordinal preference" (to use a common term for the preference structure approach) and "revealed preference," is that one must be careful always to use the best available tool for the problem at hand; to discard one approach entirely in favor of the other would be sheer waste.

In order to introduce the axiomatic study of choice behavior, we shall rework the standard two-commodity example we have used already in preference structure theory, and employ the choice behavior approach to examine the validity of the "Law of Demand." The assumptions about choices that this example requires will be set out as *preliminary* axioms for the general n-dimensional theory of choice; but of course the final version of the axiom system for the general theory will be much more orderly and coherent than this present highly informal list. In particular, the axioms that we give now are not necessarily logically independent of each other. Even this simple example, however, will bring out the roles that the various preliminary axioms play in arriving at the conclusions of demand theory.

The first axiom simply formalizes the basic assumption that we make concerning the market situation facing the consumer.

PRELIMINARY AXIOM 1. The consumer is always faced with a positive market price for each commodity, which he cannot change by his own action.

This axiom really has two parts, the last of which asserts something about individual behavior alone, namely that Adam cannot change the market prices. The first part, that a set of (positive) market prices actually exists, is apparently so obvious that probably many readers will find it gratuitous. Yet, on reflection, it is not so trivial after all; indeed to a man from Mars, the ingenious human device of market prices might seem a phenomenon strange beyond belief.

Since we are now not assuming that any individual has a preference structure, we cannot *prove* the existence of a set of equilibrium prices in the same way that we did in exchange theory. What we shall in fact do, with the first part of the axiom, is to assume such existence, and hope that the reader will find it a reasonable enough proposition. It should be noted that this first part, like the second, asserts something about human behavior and not about commodities. It assumes that the interplay between people's tastes and endowments is such that exchange takes place at fixed positive prices and so is a restriction on the behavior of *all* the individuals concerned on every commodity market; the second part is a restriction on Adam's behavior alone.

In Fig. 6.2 we consider the previous situation of Adam's having income M, and facing market prices p_a and p_b, giving him an attainable set of OAB. So that this may be a typical example, we shall assume that the theory applies for all possible sets of positive prices and any (positive) income, just as we

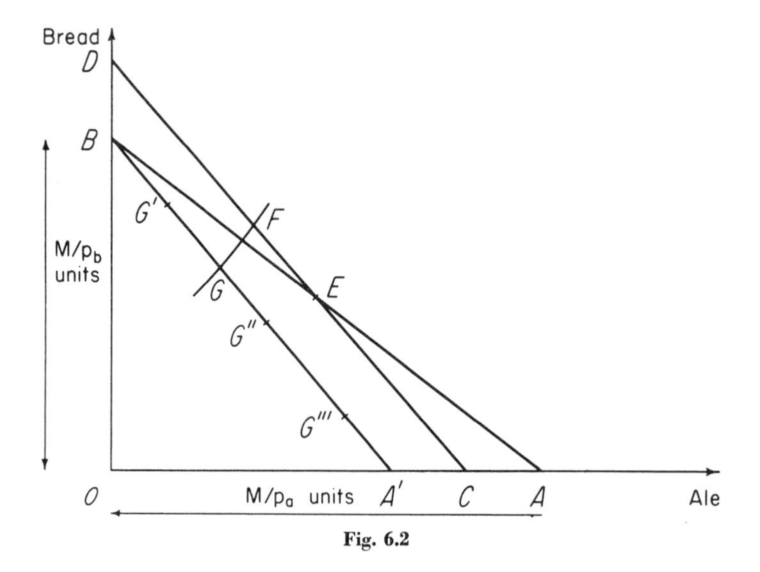

Fig. 6.2

took (and take) all commodities to be divisible. Like the latter, the former "divisibility" assumption about prices and income is not an assertion about human behavior, and so is not expressed as an axiom.

Now if any progress at all is to be made with the choice function approach, we must obviously assume that choice functions exist. This means that, given any attainable set facing him, the consumer will select a unique bundle from it; for otherwise a second "run" of the example might produce a different batch, making it difficult to talk about consistent choices. We therefore adopt the following

Preliminary Axiom 2. Given any attainable set, the consumer chooses a unique bundle from it.

Looking at Fig. 6.2, it is clear that the theory will be much easier to manage if we can assume that the bundle selected will, like E in this case, always lie on the budget line. Therefore, bearing in mind the properties of this line, we put forward

Preliminary Axiom 3. The consumer always spends the whole of his income.

Among other things, this axiom states that the consumer does not save, which is surely unreasonable. This defect can be overcome in a purely formal way by defining the various avenues for the consumer's saving as so many different "goods," with the corresponding prices being "one minus the appropriate interest rate for the period and commodity in question." But it is probably better to regard our "income" M as in fact total expenditure, and to admit frankly that we should have a separate theory for savings decisions, which to be satisfactory would really have to belong in the class of theories concerned with optimal behavior under *uncertainty*. Of course the dichotomy between these two types of decision is by no means quite as sharp as this, but perhaps as a first approximation such an approach is tolerable; we shall deal here only with the first type of theory.

A further implication of this äxiom is that the consumer should still find at least one of the available commodities useful, so that he has a motive for spending all his income; and in this regard it appears as a version of the Axiom of Dominance, which also suffers a similar weakness regarding the role of saving. Indeed this Preliminary Axiom 3 is essentially an axiom of dominance for *incomes*, asserting that a larger income will always be chosen rather than a smaller income, provided prices remain fixed.

Now let us assume that the price of ale is increased to $p_a' \, (> p_a)$, so that the new budget line becomes $A'B$, and the new attainable set $OA'B$. Adam is clearly worse off in this new situation, since he can no longer afford to buy his previous selection E. Remembering that we are now not assuming that he has a preference structure, can we say where his new choice will be on $A'B$? In order to answer this rather difficult question, let us first carry out the hypothetical experiment of offering the consumer enough extra income to enable him to continue the purchase of E at the new prices p_a' and p_b. This will result in the new budget line becoming CD, and we now have to determine where on CD his new choice will lie.

Obviously he is no worse off in this hypothetical situation than he was originally, since he can still continue to buy the batch E; and it is indeed quite possible that E will be chosen again, just as before. But if this were not the case, where else on CD would the new batch F be located? To find this, observe that each batch on CD lying below E was available when the attainable set was OAB but *was not bought*; thus Adam "revealed" E to be better —for him—than any such batch. Now in the hypothetical situation, with attainable set OCD, these bundles continue to be available but E is also still available, and Adam would therefore betray inconsistency if he bought any batch on CE except E. Therefore his new choice must necessarily lie somewhere on the segment ED.

This very simple requirement for consistent choice behavior, first emphasized by Samuelson, is in fact the key to the whole theory of demand. The axiom for the general theory will be very slightly different in wording, but the present version of this consistency axiom is

PRELIMINARY AXIOM 4. If a bundle x^0 is chosen in a price-income situation when another batch x^1 is available, then in any other price-income situation in which both x^C and x^1 are available, x^1 must not be chosen.

Now that we have conducted Adam to the bundle F by our hypothetical experiment, let us gradually take away the extra income that we gave to him, but still keep money prices at p_a' and p_b, until the original income M is regained. As we do this, Adam will reduce his purchases in the manner determined by the Engel curve through F.*

If ale is a noninferior good over the range of incomes concerned, the Engel curve will either have the shape actually drawn in Fig. 6.2 or will follow some locus such as FG', which implies that bread is inferior over the range. In either event the "final" batch will lie to the left of F, which cannot be to the right of E. Therefore the chosen batch will lie to the left of E, implying that the quantity of ale that Adam brings is actually *less* in the new situation. If ale is inferior over this income range, however, then the Engel curve might cut at a point such as G'' or—much less likely—G'''. In the first case, G'' is to the right of F but still to the left of E, so that the quantity of ale bought is still less than in the old situation. In the second case, corresponding to ale being extremely inferior, G''' is to the right both of F and of E, so that the quantity of ale purchased would rise as the price rises, thus contradicting the "Law of Demand." It is easy to see that, if F and E coincide, then the "Law" is more likely to be violated than otherwise.

So we have demonstrated that the choice behavior approach can rapidly and easily deduce important conclusions of demand theory, without using all the formal apparatus of preference structures. The question remains whether the assumptions that we have imposed on the choice functions are in fact "equivalent" to those implied by the preference approach; to this question we now turn—after an essential digression on some new notation.

(ii) A Digression on Vectors

We are going to construct our theory of choice behavior for the general n-commodity case, and so we have to develop an appropriate notation. At the end of Chapter 2 we observed that, in this general case, a commodity bundle can be regarded as an ordered n-tuple of nonnegative numbers, once we have assigned an arbitrary numbering to the commodities in the field of choice. Thus in two dimensions a bundle is a couple (x_1, x_2); in three dimensions it is a triple (x_1, x_2, x_3), and so on, while we denote different bundles by different superscripts, such as x^0, x^1, and x^2.†

In order to take these concepts further, we have to give *rules* by which these n-tuples may be combined algebraically, and in particular we need to give meaning in this context to such fundamental operations as addition and multiplication. In doing so we impart a certain algebraic structure to these

* This Engel curve may be discontinuous, but that does not matter, since Preliminary Axiom 3 ensures that the chosen bundle will change with each fall in M, which is all that we need to establish our results. In the text we shall, for simplicity's sake, argue as if it were continuous.

† A defect of this notation is that symbols such as x^2 might suggest "x squared" and so on; as we shall almost never form such polynomial expressions—and use different notation when we do—no confusion should arise.

n-tuples, and they then cease to be merely ordered arrays of numbers. We mark this change in status by a new name, calling all n-tuples satisfying the following rules *vectors*, and the set of all such n-tuples a *vector space*. We shall denote such vectors by a boldface lower-case letter, such as $\mathbf{x}$, whose components are written $x_1, x_2, \ldots, x_n$; thus $\mathbf{x}$ and $(x_1, x_2, \ldots, x_n)$ are two symbols for the same mathematical object, and each of them has its uses.

Addition of Vectors. The *sum* of two vectors $\mathbf{x}^0$ and $\mathbf{x}^1$ is defined by the set of equations

$$\left.\begin{aligned} x_1^0 + x_1^1 &= (x_1^0 + x_1^1) \\ x_2^0 + x_2^1 &= (x_2^0 + x_2^1) \\ &\vdots \\ x_i^0 + x_i^1 &= (x_i^0 + x_i^1) \\ &\vdots \\ x_n^0 + x_n^1 &= (x_n^0 + x_n^1) \end{aligned}\right\} \quad (1)$$

where, by convention, we denote the typical component of each vector by x_i. The set of equations (1) may be written equivalently either in the "row" form

$$(x_1^0, x_2^0, \ldots, x_i^0, \ldots, x_n^0) + (x_1^1, x_2^1, \ldots, x_i^1, \ldots, x_n^1) = (x_1^0 + x_1^1, x_2^0 + x_2^1, \ldots, x_i^0 + x_i^1, \ldots, x_n^0 + x_n^1)$$

or in the compact vector notation

$$\mathbf{x}^0 + \mathbf{x}^1 = (\mathbf{x}^0 + \mathbf{x}^1)$$

which reads: "the vector $\mathbf{x}^0$ added to the vector $\mathbf{x}^1$ results in a vector, each of whose elements is the sum of corresponding terms in each of the other two vectors." Notice that in order for this operation to have meaning, the two vectors must have the *same* number of components.

Vector addition is reversible, or *commutative*, by which we mean that $\mathbf{x}^0 + \mathbf{x}^1 = \mathbf{x}^1 + \mathbf{x}^0$; it is also *associative*, i.e., $\mathbf{x}^0 + (\mathbf{x}^1 + \mathbf{x}^2) = (\mathbf{x}^0 + \mathbf{x}^1) + \mathbf{x}^2$, so that the order in which vectors are added is irrelevant to the final result. One example of vector addition is of particular importance, for essentially it defines subtraction. If we define the vector, each of whose components is the number zero by $\mathbf{0}$, then we have

$$\mathbf{x} + (-\mathbf{x}) = \mathbf{0}$$

It follows that $\mathbf{x} + \mathbf{0} = \mathbf{0} + \mathbf{x} = \mathbf{x}$, and that $-(-\mathbf{x}) = \mathbf{x}$.

Multiplication of Vectors by Numbers. We now have two quite distinct kinds of mathematical object on the scene, ordinary numbers and vectors, and we can therefore envisage any vector being multiplied by either of these types.* The first kind of operation, vectors by numbers, is defined for any number k by the *vector* equation

$$k(x_1^0, x_2^0, \ldots, x_n^0) = (kx_1^0, kx_2^0, \ldots, kx_n^0)$$

or

$$k\mathbf{x}^0 = (k\mathbf{x}^0)$$

Note that this type of multiplication results in a new vector, not another number. By its definition, the operation is *distributive*, both with respect to vectors (i.e., $k(\mathbf{x}^0 + \mathbf{x}^1) = (k\mathbf{x}^0) + (k\mathbf{x}^1)$), and with respect to numbers (i.e., $(h + k)\mathbf{x}^0 = (h\mathbf{x}^0) + (k\mathbf{x}^0)$); it is also commutative ($k\mathbf{x}^0 = \mathbf{x}^0 k$).

An important application of this type of multiplication is the formation of a *convex combination* (*c.c.*) of two vectors, which involves both vector addition and multiplication by numbers. Let k be any real number such that $0 \leqq k \leqq 1$. Then a convex combination of $\mathbf{x}^0$ and $\mathbf{x}^1$ is the vector $k\mathbf{x}^0 + (1 - k)\mathbf{x}^1$; i.e., it is the vector whose typical element is $kx_i^0 + (1 - k)x_i^1$, so that it is a *weighted average*—with weights k, $1 - k$—of the two vectors. Geometrically speaking, this corresponds to a point on the "straight line" (in n-dimensional space) joining $\mathbf{x}^0$ and $\mathbf{x}^1$, as in the two-dimensional budget line discussed earlier.†

This operation can be easily generalized by considering any set of $(T + 1)$ real numbers $k_0, k_1, \ldots, k_T$, such that each of them is nonnegative and less than or equal to 1, and their sum exactly 1. Then a convex combination of the $(T + 1)$ vectors $\mathbf{x}^0, \mathbf{x}^1, \ldots, \mathbf{x}^T$ is the vector $k_0\mathbf{x}^0 + k_1\mathbf{x}^1 + \ldots + k_T\mathbf{x}^T$). The geometrical interpretation of this general formula—which is said to define a T-simplex in the n-dimensional space—is not quite so easy to visualize as before; but this need not detain us, since we are not really concerned with it in what follows.‡

* Most of what follows applies whether the numbers are real or complex, which is why this operation is often called *scalar* multiplication, a scalar being a real *or* a complex number. But our whole demand theory will be couched in terms of real numbers, so that we will be thinking only of those. In some cases the mathematical development itself requires *real* numbers, as distinct from general scalars, and in such an event we will indicate this by prefixing "real" to "numbers."

† In spite of this reference to a two-dimensional example, the reader will find it more useful, in thinking of these concepts intuitively, to keep in his "mind's eye" the picture of a vector as a point in "ordinary" three-dimensional space. Many important and subtle relationships, especially in the theory of choice functions, are lost if attention is paid only to two-dimensional pictures.

By pointing this out, we are implicitly assuming that the n-dimensional vector space we are talking about is in fact "Euclidean" n-space; and so it will be if we agree to use the "Pythagorean" definition of the distance of a vector from the origin. Thus, in two dimensions this distance is $\{(x_1 \times x_1) + (x_2 \times x_2)\}^{1/2}$, in three dimensions it is $\{(x_1 \times x_1) + (x_2 \times x_2) + (x_3 \times x_3)\}^{1/2}$, and so on for n dimensions in general.

‡ As a rough guide to this visualization, in three-dimensional space the 0-simplex, 1-simplex, 2-simplex, and 3-simplex correspond to point, line, triangle, and tetrahedron, respectively. Simplexes of dimension $T > n$, where n is the dimension of the "containing" space, are of no great importance, since their study can be reduced effectively to that of n-dimensional simplexes.

We can now define what we mean by a convex set of vectors. A set $\boldsymbol{Z}$ of vectors is said to be *convex* if, given any two vectors $\mathbf{x}^0$ and $\mathbf{x}^1$ in $\boldsymbol{Z}$, every *c.c.* of $\mathbf{x}^0$ and $\mathbf{x}^1$ is also in $\boldsymbol{Z}$; the reader will note the strong analogy of this with Definition 21 of Chapter 2.*

Multiplication of Vectors by Vectors. We now have to define multiplication of vectors by the second type of object, namely vectors themselves; and here, for the first time, we need something a little different from ordinary algebra. We define the *inner product* (written $\mathbf{x}^0\mathbf{x}^1$) of two n-dimensional vectors $\mathbf{x}^0$ and $\mathbf{x}^1$ by the vector equation

$$\mathbf{x}^0\mathbf{x}^1 = x_1^0x_1^1 + x_2^0x_2^1 + \ldots + x_i^0x_i^1 + \ldots + x_n^0x_n^1 \tag{2}$$

so that $\mathbf{x}^0\mathbf{x}^1$ is a *number*. Notice that with this type of multiplication, two vectors produce a number, while with the other type, a number and a vector produce a vector.

An alternative way to write (2) is to use the standard symbol Σ to denote "the sum of"; then we can write $\mathbf{x}^0\mathbf{x}^1$ as the sum of "cross products" of the form $x_i^0x_i^1$, or

$$\mathbf{x}^0\mathbf{x}^1 = \sum_{i=1}^{i=n} x_i^0x_i^1$$

where i, running from 1 to n, serves as the index of summation.†

Let us check some of the properties of this operation. It is commutative ($\mathbf{x}^0\mathbf{x}^1 = \mathbf{x}^1\mathbf{x}^0$) and distributive ($\mathbf{x}^0(\mathbf{x}^1 + \mathbf{x}^2) = \mathbf{x}^0\mathbf{x}^1 + \mathbf{x}^0\mathbf{x}^2$), but it is not associative. For $\mathbf{x}^0(\mathbf{x}^1\mathbf{x}^2)$ signifies that the vector $\mathbf{x}^0$ is to be multiplied by the *number* $\mathbf{x}^1\mathbf{x}^2$, and therefore the typical element of this "scalar product" is $x_i^0(\Sigma x_i^1x_i^2)$. But $(\mathbf{x}^0\mathbf{x}^1)\mathbf{x}^2$ is the vector $\mathbf{x}^2$ multiplied by the number $\mathbf{x}^0\mathbf{x}^1$, and so *its* typical element is $(\Sigma x_i^0x_i^1)x_i^2$, which is quite different from the previous expression.‡

Some special examples of this operation are $\mathbf{0x} = 0$ for any vector $\mathbf{x}$, while if $\mathbf{1}$ is the vector whose typical ith element is 1, than $\mathbf{1x} = \Sigma x_i$. Notice that, as for vector addition, the operation of multiplication of two vectors is only defined if they have the same number of components; thus no meaning is usually attached to an m-dimensional vector being multiplied by an n-dimensional vector, unless $m = n$.

* We are here adopting the notational convention of referring to *sets* of vectors by upper case boldface italic letters, *vectors* by lower case boldface letters; numbers have been in italic type throughout.

† Since we will usually only form sums over n variables, we shall normally omit the limits of summation on Σ. Thus Σx_i will stand simply for the sum of the x_i's from 1 to n.

Using this concept of inner product, we can write the Pythagorean formula for the distance of any $\mathbf{x}$ from the origin $\mathbf{O}$ by $\sqrt{\Sigma(x_i)^2}$, or simply by $(\mathbf{x}\,\mathbf{x})^{1/2}$. Similarly, the distance of any vector $\mathbf{x}^0$ from any other vector $\mathbf{x}^1$ is $[(\mathbf{x}^0 - \mathbf{x}^1)(\mathbf{x}^0 - \mathbf{x}^1)]^{1/2}$. Obviously, this distance is always nonnegative, and only zero if $\mathbf{x}^0 = \mathbf{x}^1$.

‡ Remember that here x_i^2 is "x-eye-two," not "x-eye-squared," which would be written $(x_i)^2$.

With this mathematical equipment, we may now set out our theory of choice behavior in full n-dimensional generality. But first it will prove useful to add two further pieces of notation. We often want to talk about "the set of $\mathbf{x}$ such that such-and-such a property is true"; but it is cumbersome always to write out such a lengthy phrase, so a shorthand notation is in common use. Instead of "such that" we use a colon, and place the property concerned after the colon, the whole statement being enclosed in curly brackets. Thus $\{\mathbf{x}: 0 \leqq x \leqq 2\}$ is the set of all real numbers between 0 and 2, including the end-points, while $\{\mathbf{x}: \mathbf{p}^0\mathbf{x} \leqq M^0\}$ is the set of all n-vectors $\mathbf{x}$, whose inner product with $\mathbf{p}^0$—which is some previously specified n-vector—is no greater than some specified number M^0.

If we want to consider a set of all objects having more than one property, we may proceed in either of two ways. We can either place all the properties after the colon, separating them by commas; or we can place one of them (preferably a rather general property) before it, the rest after. Thus if we want to denote the set of all *nonnegative* vectors $\mathbf{x}$ satisfying the previous requirement,* we can write either $\{\mathbf{x}: \mathbf{x} \geqq \mathbf{0},\ \mathbf{p}^0\mathbf{x} \leqq M^0\}$, or $\{\mathbf{x} \geqq \mathbf{0}: \mathbf{p}^0\mathbf{x} \leqq M^0\}$; we will use each notation as it seems appropriate.

As a final piece of conventional shorthand, instead of writing in English that "the vector $\mathbf{x}$ belongs to the set X," we will write the term $\mathbf{x} \in X$, where the symbol "$\in$" should be read "belongs to" or "is a member of"; similarly, we use $\mathbf{x} \notin X$ to mean that $\mathbf{x}$ does *not* belong to the set X.

(iii) An Axiom System for Choice Behavior

We will now present a list of formal axioms for choice behavior, which will be shown to be essentially "equivalent" to the axiom system for preferences presented in Chapter 2. Since B(i) has already discussed preliminary versions of most of those axioms, we will not spend much time on their rationale or on their role in producing restrictions on demand functions ("demand theory proper") but will concentrate instead on their interrelations with each other and with the axioms of the theory of preference structures. In order to facilitate this last comparison, these "choice" axioms will be labeled C1, C2, and so on, while the "preference" axioms will be prefixed by P, so that, for example, Axiom I becomes Axiom PI.

First we need to set out some of the basic concepts we shall use, dressed up in the "n-dimensional" notation developed in the last subsection. The *commodity space* X is now $\{\mathbf{x}: \mathbf{x} \geqq \mathbf{0}\}$, where all $\mathbf{x}$'s are n-dimensional vectors; occasionally we shall restrict attention only to the set of all *positive* commodity bundles, i.e., $X^+ = \{\mathbf{x}: \mathbf{x} > \mathbf{0}\}$. Any $\mathbf{x} \in X$ will be called a "bundle" or

* In this example we are recalling Definitions 7a and 8a of Chapter 2, which together with the associated footnote defined what is meant by the symbol $\geqq$ in this context. Briefly, $\mathbf{x}^0 \geqq \mathbf{x}^1$ means $x_i^0 \geqq x_i^1$ for all i; $\mathbf{x}^0 > \mathbf{x}^1$ means $x_i^0 \geqq x_i^1$ for all i with *strict* inequality ($x_i^0 > x_i^1$) holding at least once; and $\mathbf{x}^0 \gg \mathbf{x}^1$ means $x_i^0 > x_i^1$ for all i. Note that we use different symbols for inequalities between *numbers*.

"batch," and any $\mathbf{x} \in X^+$ a p-bundle; a vector in X but not in X^+ will be called a b-bundle ("b" being mnemonic for "boundary," and "p" for "positive").

To each commodity i in a bundle there corresponds a positive money price p_i, and so we are lead naturally to the n-dimensional positive price vectors $\mathbf{p}$. A *price-income situation* or, more briefly, just a **situation**, is then an $(n + 1)$-dimensional vector $\mathbf{s}$, given by the vector identity $\mathbf{s} \equiv (\mathbf{p}, M)$, where $\mathbf{p} \gg \mathbf{0}$ and $M > 0$. The set of all **situations** $\mathbf{s}$ will be denoted by S.

We can now define attainable sets in this n-dimensional problem. Given any **situation** $\mathbf{s}^0 (\equiv (\mathbf{p}^0, M))$, the *attainable set corresponding to* $\mathbf{s}^0$, denoted by $A(\mathbf{s}^0)$, is $\{\mathbf{x} \in X : \mathbf{p}^0\mathbf{x} \leqq M^0\}$. In two dimensions $A(\mathbf{s}^0)$ is simply a triangle, as with OAB in Fig. 6.1, in three dimensions it is a tetrahedron, with vertices on each axis and at the origin, and in general it is an n-simplex in the n-dimensional space X.

Notice that this definition, although it assigns a unique set of attainable bundles for a given $\mathbf{s}^0$, does not work the other way round, assigning a unique $\mathbf{s}$ for a given attainable set. For if we consider the set of price-income situations given by $r\mathbf{s}^0$, where r is any positive number, then the set of $\mathbf{x} \in X$ which satisfies $\mathbf{p}^0\mathbf{x} \leqq M^0$ will obviously satisfy $r\mathbf{p}^0\mathbf{x} \leqq rM^0$ as well; thus, for $r > 0$, $A(\mathbf{s}^0) = A(r\mathbf{s}^0)$. The economic meaning of this is simply that, by raising or lowering all prices *and* income by a given "scale" factor r, we will not alter the individual's opportunities at all, since he can still continue to buy exactly the same bundles as before.

Associated with each attainable set, and therefore with each **situation** $\mathbf{s}$, is the budget plane forming the "upper boundary" or *frontier*, as it were, of $A(\mathbf{s})$; in two dimensions this is the budget *line*, in three dimensions it is a triangle, and in n dimensions it is an n-dimensional "hyperplane." A more formal definition is that the *frontier* F^0 of any attainable set $A(\mathbf{s}^0)$ is the set $\{\mathbf{x} \in X : \mathbf{p}^0\mathbf{x} = M\}$. Sometimes we shall short-circuit this description, and refer to the frontier F^0 associated with the **situation** $\mathbf{s}^0$; note that the frontier associated with $\mathbf{s}^0$ and that with $r\mathbf{s}^0$ are the same, for any $r > 0$.

Finally, we can make precise what we mean by an Engel curve in this n-dimensional situation. As before, it is simply the set of batches which are bought at a *fixed* set of money prices $\mathbf{p}$, and at all possible incomes M. Formally, the *Engel curve* $\mathbf{E}^0$ *associated with a price vector* $\mathbf{p}^0$ is defined to be the *set*

$$\{\mathbf{x} \in X : \mathbf{p}^0\mathbf{x} = M, \qquad \text{for all } M > 0\}.$$

Notice that, just as in two dimensions, this set is truly a curve in the n-dimensional space X, i.e., a "one-parameter" locus of batches, the parameter being M itself. It does not follow from the definition that it is necessarily a *continuous* curve; but the complete axiom system will in fact ensure this.

With these notational conventions agreed upon, we can now formulate the first axiom, which corresponds with Preliminary Axiom 1; this simply formalizes the market situation and needs no further discussion.

Axiom C1. The consumer always faces a **situation** and cannot change the prices in that **situation** by his own action.

The second axiom is a much milder version of Preliminary Axiom 2.

Axiom C2. A bundle is always chosen by the consumer in any **situation.**

This postulate is about as innocuous as an axiom can be. It asserts only that, in any market situation, Adam will not hesitate indefinitely like Buridan's ass but will actually buy *something*. It is therefore strongly reminiscent of Axiom PIII, which assumed merely that any individual selects a bundle from the maximal class of any attainable set. Notice that C2 is less restrictive than its preliminary version, which stated that a *unique* bundle is chosen in any $\mathbf{s}^0$, so that choice *functions* exist; that stronger version will be derived as a simple consequence of part of the present axiom system.

Now we come to the idea that Adam spends all his income, an idea formalized by

Axiom C3. In any **situation** $\mathbf{s}^0$, the bundle chosen by the consumer always belongs to the frontier $\boldsymbol{F}^0$.

This axiom is the same—apart from the choice of language—as Preliminary Axiom 3, which was discussed at some length; we can therefore proceed immediately to the next axiom, which has not been mentioned before because it was not needed in the example we gave.

Since the preference structures of Chapter 2 cover the whole of $\boldsymbol{X}$, if we are to obtain *any* kind of equivalence between the two approaches, we need to bring *every* bundle in $\boldsymbol{X}$ into the orbit of choice theory. This amounts to saying that each bundle is bought in *some* price-income situation, an assumption that we will formalize as

Axiom C4. For each bundle $\mathbf{x}$, there exists a **situation** at which the consumer chooses $\mathbf{x}$.

Notice that we do not say that the **situation** is unique, which would be much stronger, but merely that at least one such $\mathbf{s}$ exists. Since it brings every bundle within the rubric of choice theory, this axiom *appears* to be closely analogous to PI, the Axiom of Comparability. But, as we shall see, it has in fact more affinities with PVI, the Axiom of Convexity, for if the latter holds, then C4 would certainly be true, as the reader may check by means of two- or three-dimensional illustrations.

We come now to the key axiom in the theory of choice behavior, which Samuelson calls the "Weak Axiom of Revealed Preference," but which we shall call the *Axiom of Consistency of Choice,* for reasons that will become apparent. First, we need to introduce the idea of a bundle $\mathbf{x}^0$ being "chosen rather than" another bundle $\mathbf{x}^1$. If $\mathbf{x}^0$ is chosen in a given $\mathbf{s}^0$, and $\mathbf{x}^1$ is *any* other bundle in $A(\mathbf{s}^0)$, then we say that $\mathbf{x}^0$ is *chosen rather than* $\mathbf{x}^1$, a relation between *pairs* of commodity bundles which we will denote by $\mathbf{x}^0C\mathbf{x}^1$.* Note carefully that in order for two bundles $\mathbf{x}^0$ and $\mathbf{x}^1$ to be related by C, it is not enough that, valued at any old prices $\mathbf{p}$, we have $\mathbf{px}^0 \geqq \mathbf{px}^1$. The valuation must be performed *at the prices at which* $\mathbf{x}^0$ *is actually bought.* We now postulate

AXIOM C5. C is an asymmetric relation in X.

This means that for all pairs of bundles $\mathbf{x}^0$ and $\mathbf{x}^1$ such that $\mathbf{x}^0C\mathbf{x}^1$, we have $\sim(\mathbf{x}^1C\mathbf{x}^0)$. This basic consistency condition may be expressed in "inner product" terms as follows: if $\mathbf{x}^0C\mathbf{x}^1$, this means that $\mathbf{p}^0\mathbf{x}^0 \geqq \mathbf{p}^0\mathbf{x}^1$, and similarly, $\mathbf{x}^1C\mathbf{x}^0$ corresponds to $\mathbf{p}^1\mathbf{x}^1 \geqq \mathbf{p}^1\mathbf{x}^0$. Therefore, C5 asserts that the statement $\mathbf{p}^0\mathbf{x}^0 \geqq \mathbf{p}^0\mathbf{x}^1$ implies the statement $\mathbf{p}^1\mathbf{x}^0 > \mathbf{p}^1\mathbf{x}^1$, *given* that $\mathbf{x}^0$ was bought at $\mathbf{s}^0$, and $\mathbf{x}^1$ at $\mathbf{s}^1$. Observe that this axiom requires C4 if it is to have real meaning, for without C4 we are not sure that *any* of the bundles $\mathbf{x}^1$ satisfying the relation $\mathbf{x}^0C\mathbf{x}^1$ are ever bought at all.

Axiom C5 is certainly implied by the set of axioms for a preference structure, for with strict convexity of preference any bundle selected in a given market situation, say $\mathbf{x}^0$ bought at $\mathbf{s}^0$, is strictly *preferred* to any other bundle, say $\mathbf{x}^1$, in the relevant attainable set, *i.e.*, $\mathbf{x}^0P\mathbf{x}^1$. If now C5 is false, and $\mathbf{x}^1$ can be selected when $\mathbf{x}^0$ is available, this means that $\mathbf{x}^1P\mathbf{x}^0$, which by the transitivity of P—deduced from Axiom PII—implies that $\mathbf{x}^0P\mathbf{x}^0$, contrary to the definition of P. Therefore failure of C5 is akin to failure of PII, which is a good reason for calling both of them consistency axioms. It must be made clear, however, that C5 does not by itself assert the transitivity of any relation, but only the asymmetry of C.

Extension of the Choice Relation

One drawback of C is that it is *not* true that for any pair of bundles $\mathbf{x}^0$ and $\mathbf{x}^1$, either $\mathbf{x}^0C\mathbf{x}^1$ or $\mathbf{x}^1C\mathbf{x}^0$. This is basically because C is a relation defined to hold only between a bundle $\mathbf{x}^0$ bought in any **situation** $\mathbf{s}^0$ and all other bundles achievable in that **situation**; and of course no attainable set can cover the whole unbounded space X.

Thus in Fig. 6.3, the bundles $\mathbf{x}^0$ and $\mathbf{x}^2$ are such that neither $\mathbf{x}^0C\mathbf{x}^2$ nor $\mathbf{x}^2C\mathbf{x}^0$; the two batches are *incomparable* with respect to the relation C.

* In Chapter 2 and beyond, we used a subscript with each relational symbol (e.g., R_A) to indicate that the ordering concerned referred to a particular individual, such as Adam. In this chapter we are concerned only with one individual throughout, so for simplicity of notation we shall not employ subscripts for any relational symbol, either for the choice relations, or for the preference relations, which previously had them; thus R_A, P_A, and I_A become R, P, and I, respectively.

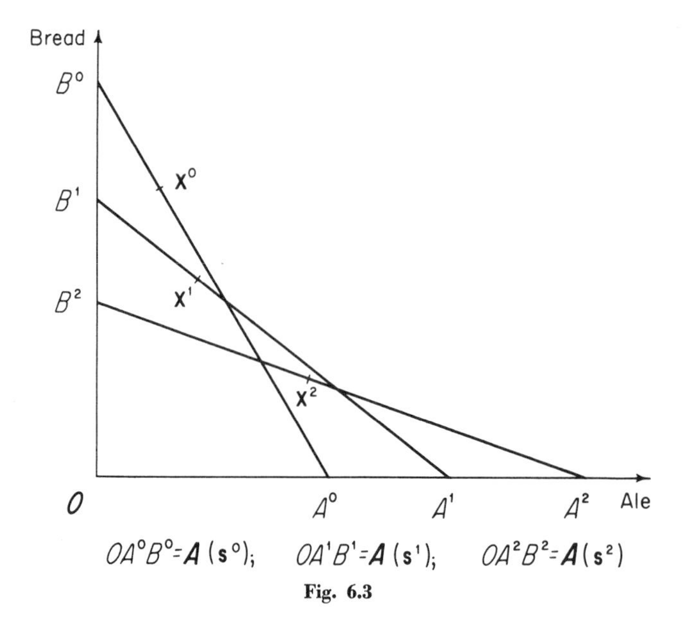

Fig. 6.3

Further—and for basically the same reason—the relation C is not transitive either. In the diagram, $\mathbf{x}^0 C \mathbf{x}^1$ and $\mathbf{x}^1 C \mathbf{x}^2$, but $\sim(\mathbf{x}^0 C \mathbf{x}^2)$, even though the consistency axiom C5 holds throughout, since $\mathbf{x}^0 \notin \boldsymbol{A}(\mathbf{s}^1)$ and $\mathbf{x}^1 \notin \boldsymbol{A}(\mathbf{s}^2)$.

The relation C is therefore inadequate as an instrument by which to establish a complete—or even a partial*—ordering of $\boldsymbol{X}$; yet a complete ordering of some kind is necessary if we are to establish anything like equivalence of the set of choice axioms and the set of preference axioms. Therefore we have to search for another candidate for the job of ordering relation.

It seems sensible first of all to try to *extend* the choice relation C in such a way that the new version takes on at least one of the desirable properties of an ordering relation, namely, transitivity. Therefore we shall define a new relation based on C, as it were, which will be shown to have potentially a wide range of application in $\boldsymbol{X}$. We shall say that a bundle $\mathbf{x}^0$ is *sequentially chosen rather than* another bundle $\mathbf{x}^1$ if there exists a *finite* chain of bundles $\mathbf{x}^{(1)}, \mathbf{x}^{(2)}, \ldots, \mathbf{x}^{(T-1)}, \mathbf{x}^{(T)}$, where T can be any positive integer, such that $\mathbf{x}^0 C \mathbf{x}^{(1)}, \mathbf{x}^{(1)} C \mathbf{x}^{(2)}, \ldots, \mathbf{x}^{(T-1)} C \mathbf{x}^{(T)}$, and $\mathbf{x}^{(T)} C \mathbf{x}^1$. If $\mathbf{x}^0$ is sequentially chosen rather than $\mathbf{x}^1$, then we shall write $\mathbf{x}^0 Q \mathbf{x}^1$, where Q is mnemonic for "queue"

* Let us recall some definitions from Chapter 2. A set $\boldsymbol{Z}$ is said to be *partially ordered* by a relation R if *some* pairs of elements of $\boldsymbol{Z}$ are ordered by R, and R obeys Axiom PII; it is *completely ordered* by R if R obeys PII, and *all* pairs of elements from $\boldsymbol{Z}$ are ordered by R. If R is reflexive as well, it is called a "weak" complete ordering, and if it is irreflexive, then it is a "strong" complete ordering; it follows that strong orderings are necessarily asymmetric.

and—by association—for "sequential"; any finite "connecting" sequence such as $\mathbf{x}^{(1)}, \mathbf{x}^{(2)}, \ldots, \mathbf{x}^{(T)}$ will be termed a *Q-sequence.**

This new relation is certainly transitive, for if $\mathbf{x}^0 Q \mathbf{x}^1$ and $\mathbf{x}^1 Q \mathbf{x}^2$, then we need only connect the Q-sequence from $\mathbf{x}^0$ to $\mathbf{x}^1$ with that from $\mathbf{x}^1$ to $\mathbf{x}^2$ in order to obtain a finite chain linking $\mathbf{x}^0$ to $\mathbf{x}^2$; hence $\mathbf{x}^0 Q \mathbf{x}^2$. It looks as though we are on the right track in our search for an ordering relation.

The next step is to point out an interesting consequence of the axiom system that has been constructed so far, namely that if $\mathbf{x}^0 C \mathbf{x}^1$, then $\mathbf{x}^0 Q \mathbf{x}^1$. In words, if a batch $\mathbf{x}^0$ is chosen rather than $\mathbf{x}^1$, then we can always find a finite sequence which will link the two, so that Q is truly an *extension* of C. This result is reached as the last of three little theorems on choice behavior, which are the earliest examples of a whole series of *demand theorems* that we shall prove and which we shall label D1, D2, and so on.

THEOREM D1. If $\mathbf{x}^k$ is a convex combination of any two batches $\mathbf{x}^0$ and $\mathbf{x}^1$, and $\mathbf{x}^0 \neq \mathbf{x}^k \neq \mathbf{x}^1$, then either $\mathbf{x}^k C \mathbf{x}^0$ or $\mathbf{x}^k C \mathbf{x}^1$ (both may occur).

PROOF: By hypothesis

$$\mathbf{x}^k = k\mathbf{x}^0 + (1 - k)\mathbf{x}^1, \qquad 0 < k < 1 \tag{3}$$

By Axiom C4, there exists a price vector, $\mathbf{p}^k$ say, at which $\mathbf{x}^k$ is bought, with income $M^k = \mathbf{p}^k\mathbf{x}^k$. Then it follows from (3) that

$$\mathbf{p}^k\mathbf{x}^k = k\mathbf{p}^k\mathbf{x}^0 + (1 - k)\mathbf{p}^k\mathbf{x}^1$$

which means that, since the left-hand side is a weighted average of the two inner products on the right-hand side, either $\mathbf{p}^k\mathbf{x}^k \geqq \mathbf{p}^k\mathbf{x}^0$, or $\mathbf{p}^k\mathbf{x}^k \geqq \mathbf{p}^k\mathbf{x}^1$ (or both). Since $\mathbf{x}^k$ is actually bought at prices $\mathbf{p}^k$, the result follows. *Q.E.D.*†

THEOREM D2. If $\mathbf{x}^k$ is a convex combination of two batches $\mathbf{x}^0$ and $\mathbf{x}^1$ such that $\mathbf{x}^0 C \mathbf{x}^1$, and $\mathbf{x}^0 \neq \mathbf{x}^k$, then $\mathbf{x}^0 C \mathbf{x}^k$.

PROOF: Assume the result to be false, so that $\mathbf{p}^0\mathbf{x}^0 < \mathbf{p}^0\mathbf{x}^k$. Then, using the definition (3) of $\mathbf{x}^k$, this implies that

$$\mathbf{p}^0\mathbf{x}^0 < k\mathbf{p}^0\mathbf{x}^0 + (1 - k)\mathbf{p}^0\mathbf{x}^1$$

from which, since $0 \leqq k < 1$, $\mathbf{p}^0\mathbf{x}^0 < \mathbf{p}^0\mathbf{x}^1$. But this means that $\sim(\mathbf{x}^0 C \mathbf{x}^1)$, contrary to hypothesis. Therefore the assumption that D2 is false gives a contradiction, so it must be true. *Q.E.D.*

* Most discussions of the choice behavior approach use the words "revealed preferred" for the relation "chosen," and "indirectly revealed preferred" for "sequentially chosen." The present terminology is meant to emphasize that "chosen" refers to comparisons between pairs of bundles which are *simultaneously* available in a market **situation**, whereas "sequentially chosen" refers to comparisons based on a *chain* of such **situations** which obviously cannot all coexist.

† In order to avoid any possible misunderstanding, we will always be careful to signal the end of a proof, using this classical formula to do so. The reader will probably find it useful, in following the simple proofs of this section, to draw his own two- or three-dimensional illustrations, though the proofs are of course self-contained without them.

THEOREM D3. If two bundles $\mathbf{x}^0$ and $\mathbf{x}^1$ are such that $\mathbf{x}^0 C \mathbf{x}^1$, then $\mathbf{x}^0 Q \mathbf{x}^1$.

PROOF: Let $\mathbf{x}^k$ be any *c.c.* of $\mathbf{x}^0$ and $\mathbf{x}^1$ such that $\mathbf{x}^0 \neq \mathbf{x}^k \neq \mathbf{x}^1$. Then by D2, $\mathbf{x}^0 C \mathbf{x}^k$ which by Axiom C5 implies that $\sim(\mathbf{x}^k C \mathbf{x}^0)$. Therefore it follows from D1 that $\mathbf{x}^k C \mathbf{x}^1$; but this gives us $\mathbf{x}^0 C \mathbf{x}^k$ and $\mathbf{x}^k C \mathbf{x}^1$, which by definition of Q means $\mathbf{x}^0 Q \mathbf{x}^1$. *Q.E.D.* The "contrapositive" of D3 is that if $\sim(\mathbf{x}^1 Q \mathbf{x}^0)$, then $\sim(\mathbf{x}^1 C \mathbf{x}^0)$.

It is convenient at this stage to introduce a "sub-relation," as it were, which will prove very useful. Let $\mathbf{x}^0$ and $\mathbf{x}^{00}$ be any two different batches on the *same* Engel curve $\boldsymbol{E}^0$ in X^0, and let M^0 and M^{00} be the respective associated incomes; then either $M^0 > M^{00}$ or $M^{00} > M^0$. Now introduce the relation "higher than on the same Engel curve" (written $\mathbf{x}^0 H \mathbf{x}^{00}$) by the definition: $\mathbf{x}^0 H \mathbf{x}^{00}$ if $\mathbf{x}^0$ and $\mathbf{x}^{00}$ are both bought at prices $\mathbf{p}^0$, and $M^0 > M^{00}$. Obviously $\mathbf{x}^0 H \mathbf{x}^{00}$ implies $\mathbf{x}^0 C \mathbf{x}^{00}$ which, in turn, because of D3, implies $\mathbf{x}^0 Q \mathbf{x}^{00}$. Moreover, $\sim(\mathbf{x}^0 H \mathbf{x}^{00})$ implies $(\mathbf{x}^{00} H \mathbf{x}^0)$, unless $\mathbf{x}^0$ and $\mathbf{x}^{00}$ are identical.

Equipped with Theorems D1 to D3, we can now fulfil an earlier promise to show that choice behavior is "convex" in the following precise sense:

THEOREM D4. For any bundle $\mathbf{x}^0$, the set $\{\mathbf{x} \in X : \mathbf{x} Q \mathbf{x}^0\}$ is convex.

PROOF: We have only to show that for any pair of bundles $\mathbf{x}^1$ and $\mathbf{x}^2$ such that $\mathbf{x}^1 Q \mathbf{x}^0$ and $\mathbf{x}^2 Q \mathbf{x}^0$, any *c.c.* $\mathbf{x}^k$ of $\mathbf{x}^1$ and $\mathbf{x}^2$ such that $\mathbf{x}^1 \neq \mathbf{x}^k \neq \mathbf{x}^2$ is also such that $\mathbf{x}^k Q \mathbf{x}^0$. By D1, either $\mathbf{x}^k C \mathbf{x}^1$ or $\mathbf{x}^k C \mathbf{x}^2$, which by D3 implies that either $\mathbf{x}^k Q \mathbf{x}^1$ or $\mathbf{x}^k Q \mathbf{x}^2$. In the one case we have $\mathbf{x}^k Q \mathbf{x}^1$ and $\mathbf{x}^1 Q \mathbf{x}^0$, and in the other, $\mathbf{x}^k Q \mathbf{x}^2$ and $\mathbf{x}^2 Q \mathbf{x}^0$; in either event $\mathbf{x}^k Q \mathbf{x}^0$, so that the set is convex. *Q.E.D.* Notice that the chief axioms used are C4 (for the proof of D1), and C5 (for D3); both together give the convexity.

Inaccessible Pairs of Bundles. Thus on the strength of this result, we can expect that the relation Q will apply to quite a wide range of pairs of bundles in X. In order to delimit what this domain of Q is to be, let us first introduce two more concepts. We shall say that a pair of bundles $\mathbf{x}^0$ and $\mathbf{x}^1$ is *accessible* if either $\mathbf{x}^0 Q \mathbf{x}^1$ or $\mathbf{x}^1 Q \mathbf{x}^0$; and that the pair is *inaccessible* (written $\mathbf{x}^0 In \mathbf{x}^1$) if this is not the case.* This means that a pair $\mathbf{x}^0$ and $\mathbf{x}^1$ in X is inaccessible only if $\sim(\mathbf{x}^0 Q \mathbf{x}^1$ or $\mathbf{x}^1 Q \mathbf{x}^0)$, i.e., if we cannot find a Q-sequence (which by definition must be finite) from $\mathbf{x}^0$ to $\mathbf{x}^1$, *and* we cannot find a Q-sequence going in the reverse direction, from $\mathbf{x}^1$ to $\mathbf{x}^0$.

By their definitions, both "accessibility" and "inaccessibility" are symmetric relations, but we know nothing about any other properties that they

* These useful terms are borrowed from thermodynamics, for there is a quite striking parallelism between our theory and Carathéodory's axiomatic formulation of the second law of thermodynamics. To avoid mystical overtones, let us be clear that it is only the *mathematical structures* of the problems that are so close, and not the actual contents of the two theories.

might have. In particular, *In* might be a completely vacuous relation in X, by which we mean that *all* pairs of bundles might be accessible and none inaccessible. This state of affairs would not upset most of demand theory proper but would make it impossible to prove equivalence of the two axiom systems. For let us suppose—to anticipate things a little—that the Q-relation in choice theory *implies* the P relation in preference theory. Then if all pairs of bundles in X are accessible, there is no possibility that $\mathbf{x}^0 R \mathbf{x}^1$ and *not* $\mathbf{x}^0 P \mathbf{x}^1$, i.e., no possibility that "indifferent" pairs of bundles can exist.

The reader will remember that a similar problem arose in preference theory, where we had to introduce a special "continuity" axiom on preferences in order to ensure that batches indifferent to a given bundle $\mathbf{x}^0$ actually existed. So now in choice theory we have to postulate some kind of continuity condition on the sequential choice relation Q, in order to assert with confidence the existence of inaccessible pairs of batches in X. As before, there are a number of equivalent statements of this continuity axiom, and—once again—we choose the frankest version, which *is* simply to assert the existence of a class of inaccessible batches for any bundle $\mathbf{x}^0$. The formal postulate is

Axiom C6. For any two distinct Engel curves E^0 and E^1, and any $\mathbf{x}^0$ on E^0, there exists a unique batch $\mathbf{x}^{01}$ on E^1 such that $\mathbf{x}^0 In \mathbf{x}^{01}$.

This says that any Engel curve whatever—apart from E^0—contains a batch inaccessible from $\mathbf{x}^0$. This in turn implies that we could never, by any conceivable chain of observable market situations, find out whether $\mathbf{x}^0$ is sequentially chosen rather than $\mathbf{x}^{01}$, or conversely, because only an unlimited sequence of batches could do that, and the observable sequences would necessarily have to be finite.

The power of this seemingly innocuous axiom may be gauged by noting that it is true by Axiom C4 and definition of the terms involved that either a pair of bundles is accessible or it is inaccessible; this axiom then says that only a rather small—but definite—class of batches is inaccessible "with" a given $\mathbf{x}^0$, namely just one batch on each Engel curve. Hence the relation of accessibility, and therefore of Q, must cover the whole of the rest of X, so that it has a very large domain.

As with many axioms about preferences or behavior, it is difficult to judge the "realism" of C6 until its full consequences are known, so it is best to postpone such discussion until the theory has been more fully developed. It will turn out to be an essential axiom in the proof of "equivalence," being neither too strong nor too weak; in fact many of the comments about its preference "sister," Axiom PV, are just as relevant here.

Several important results become more or less immediate consequences of the addition of C6 to the axiom system. The first three deal with properties of Q, and in fact could equally well be proved (as the reader may check) by using a weaker assumption than C6, to the effect that *at least* one batch

$\mathbf{x}^{01}$ exists on $\mathbf{x}^0$ such that $\mathbf{x}^0 In \mathbf{x}^{01}$; the proofs would proceed exactly as they do here.

THEOREM D5. Q is an asymmetric relation in X.

PROOF: We have to show that for any two bundles $\mathbf{x}^0$ and $\mathbf{x}^1$ such that $\mathbf{x}^0 Q \mathbf{x}^1$, (where $\mathbf{x}^1$ is bought at prices $\mathbf{p}^1$), we have $\sim(\mathbf{x}^1 Q \mathbf{x}^0)$. Let $\mathbf{x}^{01}$ be a batch on E^1 such that $\mathbf{x}^0 In \mathbf{x}^{01}$; such a batch necessarily exists because of C6. Then $\sim(\mathbf{x}^1 Q \mathbf{x}^{01})$, for, otherwise, $\mathbf{x}^0 Q \mathbf{x}^1$ and $\mathbf{x}^1 Q \mathbf{x}^{01}$ would yield the false conclusion $\mathbf{x}^0 Q \mathbf{x}^{01}$. Since $\sim(\mathbf{x}^1 Q \mathbf{x}^{01})$, by D3 we have $\sim(\mathbf{x}^1 C \mathbf{x}^{01})$, which means—since $\mathbf{x}^1$ and $\mathbf{x}^{01}$ are both on E^1—that $\sim(\mathbf{x}^1 H \mathbf{x}^{01})$, or $\mathbf{x}^{01} H \mathbf{x}^1$. But then $\mathbf{x}^{01} C \mathbf{x}^1$, which by D3 again yields $\mathbf{x}^{01} Q \mathbf{x}^1$. This in turn implies $\sim(\mathbf{x}^1 Q \mathbf{x}^0)$, for, otherwise, $\mathbf{x}^{01} Q \mathbf{x}^1$ and $\mathbf{x}^1 Q \mathbf{x}^0$ yield $\mathbf{x}^{01} Q \mathbf{x}^0$, contrary to hypothesis. Therefore, $\mathbf{x}^0 Q \mathbf{x}^1$ implies $\sim(\mathbf{x}^1 Q \mathbf{x}^0)$. *Q.E.D.*

Note that Theorem D5 *proves* for Q the same property that Axiom C5 *asserts* for C. Most expositions of the relation between "choice" theory and preference theory in fact replace C5 by this condition on Q which is called the "Strong Axiom of Revealed Preference," and then add certain essential continuity conditions on the choice functions themselves in order to prove "equivalence" with the preference axioms. The present approach is apparently less satisfactory in that, in a sense, it cuts the Gordian knot of the problem by frankly assuming the powerful Axiom C6; but it does have two important advantages. First, it is much simpler than the other method, which involves a rather lengthy and inelegant detour into the differential calculus and out again.* Secondly, the present approach places conditions directly on the choice *relations* themselves and not explicitly on the choice *functions*, which indeed have not yet been shown even to exist, let alone to have continuity properties.

THEOREM D6. Q is an irreflexive relation in X.

PROOF: We have to show that $\sim(\mathbf{x}^0 Q \mathbf{x}^0)$ for all bundles $\mathbf{x}^0$. Suppose the result to be false for at least one bundle $\mathbf{x}^0$, and let $\mathbf{x}^1$ be any batch in a Q-sequence from $\mathbf{x}^0$ to $\mathbf{x}^0$. Then either $\mathbf{x}^0 C \mathbf{x}^1$ or $\mathbf{x}^0 Q \mathbf{x}^1$. Because of D3, we have $\mathbf{x}^0 Q \mathbf{x}^1$ in either case; similarly, $\mathbf{x}^1 Q \mathbf{x}^0$. But then $\mathbf{x}^0 Q \mathbf{x}^1$ and $\mathbf{x}^1 Q \mathbf{x}^0$ contradicts D5, so Q must be irreflexive. *Q.E.D.*

Hence Q—like P—is a strong ordering relation, for by definition it is transitive, and we have just proved that it is asymmetric and irreflexive.

THEOREM D7. For any bundle $\mathbf{x}^0$, the set $\{\mathbf{x} \in X: \sim(\mathbf{x}^0 Q \mathbf{x})\}$ is convex.

PROOF: Let $\mathbf{x}^1$ and $\mathbf{x}^2$ be any two distinct bundles in the set, and let $\mathbf{x}^k$ be any *c.c.* of $\mathbf{x}^1$ and $\mathbf{x}^2$ not equal to either of them. Then there are four

* This implies the additional advantage of not needing to assume that the theory applies only to X^+, and not to X, which is necessary if one uses a calculus approach.

cases to deal with: (1) $\mathbf{x}^1 Q \mathbf{x}^0$ and $\mathbf{x}^2 Q \mathbf{x}^0$; (2) $\mathbf{x}^1 In \mathbf{x}^0$ and $\mathbf{x}^2 In \mathbf{x}^0$; (3) $\mathbf{x}^1 Q \mathbf{x}^0$ and $\mathbf{x}^2 In \mathbf{x}^0$; and (4) $\mathbf{x}^1 In \mathbf{x}^0$ and $\mathbf{x}^2 Q \mathbf{x}^0$; we prove the result for each in turn. (1) From D4 we have $\mathbf{x}^k Q \mathbf{x}^0$, which by D5 implies $\sim(\mathbf{x}^0 Q \mathbf{x}^k)$. (2) Suppose the result false, so that $\mathbf{x}^0 Q \mathbf{x}^k$. Then from D1 we have either $\mathbf{x}^k C \mathbf{x}^1$ or $\mathbf{x}^k C \mathbf{x}^2$, so that either $\mathbf{x}^0 Q \mathbf{x}^1$ or $\mathbf{x}^0 Q \mathbf{x}^2$, contrary to hypothesis. Therefore, $\sim(\mathbf{x}^0 Q \mathbf{x}^k)$. (3) Suppose $\mathbf{x}^0 Q \mathbf{x}^k$. Then $\mathbf{x}^1 Q \mathbf{x}^0$ and $\mathbf{x}^0 Q \mathbf{x}^k$ imply $\mathbf{x}^1 Q \mathbf{x}^k$, which by D5 yields $\sim(\mathbf{x}^k Q \mathbf{x}^1)$ and by D3 in turn implies $\sim(\mathbf{x}^k C \mathbf{x}^1)$. Then from D1 we can conclude that $\mathbf{x}^k C \mathbf{x}^2$, so that we have $\mathbf{x}^0 Q \mathbf{x}^k$ and $\mathbf{x}^k C \mathbf{x}^2$, yielding $\mathbf{x}^0 Q \mathbf{x}^2$, contrary to hypothesis. Therefore, $\sim(\mathbf{x}^0 Q \mathbf{x}^k)$. (4) Exactly as for (3). *Q.E.D.*

We now prove some results about the relation *In* which, unlike the last three, depend essentially upon the full force of C6, namely, that the batch inaccessible from $\mathbf{x}^0$ on any Engel curve be actually *unique.*

THEOREM D8. *In* is a transitive relation in X.

PROOF: We have to show that if $\mathbf{x}^0$, $\mathbf{x}^{01}$, and $\mathbf{x}^{012}$ on E^0, E^1, and E^2, respectively are such that $\mathbf{x}^0 In \mathbf{x}^{01}$ and $\mathbf{x}^{01} In \mathbf{x}^{012}$, then $\mathbf{x}^0 In \mathbf{x}^{012}$. Because of the symmetry of *In*, this means that the batch $\mathbf{x}^{20}$ on E^0 such that $\mathbf{x}^{012} In \mathbf{x}^{20}$ must be *identical* to $\mathbf{x}^0$; it will be useful to provide an explicit three-dimensional illustration of this construction, in Fig. 6.4.

Suppose the conclusion to be false, so that $\mathbf{x}^0 \neq \mathbf{x}^{20}$; there are then two cases: (1) $\mathbf{x}^{20} H \mathbf{x}^0$ or (2) $\mathbf{x}^0 H \mathbf{x}^{20}$; we shall take (1) first. Let $\mathbf{x}^{00}$ be a batch on E^0 *between* $\mathbf{x}^{20}$ and $\mathbf{x}^0$ (i.e., $M^{20} > M^{00} > M^0$), so that $\mathbf{x}^{20} H \mathbf{x}^{00}$ and $\mathbf{x}^{00} H \mathbf{x}^0$. Then $\mathbf{x}^{00} Q \mathbf{x}^{01}$; for *(1)* if $\mathbf{x}^{01} Q \mathbf{x}^{00}$, then the fact that $\mathbf{x}^{00} H \mathbf{x}^0$ means that $\mathbf{x}^{01} Q \mathbf{x}^0$, contrary to hypothesis; and *(2)* $\sim(\mathbf{x}^{00} In \mathbf{x}^{01})$, because of the uniqueness of $\mathbf{x}^0$'s inaccessibility to $\mathbf{x}^{01}$; hence the only possibility left is $\mathbf{x}^{00} Q \mathbf{x}^{01}$. Similarly, we have $\mathbf{x}^{012} Q \mathbf{x}^{00}$; for *(3)* if $\mathbf{x}^{00} Q \mathbf{x}^{012}$, then $\mathbf{x}^{20} H \mathbf{x}^{00}$ means that $\mathbf{x}^{20} Q \mathbf{x}^{012}$, contrary to hypothesis; and *(4)* $\sim(\mathbf{x}^{00} In \mathbf{x}^{012})$, because of the uniqueness of $\mathbf{x}^{20}$'s inaccessibility to $\mathbf{x}^{012}$; hence the only possibility left is $\mathbf{x}^{012} Q \mathbf{x}^{00}$.

But $\mathbf{x}^{012} Q \mathbf{x}^{00}$ and $\mathbf{x}^{00} Q \mathbf{x}^{01}$ imply $\mathbf{x}^{012} Q \mathbf{x}^{01}$, contrary to hypothesis. Therefore we cannot have $\mathbf{x}^0 \neq \mathbf{x}^{20}$.

(2) This case is proved just as for (1), showing first that $\mathbf{x}^{01} Q \mathbf{x}^{00}$ and then that $\mathbf{x}^{00} Q \mathbf{x}^{012}$, yielding the contradiction that $\mathbf{x}^{01} Q \mathbf{x}^{012}$. *Q.E.D.*

THEOREM D9. *In* is a reflexive relation in X.

PROOF: This follows immediately from the symmetry of *In* (which is true by definition) and its transitivity (from D8), since if $\mathbf{x}^0 In \mathbf{x}^1$ and $\mathbf{x}^1 In \mathbf{x}^0$, then $\mathbf{x}^0 In \mathbf{x}^0$. Note that C6 is also needed to assure us that there *is* at least one $\mathbf{x}^1$ such that $\mathbf{x}^0 In \mathbf{x}^1$, so that symmetry may be invoked. *Q.E.D.*

We have therefore shown that *In*—like the relation I in preference theory—is reflexive, symmetric, and transitive, so that it is indeed an equivalence

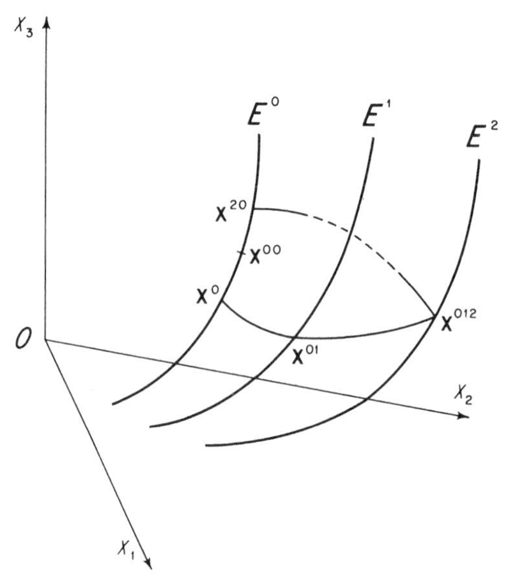

Fig. 6.4

relation. We can now prove three simple results concerning the interrelation of Q and In.

THEOREM D10. For all $\mathbf{x}^0$, $\mathbf{x}^1$, and $\mathbf{x}^2$ in X such that $\mathbf{x}^0 Q \mathbf{x}^1$ and $\mathbf{x}^1 In \mathbf{x}^2$, we have $\mathbf{x}^0 Q \mathbf{x}^2$.

PROOF: Suppose the result to be false, so that (a) either $\mathbf{x}^2 Q \mathbf{x}^0$ or (b) $\mathbf{x}^2 In \mathbf{x}^0$. If (a), then $\mathbf{x}^2 Q \mathbf{x}^1$ as well, contrary to hypothesis. If (b), then by D8 we have $\mathbf{x}^1 In \mathbf{x}^0$, contrary to hypothesis. Thus $\mathbf{x}^0 Q \mathbf{x}^2$. We may prove in a precisely similar way that $\mathbf{x}^0 In \mathbf{x}^1$ and $\mathbf{x}^1 Q \mathbf{x}^2$ imply $\mathbf{x}^0 Q \mathbf{x}^2$.

THEOREM D11. If $\mathbf{x}^0$, $\mathbf{x}^1$, and $\mathbf{x}^2$ are three distinct bundles such that $\mathbf{x}^0 In \mathbf{x}^1$ and $\mathbf{x}^0 In \mathbf{x}^2$, then for any *c.c.* $\mathbf{x}^k$ of $\mathbf{x}^1$ and $\mathbf{x}^2$ such that $\mathbf{x}^1 \neq \mathbf{x}^k \neq \mathbf{x}^2$, we have $\mathbf{x}^k Q \mathbf{x}^0$.

PROOF: From D7 we know that $\sim(\mathbf{x}^0 Q \mathbf{x}^k)$, so that we only have to show that $\sim(\mathbf{x}^0 In \mathbf{x}^k)$. If this were false, then from D9 we could conclude that $\mathbf{x}^1 In \mathbf{x}^0$ and $\mathbf{x}^0 In \mathbf{x}^k$ imply $\mathbf{x}^1 In \mathbf{x}^k$, and similarly $\mathbf{x}^2 In \mathbf{x}^k$, so that by symmetry $\mathbf{x}^k In \mathbf{x}^1$ and $\mathbf{x}^k In \mathbf{x}^2$. But from D1 we know that either $\mathbf{x}^k C \mathbf{x}^1$ or $\mathbf{x}^k C \mathbf{x}^2$, which from D3 means that either $\mathbf{x}^k Q \mathbf{x}^1$ or $\mathbf{x}^k Q \mathbf{x}^2$. This contradicts the previously established inaccessibility of *both* the pairs $\mathbf{x}^k$ and $\mathbf{x}^1$, and $\mathbf{x}^k$ and $\mathbf{x}^2$, so we must have $\sim(\mathbf{x}^0 In \mathbf{x}^k)$, which implies $\mathbf{x}^k Q \mathbf{x}^0$. *Q.E.D.*

THEOREM D12. If $\mathbf{x}^0$ is any bundle, and $\boldsymbol{E}^1$ any Engel curve, let $\mathbf{x}^{01}$ be the batch on $\boldsymbol{E}^1$ such that $\mathbf{x}^{01} In \mathbf{x}^0$. Then all batches $\mathbf{x}^1$ on $\boldsymbol{E}^1$ higher than

$\mathbf{x}^{01}$ are such that $\mathbf{x}^1 Q\mathbf{x}^0$; and all batches $\mathbf{x}^1$ on E^1 which are lower than $\mathbf{x}^{01}$ are such that $\mathbf{x}^0 Q\mathbf{x}^1$.

PROOF: To prove the first part, suppose instead that, for some $\mathbf{x}^1 H\mathbf{x}^{01}$, we had $\mathbf{x}^0 Q\mathbf{x}^1$; then $\mathbf{x}^0 Q\mathbf{x}^{01}$, contrary to hypothesis. By C6 we cannot have $\mathbf{x}^1 In\mathbf{x}^0$, so the only alternative left is $\mathbf{x}^1 Q\mathbf{x}^0$. The second part is proved similarly. If $\mathbf{x}^{01} H\mathbf{x}^1$ and $\mathbf{x}^1 Q\mathbf{x}^0$, then $\mathbf{x}^{01} Q\mathbf{x}^0$, while we cannot have $\mathbf{x}^1 In\mathbf{x}^0$ because of C6. *Q.E.D.*

Let us now define a new relation R^C, holding between pairs of bundles $\mathbf{x}^0$ and $\mathbf{x}^1$ in X, as follows: $\mathbf{x}^0 R^C \mathbf{x}^1$ if $\sim(\mathbf{x}^1 Q\mathbf{x}^0)$; this obviously has the equivalent form: $\mathbf{x}^0 R^C \mathbf{x}^1$ means ($\mathbf{x}^0 Q\mathbf{x}^1$ or $\mathbf{x}^0 In\mathbf{x}^1$). Then we have two results which end our search for an ordering relation, namely

THEOREM D13. R^C is a complete weak ordering of X.

PROOF: We have to show that R^C is complete, "weak," and transitive in X. *Completeness*: Obvious from C4 and the definitions of Q, In, and R^C. *Reflexivity*: If $\sim(\mathbf{x}^0 R^C \mathbf{x}^0)$ for some $\mathbf{x}^0$, then $\mathbf{x}^0 Q\mathbf{x}^0$, which contradicts D6. *Transitivity*: Suppose that we have $\mathbf{x}^0 R^C \mathbf{x}^1$, $\mathbf{x}^1 R^C \mathbf{x}^2$ and *not* $\mathbf{x}^0 R^C \mathbf{x}^2$ for some trio of bundles. Then by definition of R^C, $\mathbf{x}^2 Q\mathbf{x}^0$, and either $\mathbf{x}^0 Q\mathbf{x}^1$ or $\mathbf{x}^0 In\mathbf{x}^1$. In the first case we have $\mathbf{x}^2 Q\mathbf{x}^1$, and so we do in the second, because of D11; but $\mathbf{x}^2 Q\mathbf{x}^1$ contradicts $\mathbf{x}^1 R^C \mathbf{x}^2$, so R^C must be transitive for all trios in X. *Q.E.D.*

THEOREM D14. R^C possesses a continuous representation.

PROOF: This theorem means that there exists a continuous real-valued function w, say, defined on X, such that $w(\mathbf{x}^0) \geqq w(\mathbf{x}^1)$ if and only if $\mathbf{x}^0 R^C \mathbf{x}^1$. In Chapter 2, Section D(iii) we mentioned some conditions guaranteeing this result which, translated into this situation, read: For any bundles $\mathbf{x}^0$ and $\mathbf{x}^1$ such that $\mathbf{x}^0 Q\mathbf{x}^1$, there exists a set of bundles N^0 around $\mathbf{x}^0$, and a set of bundles N^1 around $\mathbf{x}^1$, such that for any $\mathbf{x}^{00}$ in N^0 we have $\mathbf{x}^{00} Q\mathbf{x}^1$, and for any $\mathbf{x}^{11}$ in N^1 we have $\mathbf{x}^0 Q\mathbf{x}^{11}$.*

In order to prove that these conditions hold, let $\mathbf{x}^0$ and $\mathbf{x}^1$ be such that $\mathbf{x}^0 Q\mathbf{x}^1$. There are then two cases to consider: (a) $\mathbf{x}^0$ and $\mathbf{x}^1$ are bought at the same prices, and are therefore such that $\mathbf{x}^0 H\mathbf{x}^1$, or (b) $\mathbf{x}^0$ and $\mathbf{x}^1$ are bought at different prices. If (a) holds, then take any batch $\mathbf{x}^{00}$ such that $\mathbf{x}^0 H\mathbf{x}^{00}$ and $\mathbf{x}^{00} H\mathbf{x}^1$, and let M^{00} be the associated income. Then the set of all batches on E^0 which are bought at incomes greater than M^{00} certainly contains $\mathbf{x}^0$ and is such that for any member $\mathbf{x}$, we have $\mathbf{x}Q\mathbf{x}^1$; we can then call this set an N^0. Similarly, the set of all batches on E^0 which are bought at

* In technical language, we require that N^0 and N^1 be *open sets* of bundles containing x^0 and x^1, respectively, and satisfying the properties mentioned. The sets obtained in the proof are all open intervals of Engel curves (i.e., open sets) around the respective batches.

incomes less than M^{00} contains $\mathbf{x}^1$, and for any $\mathbf{x}$ in it we have $\mathbf{x}^0 Q\mathbf{x}$, so it qualifies as an N^1.

If (b) holds, then let $\mathbf{x}^{01}$ on E^1 be the batch such that $\mathbf{x}^0 In\mathbf{x}^{01}$, and $\mathbf{x}^{10}$ the batch on E^0 such that $\mathbf{x}^1 In\mathbf{x}^{10}$. Then $\mathbf{x}^0 H\mathbf{x}^{10}$, for if $\mathbf{x}^{10} H\mathbf{x}^0$, then $\mathbf{x}^0 Q\mathbf{x}^1$ implies $\mathbf{x}^{10} Q\mathbf{x}^1$, contrary to hypothesis; similarly we may show that $\mathbf{x}^{01} H\mathbf{x}^1$. Consider now the set of all batches on E^0 higher than $\mathbf{x}^{10}$; this contains $\mathbf{x}^0$, as we have just proved, and by D12 every batch $\mathbf{x}$ in it is such that $\mathbf{x}Q\mathbf{x}^1$; thus this set is an N^0. Similarly, consider the set of all batches on E^1 such that $\mathbf{x}^{01}$ is higher than they. Then this set contains $\mathbf{x}^1$, and by D12 again we have $\mathbf{x}^0 Q\mathbf{x}$ for every batch in the set; therefore this set is an N^1.

In both cases (a) and (b), therefore, we have found sets N^0 and N^1 satisfying the "continuity" requirements on Q, so that a continuous representation of R^C exists. *Q.E.D.*

(iv) Comparison of the Axiom Systems

Let us now pause to collect our wits and to review what we have proved about choice behavior on the basis of Axioms C1 to C6. We first defined the basic choice relation C, and postulated its characteristic property of asymmetry, which was the Axiom of Consistency of Choice (C5). The relation C was then *extended* to the sequential choice relation Q, which in turn allowed us to introduce the relations of accessibility, and inaccessibility (In), holding between pairs of bundles in X. It was shown that Q is a strong ordering (i.e., transitive, asymmetric (D5) and irreflexive (D6)), and In an equivalence relation (i.e., transitive (D8), symmetric, and reflexive (D9)).

A final relation R^C, defined to mean $\sim Q$, was shown to be a complete, weak (D13), and continuous (D14) ordering of X. Moreover, a series of demand theorems ((D4), (D7), and (D11)) showed that, for any $\mathbf{x}^0$, the set of all bundles $\mathbf{x}$ such that $\mathbf{x}R^C\mathbf{x}^0$, is convex, and indeed *strictly* convex, by which we mean that all *c.c.*'s $\mathbf{x}^k$ of any two bundles in the set are such that $\mathbf{x}^k Q\mathbf{x}^0$, so that the boundary surface through $\mathbf{x}^0$ is itself strictly convex. It follows obviously from these results that all the bundles $\mathbf{x}$ on this boundary or "behavior surface" are inaccessible to $\mathbf{x}^0$.

Thus the relation R^C has all the properties that Axioms PI to PIV confer on the weak preference relation R in X; and it is natural to inquire whether the two relations are in fact equivalent, in the sense that, for any two bundles $\mathbf{x}^0$ and $\mathbf{x}^1$, $\mathbf{x}^0 R^C\mathbf{x}^1$ if and only if $\mathbf{x}^0 R\mathbf{x}^1$.

Let us start with the more modest aim of proving that C—and hence Q—implies P. If Adam has a complete ordering R of X, which is strictly "convex" and continuous, then his choice of a bundle $\mathbf{x}^0$ in a given **situation** $\mathbf{s}^0$ certainly implies that $\mathbf{x}^0 P\mathbf{x}$ for all $\mathbf{x} \in A(\mathbf{s}^0)$. Therefore, if we have a Q-sequence $\mathbf{x}^{(1)}, \mathbf{x}^{(2)}, \ldots, \mathbf{x}^{(T-1)}, \mathbf{x}^{(T)}$ connecting $\mathbf{x}^0$ and $\mathbf{x}^1$, we know that $\mathbf{x}^0 P\mathbf{x}^{(1)}, \mathbf{x}^{(1)} P\mathbf{x}^{(2)}, \ldots, \mathbf{x}^{(T-1)} P\mathbf{x}^{(T)}$, and $\mathbf{x}^{(T)} P\mathbf{x}^1$, so that $\mathbf{x}^0 P\mathbf{x}^1$. Hence Q implies P and so $\sim P$ implies $\sim Q$, and it follows that all the batches in X

except those on the "behavior surface" through $\mathbf{x}^0$ are such that either $\mathbf{x}^0 P \mathbf{x}$ or $\mathbf{x} P \mathbf{x}^0$.

But we cannot prove the converse result, that P implies Q. For P and I are concepts referring to states of mind, and may not be completely testable (or "revealable") by considerations of market behavior alone, even in the extended sense of the relations Q and In. Thus there may be pairs of batches $\mathbf{x}^1$ and $\mathbf{x}^2$ on the convex behavior surface through $\mathbf{x}^0$ which are inaccessible in the market sense, but which are actually such that $\mathbf{x}^1 P \mathbf{x}^2$ or $\mathbf{x}^2 P \mathbf{x}^1$, as sufficiently close direct *questioning* of the individual would "reveal." Putting this another way, the fact that R^C is "representable" by an order-preserving continuous function does *not* rule out the possibility that the individual possessing such an R^C may be like our drunkard of Fig. 2.4, and have no representation of his *preferences*, even though one exists of his (extended) choices.

It is because of this rather delicate failure of the concepts of the two theories to correspond completely that we have spoken always of the "equivalence" of the two sets of axioms, rather than just of their equivalence. But it is clear that this is a nuance only, that it should affect demand theory proper hardly at all, and that for all practical purposes the two theories *are* identical. Because of this, it will be useful to set out the two axiom systems side by side, with an indication of the axioms in the two theories that either clearly correspond to each other or have a strong connection.

PREFERENCE THEORY	CHOICE THEORY
Axiom PI: Axiom of Comparability	Axiom C1: Existence of **situations**
Axiom PII: Axiom of Consistency of Preferences	Axiom C2: Existence of Choices
Axiom PIII: Principle of Selection	Axiom C3: Budget Identity
Axiom PIV: Axiom of Dominance	Axiom C4: Each Bundle Is Bought
Axiom PV: Axiom of Continuity of Preference	Axiom C5: Axiom of Consistency of Choices
Axiom PVI: Axiom of Convexity	Axiom C6: Existence of Inaccessible Bundles

To make the axioms correspond in this way of course does violence to the fact that each set forms an interlocking *system*, as we partially indicate by showing that PIV connects both with C1 *and* with C3, that C4 has relations with PI and PVI, and that C5 has aspects of both PII and PVI about it. Nevertheless the reader should find this schematic outline of some use in thinking about the two systems, and in particular in considering what the relaxation of an axiom in one system would correspond to in the other.

Obviously, one axiom is missing from the set on the left, namely that rather unessential one which asserts the continuity of the rate of substitution (Axiom PVII). We found this of use in exchange theory, but actually its main employment is in demand theory, where it enables us to assume suitable "smoothness" of the various substitution functions from which the demand theorems are derived. But because this derivation requires use of the differential calculus, we then have to confine the region of applicability of the theory to the *interior* of the commodity space (i.e., to X^+ rather than X), where all bundles are strictly positive.*

The assumption in choice theory that corresponds to PVII is the very simple one that for each batch there should exist a *unique* **situation** at which it is bought. This does not look like any kind of continuity condition, but it is; for it postulates in effect that a change in the bundle purchased can only be brought about by a change in the **situation**. In formal terms we have

AXIOM C7. If for any $\mathbf{x} \in X^+$ there exists a **situation** at which $\mathbf{x}$ is chosen, then that **situation** is unique, at least up to a scale factor r.

Notice that we write $\mathbf{x} \in X^+$, since this uniqueness condition obviously cannot hold for *b*-bundles, at which there are always infinitely many "touching" frontiers (*cf.*, Fig. 2.13). Therefore any choice structure satisfying C1–C7 must (unlike those obeying only C1–C6) be confined to the *interior* X^+ of the commodity space.

We should, therefore, add to our comparative list of axioms the following.

Axiom PVII:	Axiom of Continuity of Substitution	←——→	Axiom C7:	Each Bundle is Bought in a Unique **Situation**

Since Axiom C4 postulated that there *is* always a **situation s** at which $\mathbf{x}$ is bought, and since $A(\mathbf{s}) = A(r\mathbf{s})$, it follows that C4 and C7 together assert that to each *p*-bundle there corresponds one and only one attainable set from which that bundle is bought. An important alternative way of stating this is that for each *p*-bundle there is a unique frontier from which it is selected. Such a stringent condition should make it possible to derive powerful demand theorems, and so it will turn out in the next section, which is devoted to demand theory "proper."

C. THE THEORY OF CHOICE FUNCTIONS

This final section will be divided into two parts, in the first of which we present some theorems on choice functions that are derived from Axioms C1 to C5 (or the "equivalent" set of preference axioms) and so do not depend upon any "continuity" properties of preferences, choices, or substitutions; only commodities, prices, and income are assumed to be continuously divisible here, though even that is not strictly necessary for several of the results. In the second part, however, we shall prove some other theorems which depend essentially on the two continuity axioms C6 and C7 (or their

* The convention that we adopted in Chapter 2 in order to deal with continuity of substitution for *b*-bundles is not nearly so neat in $n > 2$ dimensions. If we want to keep PVII, we really have to retreat into X^+; but it should be remembered that this axiom is not at all necessary for exchange theory, although it is useful in demand analysis.

preference "equivalents" PV and PVII), and here—since the main tool used is differential calculus—the going will of necessity be mathematically a little rougher than in the rest of the book.*

(i) "Finite" Demand Theorems

The first of these theorems that depend only on C1–C5 is rather basic; it is the simple

THEOREM D15. Choice functions exist.

PROOF: This result means that in any **situation** a *unique* bundle is chosen. Now by C2, for a given $\mathbf{s}^0$ there exists at least one chosen bundle; let there be two such bundles, say $\mathbf{x}^0$ and $\mathbf{x}^{00}$. Then by definition of the relation C, $\mathbf{x}^0 C \mathbf{x}^{00}$ *and* $\mathbf{x}^{00} C \mathbf{x}^0$, contradicting C5. Therefore the chosen bundle is unique. *Q.E.D.*

We also have what is really a corollary of D15, namely

THEOREM D16. If $\mathbf{x}^0$ is chosen at $\mathbf{s}^0$, then it is also chosen at $r\mathbf{s}^0$, where r is any positive real number.

PROOF: By D15 an $\mathbf{x}^0$ is chosen uniquely at $\mathbf{x}^0$, and by definition there corresponds a unique $A(\mathbf{s}^0)$ to the **situation** $\mathbf{s}^0$; so an $\mathbf{x}^0$ is chosen uniquely in $A(\mathbf{s}^0)$. But for all $r > 0$, $A(r\mathbf{s}^0) = A(\mathbf{s}^0)$, so that $\mathbf{x}^0$ is also chosen uniquely in $A(r\mathbf{s}^0)$. *Q.E.D.*

Thus choice functions exist, and in any **situation** the chosen bundle remains chosen even if all prices *and* income are changed, provided that they all change in the same proportion. We can therefore write down n *choice functions* f_i, one for each commodity x_i, such that

$$x_i = f_i(p_i, p_2, \ldots, p_i, \ldots, p_n, M), \qquad i = 1, \ldots, n$$

This system of n equations may be expressed much more compactly in vector notation if we denote by $\mathbf{f}$ the n-dimensional vector of the choice functions f_i, so that we have†

$$\begin{aligned} \mathbf{x} &= \mathbf{f}(\mathbf{p}, M) \\ &= \mathbf{f}(\mathbf{s}) \end{aligned}$$

* The theorems given in this section are only a few of the most important results in demand analysis, since this book is concerned mainly with the theory of exchange. For more complete treatments, the reader should consult the standard works cited in the Notes at the end of this chapter.

† By writing $\mathbf{f} = (f_1, f_2, \ldots, f_i, \ldots, f_n)$, we are following the modern practice of treating a whole function f_i as a single mathematical object, just as a real or a complex number, or a vector or a point in n-space is a single such object.

Because of D16, the f_i have the property that, if $\mathbf{x}^0 = \mathbf{f}(\mathbf{s}^0)$, then

$$\mathbf{x}^0 = \mathbf{f}(r\mathbf{s}^0), \qquad \text{for } r > 0 \tag{4}$$

The mathematical name for this property is that the choice functions are *positively homogeneous of degree zero* in money prices and money income.* Because of this fact, demand theory cannot distinguish between a **situation** $\mathbf{s}^0$ and any positive multiple $r\mathbf{s}^0$ of that situation; the choice behavior in each is precisely the same.

Since it is a great nuisance to have to talk always about "the price-income situation **s** or any positive multiple of it," we shall adopt the convention of understanding that, when we refer to any **s**, we are also including the set of all its positive scale changes. In particular, if we say that **s** is unique in some respect, it will be understood that this uniqueness is determined only up to a positive scale factor. What is unique about **s** then, is not its level, but the *ratios* between the components of **s**, e.g., the ratios $p_2/p_1, p_3/p_1, \ldots, p_n/p_1, M/p_1$. At what level of p_1 these ratios are set is purely a matter of convenience, depending on the problem at hand.

One common device for choosing this level of p_1 is known by the rather misleading description of "setting p_1 equal to unity." Now p_1 is the market price of commodity x_1 and is what it is; by explicit assumption (C1), Adam cannot change that market price by his own action—and neither can the economic theorist. What this device really means is that we change our system of *physical* units of measurement of each commodity in such a way that one (new) unit of x_1 sells for one unit of money ($p_1/p_1 \equiv 1$), one (new) unit of x_2 sells for p_2/p_1 units of money, and so on, until total expenditure valued at the new prices is equal to M/p_1 units of money. It follows that, if the market price of p_1 changes, then *all* the measurement units of physical quantity have to be changed, since p_1 enters the denominator of each of the new prices; but if any of the other prices, or income, is changed, then the measurement units need not be altered. Obviously, the choice of p_1 rather than any other price p_i is quite arbitrary, as a renumbering of the n commodities would show immediately.†

What this device means, mathematically speaking, is that we are choosing a *normalization* (the "p_1-normalization") of the components of **s** in such a way as to produce a unique set of prices and income. In Equation (4), we

* A set of functions **g** is said to be positively homogeneous of degree k if, for every possible set of values for the argument vector **z**, we have the vector equation $\mathbf{g}(r\mathbf{z}) = r^k\mathbf{g}(\mathbf{z})$, where k and r are any positive numbers. In this definition, **g** and **z** need not have the same number of components; if **g** has just one, then of course it reduces to an ordinary "scalar" function.

† The reader should be careful not to identify this device with the superficially similar device discussed in Section D(ii) of Chapter 3. There we set the *accounting* price of ale equal to one, which was something that the mere *definition* of accounting prices enabled us to do. Here we are arranging that the *money* price of "ale" be equal to one. This we are permitted to do on the strength of Theorem D16, which itself is deduced from our *assumptions* (actually C2 and C5) about choice behavior.

are putting r equal to the *number* $1/p_1$, and so producing a *particular* "normalized" **situation** $((1/p_1)\mathbf{s})$. Notice that the "dimensions" of this normalized vector are the same as before, each component having the "dimension" units of money, since the division is by the dimensionless pure number $1/p_1$.

A more symmetrical normalization, which we will also find useful in sub-section (ii) below, is to put r equal to the number $1/M$, so that the normalized **situation** vector becomes $(p_1/M, p_2/M, \ldots, p_n/M, 1)$—again in units of money. This normalization implies that the consumer's income is always ("identically") equal to one unit of money and, like all such normalizations, corresponds to the choice of an appropriate set of physical units of measurement for each commodity. In this case, these units must be such that the new unit prices become $p_1/M, p_2/M, \ldots,$ and so on.

Axiom C3 places a further restriction on $\mathbf{f}$, for these choice functions must be such that the values of x_i which they produce satisfy the budget identity $\mathbf{px} = M$, which means that

$$\mathbf{pf}(\mathbf{s}) \equiv M \tag{5}$$

This implies that not all the f_i are *independent* of each other. For if, say, the first $(n-1)$ choice functions are allowed to assume their "chosen" values, then the value assumed by the nth choice function is completely determined by the actual *identity*

$$x_n \equiv \frac{1}{p_n}\left(M - \sum_{i=1}^{i=(n-1)} p_i x_i\right) \tag{6}$$

Because of (6), we shall in the future always understand the nth choice function actually to *be* the right-hand side of (6); this is clearly a function of $\mathbf{s}$ alone, as are all the other $(n-1)$ functions. Using this interpretation, the n choice functions lose their previous functional dependence, the explicit incorporation of the budget identity (5) into the previously dependent set producing a new set of n independent functions.*

We have now proved two rather general statements about choice functions, to the effect that they exist and are "homogeneous"; other general properties, such as continuity, depend upon C6 and C7, and their derivation will be given in sub-section (ii) below. But meanwhile we can generalize our graphical treatment of the "Law of Demand" very easily to the n-commodity case. To do so we start, as usual, with a bundle $\mathbf{x}^0$ bought in a **situation** $\mathbf{s}^0$ $(\equiv(\mathbf{p}^0, M^0))$. We now change the price vector to $\mathbf{p}^1$, and inquire about the relation between $\mathbf{x}^0$ and $\mathbf{x}^1$, where $\mathbf{x}^1 = \mathbf{f}(\mathbf{p}^1, M^0)$.

As in the two-dimensional case, we consider a hypothetical **situation** $\mathbf{s}^{10}$, consisting of the vector $(\mathbf{p}^1, M^{10})$, where M^{10} in turn is defined to be equal

* Strictly speaking, this device only removes the dependence caused by the budget restriction but does not of itself ensure that the new set is functionally independent. As we shall see in C(ii) however, the full axiom system C1–C7 does in fact "almost" guarantee that this is the case.

to $\mathbf{p}^1\mathbf{x}^0$. This means that we give the consumer enough extra income ΔM ($\equiv(M^{10} - M^0)$) to enable him to continue the purchase of $\mathbf{x}^0$ at the new prices $\mathbf{p}^1$ if he so wishes. Let us denote the bundle which he selects from $A(\mathbf{s}^{10})$ by $\mathbf{x}^{10}$, so that $\mathbf{x}^{10} = \mathbf{f}(\mathbf{p}^1, M^{10})$; it is, of course, possible, though unlikely, that $\mathbf{x}^0 = \mathbf{x}^{10}$.

Then, by construction, $\mathbf{p}^1\mathbf{x}^{10} = \mathbf{p}^1\mathbf{x}^0$, and since $\mathbf{x}^{10}$ is bought at $\mathbf{s}^{10}$, we have either $\mathbf{x}^{10}C\mathbf{x}^0$ or $\mathbf{x}^{10} = \mathbf{x}^0$. Since from C5 we have $\sim(\mathbf{x}^0C\mathbf{x}^{10})$ if the first possibility occurs, then either $\mathbf{p}^0\mathbf{x}^{10} > \mathbf{p}^0\mathbf{x}^0$ if $\mathbf{x}^{10} \neq \mathbf{x}^0$, or $\mathbf{p}^0\mathbf{x}^{10} = \mathbf{p}^0\mathbf{x}^0$ otherwise. Therefore, we have

$$\mathbf{p}^1\mathbf{x}^{10} = \mathbf{p}^1\mathbf{x}^0 \tag{7a}$$

and

$$\mathbf{p}^0\mathbf{x}^{10} \geqq \mathbf{p}^0\mathbf{x}^0 \tag{7b}$$

from which, on subtracting (7b) from (7a), we obtain

$$(\mathbf{p}^1 - \mathbf{p}^0)(\mathbf{x}^{10} - \mathbf{x}^0) \leqq 0 \tag{8}$$

with strict inequality holding if $\mathbf{x}^{10} \neq \mathbf{x}^0$. If we write $\Delta\mathbf{p}$ for $(\mathbf{p}^1 - \mathbf{p}^0)$, and $\mathbf{x}^{10}$ for $\mathbf{x}^{10} - \mathbf{x}^0$, then (8) may be written*

$$\Delta\mathbf{p}\Delta\mathbf{x}^{10} \leqq 0 \tag{8a}$$

It is natural to call the move from $\mathbf{x}^0$ to $\mathbf{x}^{10}$ the effect of an *overcompensated* price change since, as we have seen, the amount ΔM enables the consumer to continue to buy $\mathbf{x}^0$ and probably to buy an even better bundle; thus ΔM *more* than compensates him for the change in prices. This effect should be distinguished from the substitution effect, since the latter postulates that $\mathbf{x}^{10}$ is on the same indifference level as $\mathbf{x}^0$ and, therefore, that the compensation is *exact*. In deriving (8a) we have proved an important property of this "overcompensated" price change effect, which we therefore record as a formal

Theorem D17. If a price change from $\mathbf{p}^0$ to $\mathbf{p}^1$ is overcompensated, and $\mathbf{x}^{10}$ is the batch bought in the resulting **situation** $\mathbf{s}^{10}$, then $\Delta\mathbf{p}\Delta\mathbf{x}^{10} \leqq 0$, where $\Delta\mathbf{p} \equiv \mathbf{p}^1 - \mathbf{p}^0$, and $\Delta\mathbf{x}^{10} \equiv \mathbf{x}^{10} - \mathbf{x}^0$; and if $\mathbf{x}^{10} \neq \mathbf{x}^0$, then actually $\Delta\mathbf{p}\Delta\mathbf{x}^{10} < 0$.

In the case where only one price is changed from p^0 to p^1, say p_j is increased from p_j^0 to p_j^1, then (8a) reduces to

$$\Delta p_j(x_j^{10} - x_j^0) \leqq 0 \tag{9}$$

since $\Delta\mathbf{p} = (0, 0, \ldots, \Delta p_j, \ldots, 0)$. In ordinary English, the change in Adam's expenditure on the commodity whose price has risen cannot be positive, as he moves from his original position $\mathbf{x}^0$ to the "overcompensated" position $\mathbf{x}^{10}$.

* Compare the Δ-notation introduced in Chapter 2, Section D(iv).

If p_j is the only price that changes, then even more can be said. For we can always write the identity

$$x_i^1 - x_i^0 \equiv x_i^1 - x_i^{10} + x_i^{10} - x_i^0, \qquad i = 1, 2, \ldots, n$$

so that, dividing by $\Delta p_j \neq 0$, we get

$$\frac{x_i^1 - x_i^0}{\Delta p_j} = \frac{x_i^1 - x_i^{10}}{\Delta p_j} + \frac{x_i^{10} - x_i^0}{\Delta p_j}, \qquad i = 1, 2, \ldots, n \tag{10}$$

In this case of a "simple" price change affecting only p_j, we have

$$\Delta M \equiv M^{10} - M^0 \equiv \mathbf{p}^1\mathbf{x}^0 - \mathbf{p}^0\mathbf{x}^0 = \Delta p_j x_j^0$$

so that we can rewrite (10) as follows

$$\frac{x_i^1 - x_i^0}{\Delta p_j} = \frac{x_j^0(x_i^1 - x_i^{10})}{\Delta M} + \frac{(x_i^{10} - x_i^0)}{\Delta p_j}, \qquad i = 1, 2, \ldots, n \tag{11}$$

For $i = j$, (11) becomes

$$\frac{x_j^1 - x_j^0}{\Delta p_j} = \frac{x_j^0(x_j^1 - x_j^{10})}{\Delta M} + \frac{(x_j^{10} - x_j^0)}{\Delta p_j} \tag{11a}$$

In the analysis of Fig. 6.2, we saw that we could break up the effect of a simple price increase Δp_j into a movement from E to F, which was the result of the overcompensation ΔM, and then a movement back down the Engel curve from F to G (or to G', G'' or G''') as income was shrunk back from M^{10} to M^0. Now Equation (11a) says exactly the same thing. The effect of a simple price increase splits up into two additive components, the second term on the right-hand side of (11a), which is the overcompensated price effect, and the first term on the right-hand side, which is a pure income effect.*

Moreover we can conclude from (9) that if Δp_j is positive, then the overcompensated price effect is always nonpositive (as we saw in the two-dimensional case), and, if $x_j^{10} \neq x_j^0$, it is actually negative. If the income effect is nonnegative, so that the good x_j is noninferior over this range of incomes, then as we make the income reduction $-\Delta M$ from $\mathbf{s}^{10}$, the quantity of x_j bought will certainly not increase. Hence each component of the right-hand side is nonpositive, and the total effect will almost certainly be negative. Only if the income effect is very strongly negative will the first term be sufficiently positive (i.e., for a *negative* ΔM) to outweigh the nonpositive second term. Thus we have given a general proof of

THEOREM D18. ("True" Law of Demand). If a simple price increase occurs, and the commodity whose price has increased is noninferior, then the quantity of it demanded will not rise.

* Indeed, as we indicated earlier, the device of a composite commodity allows us to analyze the consequences of a *simple* price change with graphical techniques alone, even in the n-commodity case. But the present algebraic approach is almost as simple, and far more revealing of the structure of the theory.

Theorems D17 and D18 are typical of the theorems that can be obtained with the "finite" part (C1–C5) of the axiom system for choice behavior, and are in fact the most important such results.* In the next subsection we will explore some other results which depend essentially upon those continuity aspects of choice behavior which are expressed by Axioms C6 and C7.

(ii) "Continuous" Demand Theorems

The first consequence of adopting C6 and C7 is the obvious sharpening of D17 and D18 which results from the fact that, with C7, we cannot have $\mathbf{x}^{10} = \mathbf{x}^0$. Hence in the statement of D17, the expression $\Delta\mathbf{p}\Delta\mathbf{x}^{10}$ is actually always *negative*, and in D18 the words "not rise" should be replaced by "fall."

But we can do much better than that with these powerful new axioms, and for the rest of this chapter we shall investigate the main consequences for demand theory that follow from their adoption. To this end, we must first examine just what new ingredients these axioms contribute to the previous system.

The essential force of C6 in this context is to make *exact* compensation possible, provided that we reinterpret compensation in behavioristic terms. In this new interpretation, a change in income ΔM is said to be *an exact compensation for a price change* $\Delta\mathbf{p}$ *from the* **situation** $\mathbf{s}^0$ if the bundle $\mathbf{x}$ to which the consumer is led in the new **situation** $\mathbf{s}$ (i.e., $\mathbf{x} = \mathbf{f}(\mathbf{p}^0 + \Delta\mathbf{p}, M^0 + \Delta M)$), is such that $\mathbf{x} In\, \mathbf{x}^0$. Then C6 implies that the set of all exact compensations for a given $\mathbf{s}^0$ corresponds precisely to a convex surface of bundles $\mathbf{x}$ "through" $\mathbf{x}^0$.

The main force of C7, on the other hand, is to set up a one-to-one correspondence between *p*-bundles and **situations**. To every *p*-bundle there corresponds a **situation**, and vice versa, so that to every statement about either entity there corresponds a statement about the other. Such a state of affairs is often expressed by saying that there exists a relationship of *duality* between the commodity space X^+ and the **situation** space S. In what follows we shall exploit this idea to the full in order to derive our results in as logical and simple a way as we can.†

Given an $\mathbf{s}^0$, we can find an $\mathbf{x}^0$ in X^+ by the relation $\mathbf{x}^0 = \mathbf{f}(\mathbf{s}^0)$; and then to $\mathbf{x}^0$ there corresponds a **situation** $\mathbf{s}$ in S; by C7, we must have $\mathbf{s} = \mathbf{s}^0$,

* Actually C1–C5 constitute a stronger body of postulates than is necessary for the essential conclusions of those theorems; in particular, the budget restriction C3 can be weakened substantially.

† In order to help the reader follow some of the more mathematical steps, we will break our usual habit and give footnote references—wherever appropriate—to the relevant literature.

For the material of the next three paragraphs, the reader should consult Chapter 1 of the beautiful book by J. Dieudonné: *Foundations of Modern Analysis* (Academic Press, New York, 1960).

so that an application of the vector function $\mathbf{f}$ to $\mathbf{s}^0$, followed by the reverse correspondence from X^+ to S, takes one back to the original $\mathbf{s}^0$. In mathematical terms, $\mathbf{f}$ is a *mapping* from the space S to X^+, and the reverse correspondence is in fact the *inverse* mapping $\mathbf{f}^{-1}$ from X^+ to S, where $\mathbf{f}^{-1}$ is defined by the relation $\mathbf{f}^{-1}(\mathbf{f}(\mathbf{s}^0)) \equiv \mathbf{s}^0$.

Now any representation w of the ordering R^C of X^+ can be looked at in the following way. To each p-bundle $\mathbf{x}^0$, there corresponds a level c^0 of the representation, so that

$$c^0 = w(\mathbf{x}^0) \tag{12}$$

But $\mathbf{x}^0 = \mathbf{f}(\mathbf{s}^0)$, so we can write (12) as

$$c^0 = w(\mathbf{f}(\mathbf{s}^0)) \tag{13}$$

Then (13) implies that we have established a representation, say W, on S. Thus we have

$$W(\mathbf{s}) = w(\mathbf{f}(\mathbf{s}))$$

It is common mathematical usage to call the mapping W from S to the space $R^\#$ of the real numbers (the "real line"), a *composition* of two mappings, namely of the mapping $\mathbf{f}$ from S to X^+, and the mapping w from X^+ to $R^\#$. In symbols, we write $W = w \circ \mathbf{f}$. We can look at this the other way round as well, for we have a mapping $\mathbf{f}^{-1}$ from X^+ to S, and another mapping—the representation W—from S to $R^\#$. Then w is a composition of $\mathbf{f}^{-1}$ and W, so that $w = W \circ \mathbf{f}^{-1}$.

We therefore have essentially the same representation defined on the two spaces X^+ and S, and we can move between each of them quite freely. In order to make the exposition simpler, we shall refer to these representations as indicating levels of *satisfaction*, though we must be careful to note that the implication that *satisfaction* is constant on each behavior surface must be interpreted solely in behaviorist terms and not to mean that the "true" intensive magnitude of satisfaction possesses a representation (cf., the earlier discussion at the end of Section B).

In putting our theory entirely in the dual terms of X^+ and S, we apparently face the difficulty that the former is an n-space and the latter an $(n + 1)$-space. But this difficulty *is* only apparent, because the positive homogeneity of the choice functions means that it is only the *ratios* between the components of the vectors of S that are important. So we meet this problem by the simple device of choosing a normalization, and for the first part of the exposition the M-normalization is appropriate. We choose new units of measurement for the x_i, and so obtain a new price vector $\boldsymbol{\pi}$, defined by*

$$\pi_i = \mu p_i, \qquad i = 1, 2, \ldots, n$$

* We are here using the symbol π_i in a sense different from that in Chapter 3, Section D(ii).

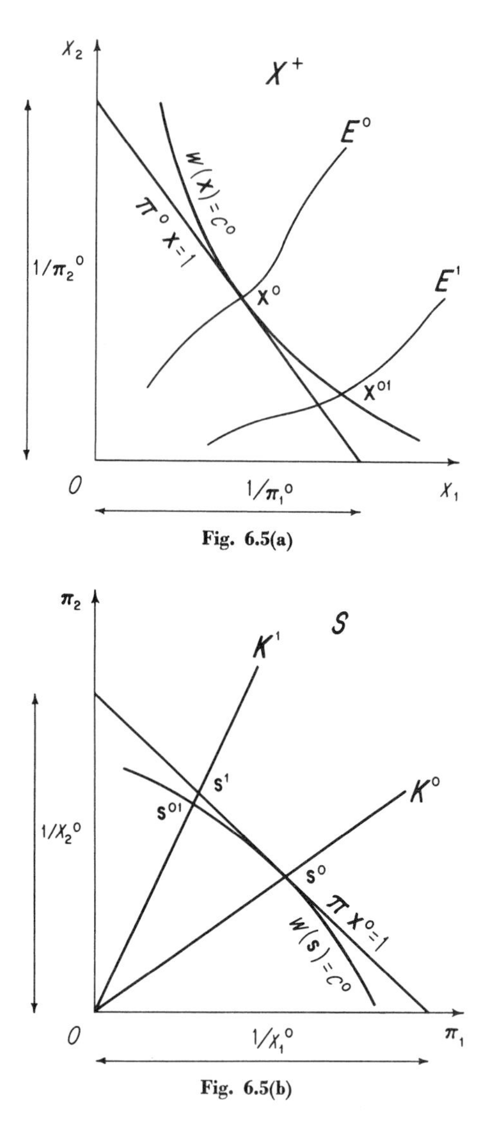

Fig. 6.5(a)

Fig. 6.5(b)

where μ is equal to the *number* $1/M$. Then if $\mathbf{x}^0$ is chosen at $\mathbf{s}^0$, we have always

$$\boldsymbol{\pi}^0\mathbf{x}^0 = 1 \tag{14}$$

where the 1 has dimension "unit of money."

It helps the following argument considerably if we illustrate it for the two-dimensional case by a parallel pair of diagrams, as in Figs. 6.5(a) and (b); but the discussion below is completely general.

Figure 6.5(a) illustrates the space X^+. The *p*-bundle $\mathbf{x}^0$ is bought at prices π^0, and the frontier F^0 (whose equation is $\pi^0\mathbf{x} = 1$) meets the axis of x^1 at a distance $1/\pi_1^0$ from $\mathbf{O}$, and the x_2-axis at a distance $1/\pi_2^0$ from the origin. Note that *neither* of the two axes (including $\mathbf{O}$) actually belongs to X^+. The convex curve through $\mathbf{x}^0$ has the equation $w(\mathbf{x}) = c^0$, where c^0 is the level of *satisfaction* appropriate to $\mathbf{x}^0$. The p-bundle x^{01} on the Engel curve E^1 is another member of this behavior curve and is, of course, bought at prices π^1. In the general case, the frontier F^0 is a hyperplane, and $w(\mathbf{x}) = c^0$ is the equation of a convex behavior surface through $\mathbf{x}^0$; to save space, we shall often denote the surface by w^0.

In Fig. 6.5(b), which depicts the **situation** space S, the point $\mathbf{s}^0$ is the **situation** at which the $\mathbf{x}^0$ of diagram (a) is bought. Then $\mathbf{s}^0$ possesses a unique frontier, say L^0, whose equation is $\pi\mathbf{x}^0 = 1$; and L^0 meets the π_1- and π_2-axes, respectively, at distances $1/x_1^0$ and $1/x_2^0$ from $\mathbf{O}$; again, neither of the two axes belongs to the space. The curve through $\mathbf{s}^0$ (a surface in the general case) is the locus of **situations** $\mathbf{s} = \mathbf{f}^{-1}(\mathbf{x})$, where $\mathbf{x}$ is any p-bundle belonging to the curve (surface) w^0 in X^+; it therefore has the equation $W(\mathbf{s}) = c^0$, and we shall for brevity often denote the surface by W^0.

Each Engel curve E in X^+ corresponds to a fixed set of price ratios in S and an increasing positive parameter M. Therefore the corresponding one-parameter family of **situations** in S is a *ray* K through (but not including) the origin. Along each such ray, the ratios $\pi_1 : \pi_2 : \ldots : \pi_n$ equal the ratios $p_1 : p_2 : \ldots : p_n$, and the further "up" the **situation** is on the ray, the higher the income. Thus, in diagram (b), the ray K^0 corresponds to E^0 in (a), and K^1 to E^1; the ray K^1 is steeper than K^0 since the frontier at $\mathbf{x}^{01}$ corresponds to a higher price π_1 than is the case at $\mathbf{x}^0$.*

THEOREM D19. The surface W^0 in S is strictly *concave* to the origin.

PROOF: We observe that to each $\mathbf{s}$ in W^0 there is a unique frontier L; it therefore follows from the theory of convex sets that W^0 is either strictly convex or strictly concave.† In order to show that W^0 is actually concave, it must be demonstrated that it lies everywhere *below* the frontier L^0, as in diagram (b).

To prove this, note that any pair of **situations** in W^0 corresponds to an

* It is interesting to note that the continuity axiom C6 has the following equivalent form in S: If $\mathbf{s}^1Q^*\mathbf{s}^0$ (where we define $\mathbf{s}^1Q^*\mathbf{s}^0$ if and only if the corresponding p-bundles $\mathbf{x}^1$ and $\mathbf{x}^0$ are such that $\mathbf{x}^1Q\mathbf{x}^0$), then there exists a unique **situation** $\mathbf{s}^{01}$ on K^1 such that $\mathbf{s}^{01}In^*\mathbf{s}^0$, where $\mathbf{s}^{01}In^*\mathbf{s}^0$ if and only if $\mathbf{x}^{01}In\mathbf{x}^0$. But this "ray condition" is completely analogous to one of the versions of PV, not given explicitly in Chapter 2, that is applicable when the commodity space is X^+. The axiom C6 therefore gains considerably greater logic—or at least clarity—if looked at as a continuity condition on the dual ordered space S rather than on the ordered space X^+.

† See, for example, Chapter 1 of H. G. Eggleston: *Convexity* (Cambridge Tracts in Mathematics and Mathematical Physics, No. 47, Cambridge U.P., New York, 1958), especially Theorem 9 and Section 11.

inaccessible pair of p-bundles. Now consider the **situation** $\mathbf{s}^1$ (illustrated in Fig. 6.5(b)) which belongs to the frontier L^0 and also to the ray K^1; we therefore have $\boldsymbol{\pi}^1\mathbf{x}^0 = 1$. This implies that, if he spent one unit of money, the consumer *could* buy $\mathbf{x}^0$ at prices $\boldsymbol{\pi}^1$, and since $\mathbf{x}^0 In\, \mathbf{x}^0$ (by the reflexivity of *In*), he would then have a p-batch satisfying the requirement necessary for it to be in w^0. Therefore, the p-batch $\mathbf{x}^{01}$ that actually *is* in w^0 cannot be bought at an income greater than one, for otherwise Adam would buy the more economical $\mathbf{x}^0$, and still stay in w^0.

But since C7 implies that he will *not* continue to buy $\mathbf{x}^0$ when prices change from $\boldsymbol{\pi}^0$ to $\boldsymbol{\pi}^1$, it follows that the batch $\mathbf{x}^{01}$ belonging to w^0 must actually cost *less* than one unit of money. Therefore, $\mathbf{s}^{01}$ lies lower down the ray K^1 than $\mathbf{s}^1$, and since K^1 was arbitrary, the *whole* of W^0 must lie below L^0. *Q.E.D.*

The whole of the succeeding theory turns on the dual facts that w^0 is convex and W^0 concave, since we can exploit many of the mathematical properties possessed by convex (and, equivalently, concave) surfaces in order to prove our economic results. We start with a purely mathematical property:

THEOREM D20. The surfaces w^0 in X^+ and W^0 in S are each continuously differentiable.

PROOF: Since to each point of each surface there is a unique frontier, (a) this is a necessary and sufficient condition for a tangent plane to exist at each such point, and the frontier actually is the tangent plane; moreover, (b) this plane is a continuous function of the points of the surface.* But the existence of a continuously turning tangent plane at every point is simply another way of saying that the surface is continuously differentiable. *Q.E.D.*

To make the exposition as self-contained as possible, we shall give a short discussion of what this means.† In brief, an ordinary "scalar" function F, defined on an n-dimensional vector space Y, is said to be *differentiable at the point* $\mathbf{y}^0$ if its behavior in a small neighborhood N around $\mathbf{y}^0$ can be approximated arbitrarily closely by a *linear* function of the difference vector $\mathbf{dy}^0 (\equiv \mathbf{y} - \mathbf{y}^0$, where $\mathbf{y}$ is any vector in N); geometrically (think of three dimensions) this means that the graph of the function F has a tangent plane at the point $\mathbf{y}^0$, the equation of the tangent plane actually being the linear function in question. In more specific algebraic terms, we say that F is differentiable at $\mathbf{y}^0$ if we can write the equation

$$F(\mathbf{y}) - F(\mathbf{y}^0) = \mathbf{D}F(\mathbf{y}^0)\mathbf{dy}^0 + o(\mathbf{dy}^0) \tag{15}$$

* These simple results are often given without proof. The only explicit statements and proofs of (a) and (b) that I know of are in T. Botts: "Convex Sets," *American Mathematical Monthly*, 49, 1942, 527–35, where they correspond to his Theorems 4.1 and 4.2, respectively.

† For a very lucid treatment of this basic concept of differentiability, see R. Courant: *Differential and Integral Calculus*, Volume II (translated by E. J. McShane, Interscience, New York, 1936), Chapter 2, especially Section 4. An equally lucid but more advanced discussion is in Sections 1 and 9 of Chapter 8 of Dieudonné, *op. cit.*

In (15), $o(\mathbf{dy}^0)$ is a notation that indicates that the (scalar) term involved is of a smaller order of magnitude than $\mathbf{dy}^0$ (i.e., the term $o(\mathbf{dy}^0)$ tends to zero faster than does the absolute value of $\mathbf{dy}^0$ itself; in old-fashioned language, it is "of the second order of small quantities"). The expression $\mathbf{D}F(\mathbf{y}^0)$ signifies an n-dimensional vector of numbers $(D_1F(\mathbf{y}^0), D_2F(\mathbf{y}^0), \ldots, D_jF(\mathbf{y}^0), \ldots, D_nF(\mathbf{y}^0))$, which are usually called the *n partial derivatives of F, evaluated at the point* $\mathbf{y}^0$.* The linear expression $\mathbf{D}F(\mathbf{y}^0)\mathbf{dy}^0$—which is a scalar and the *linear part* of the increment $(F(\mathbf{y}) - F(\mathbf{y}^0))$—is called the *differential* of F at the point $\mathbf{y}^0$, and written $dF(\mathbf{y}^0)$.

We say that F is *continuously differentiable at* $\mathbf{y}^0$ if the numbers $D_jF(\mathbf{y}^0)$ are each continuous functions of $\mathbf{y}$ at the point $\mathbf{y}^0$. A *set* $\mathbf{F}$ of m functions F_i, each defined on the same space Y, is continuously differentiable at $\mathbf{y}^0$ if each of its members F_i is continuously differentiable there. The jth *partial derivative of the set* $\mathbf{F}$ *at* $\mathbf{y}^0$, denoted by $\mathbf{D}_j\mathbf{F}(\mathbf{y}^0)$, is an m-dimensional vector of numbers $(D_jF_1(\mathbf{y}^0), D_jF_2(\mathbf{y}^0), \ldots, D_jF_i(\mathbf{y}^0), \ldots, D_jF_m(\mathbf{y}^0))$. If these vectors $\mathbf{D}_j\mathbf{F}(\mathbf{y}^0)$ are written in column (not row) form, then the collection of vectors $(\mathbf{D}_1\mathbf{F}(\mathbf{y}^0), \mathbf{D}_2\mathbf{F}(\mathbf{y}^0), \ldots, \mathbf{D}_j\mathbf{F}(\mathbf{y}^0), \ldots, \mathbf{D}_n\mathbf{F}(\mathbf{y}^0))$ is a *matrix* with m rows and n columns, and the ith row of this matrix is simply $\mathbf{D}F_i(\mathbf{y}^0)$, which is the set of n partial derivatives of the function F_i, evaluated at $\mathbf{y}^0$. The matrix is called the *Jacobian matrix of the set* $\mathbf{F}$ *at the point* $\mathbf{y}^0$, and is denoted by $J_{\mathbf{F}}(\mathbf{y}^0)$; if $m = n$, then the Jacobian matrix is *square*.

We may now apply these concepts to the surfaces w^0 and W^0, which are defined by the scalar functions $w(\mathbf{x}) - c^0 = 0$ and $W(\mathbf{s}) - c^0 = 0$, respectively, or, in the more useful *implicit* form, $v(\mathbf{x}, c^0) = 0$ and $V(\mathbf{s}, c^0) = 0$. Then Theorem D20 states that both these implicit functions v and V are continuously differentiable. For the next few paragraphs, the derivations for each of the spaces X^+ and S are so symmetrical that we shall simply write them in parallel columns, duplicating the language wherever possible.

X^+

By D20, the differential $dv(\mathbf{x}^0)$ exists, and is given by

$$dv(\mathbf{x}^0) = \mathbf{D}v(\mathbf{x}^0)d\mathbf{x}^0 \quad (16a)$$

where $\mathbf{D}v(\mathbf{x}^0)$ is the n-vector of partial derivatives of v evaluated

S

By D20, the differential $dV(\mathbf{s}^0)$ exists, and is given by

$$dV(\mathbf{s}^0) = \mathbf{D}V(\mathbf{s}^0)\mathbf{d}\pi^0 \quad (16b)$$

where $\mathbf{D}V(\mathbf{s}^0)$ is the n-vector of partial derivatives of V evaluated

* Note that since we are necessarily concerned only with small price changes $\mathbf{dp}$ where the linear approximations by differentials is valid, the whole of the remaining analysis deals only with "local" properties of the choice functions, i.e., those holding in a small neighborhood of any $\mathbf{s}^0$.

The reader is perhaps more familiar with the notation $\partial F/\partial y_1$, $\partial F/\partial y_2$, and so on, for these partial derivatives. This latter notation has the disadvantage of making it difficult to indicate explicitly that the derivatives are evaluated at a *particular* point of the space $\mathbf{Y}$, and hence are *constants* for that point, which in our case is $\mathbf{y}^0$. The notation used here is close to that of Dieudonné, *op. cit.*, Chapter 8, Section 9.

at $\mathbf{x}^0$, the typical member of which is $D_j v(\mathbf{x}^0)$.

Because the level of **satisfaction** is constant on w^0, we have that $dv(\mathbf{x}^0)$ is identically zero for all difference vectors $(\mathbf{x} - \mathbf{x}^0)$, where $\mathbf{x} \in w^0$. Hence from (16a) we have

$$\mathbf{D}v(\mathbf{x}^0)\mathbf{dx}^0 = 0 \qquad (17a)$$

Equation (17a) is the equation of the tangent plane at $\mathbf{x}^0$; but we already have a frontier $\boldsymbol{F}^0$ at $\mathbf{x}^0$, whose equation is

$$\pi^0\mathbf{x} = 1$$

or, equivalently,

$$\pi^0\mathbf{dx}^0 = 0 \qquad (18a)$$

and we have stated in D20 that the frontier $\boldsymbol{F}^0$ coincides with the (unique) tangent plane at $\mathbf{x}^0$. There must therefore be a strong relation between (17a) and (18a); in fact, they are identical save for a "dimensional" problem. The units of (17a) are units of *satisfaction*, whereas those of (18a) are units of money. So let us multiply both sides of (18a) by a parameter σ, whose magnitude is arbitrary but whose "dimension" is "units of *satisfaction* per unit of money." Then we have the *identity*

$$(\mathbf{D}v(\mathbf{x}^0) - \sigma\pi^0)\mathbf{dx}^0 \equiv 0 \quad (19a)$$

since there *can* be only one set of coefficients (apart from a scale factor), of the linear form which is the differential of v at $\mathbf{x}^0$.

at $\mathbf{s}^0$, the typical member of which is $D_j V(\mathbf{s}^0)$.

Because the level of **satisfaction** is constant on W^0, we have that $dV(\mathbf{s}^0)$ is identically zero for all difference vectors $(\mathbf{s} - \mathbf{s}^0)$, where $\mathbf{s} \in W^0$. Hence from (16b) we have

$$\mathbf{D}V(\mathbf{s}^0)\mathbf{d}\pi^0 = 0 \qquad (17b)$$

Equation (17b) is the equation of the tangent plane at $\mathbf{s}^0$; but we already have a frontier $\boldsymbol{L}^0$ at $\mathbf{s}^0$, whose equation is

$$\mathbf{x}^0\pi = 1$$

or, equivalently,

$$\mathbf{x}^0\mathbf{d}\pi^0 = 0 \qquad (18b)$$

and we have stated in D20 that the frontier $\boldsymbol{L}^0$ coincides with the (unique) tangent plane at $\mathbf{s}^0$. There must therefore be a strong relation between (17b) and (18b); in fact, they are identical save for a "dimensional" problem. The units of (17b) are units of *satisfaction*, whereas those of (18b) are units of money. So let us multiply both sides of (18b) by a parameter σ, whose magnitude is arbitrary, but whose "dimension" is "units of *satisfaction* per unit of money." Then we have the *identity*

$$(\mathbf{D}V(\mathbf{s}^0) - \sigma\mathbf{x}^0)\mathbf{d}\pi^0 \equiv 0 \quad (19b)$$

since there *can* be only one set of coefficients (apart from a scale factor), of the linear form which is the differential of V at $\mathbf{s}^0$.

From (19a) we have immediately that, for any commodity j,

$$D_j v(\mathbf{x}^0) \equiv \sigma \pi_j^0 \qquad (20a)$$

so that, for any pair of commodities j and k

$$D_j v(\mathbf{x}^0)/D_k v(\mathbf{x}^0) \equiv \pi_j^0/\pi_k^0 \quad (21a)$$

From (19b) we have immediately that, for any commodity j,

$$D_j V(\mathbf{s}^0) \equiv \sigma x_j^0 \qquad (20b)$$

so that, for any pair of commodities j and k,

$$D_j V(\mathbf{s}^0)/D_k V(\mathbf{s}^0) \equiv x_j^0/x_k^0 \quad (21b)$$

The interpretation of these results differs in each case. For $\boldsymbol{X}^+$, it is (21a) which is economically important, for it tells us that the ratio of the partial derivatives of v at $\mathbf{x}^0$, which equals the personal rate of substitution there, is identically equal to the price ratio, a result we have proved often in other ways. For $\boldsymbol{S}$, the important result is (20b), a consequence of which we state as

THEOREM D21. The choice functions are continuous in prices and income.*

PROOF: From (20b), the amount of any commodity j bought at $\mathbf{s}^0$ is identically equal to a scalar multiple $(1/\sigma)$ of $D_j V(\mathbf{s}^0)$; but the latter partial derivative is a continuous function of $\mathbf{s}$ at $\mathbf{s}^0$, since V is continuously differentiable there, by D20. Since σ and $\mathbf{s}^0$ are arbitrary, we have that each x_j is a continuous function of $\mathbf{s}$ at all points of $\boldsymbol{S}$. *Q.E.D.*

In order to make further progress, we concentrate attention now on $\boldsymbol{S}$, which is the "natural" space for the choice functions, and switch from the previous M-normalization to the p_1-normalization. We choose new units of measurement for the x_i so that we have always $p_1 \equiv 1$, and the **situation** vectors become $(1, p_2/p_1, p_3/p_1, \ldots, p_n/p_1, M/p_1)$; but in order to economize on notation, we will continue to use the same symbols p_i and M for the new normalized prices and income. The concavity property of $\boldsymbol{W}^0$ in $\boldsymbol{S}$ remains unaffected by this change of units.†

Since $V(\mathbf{s}, c^0) = 0$ is the equation of a differentiable concave surface in $\boldsymbol{S}$, it follows that for any $\mathbf{s}^0$ in $\boldsymbol{W}^0$, there exists a neighborhood $\boldsymbol{N}^0$ surrounding $\mathbf{s}^0$, and itself lying entirely in $\boldsymbol{W}^0$, such that in it we can "solve" the implicit function V for any one variable of $\mathbf{s}$, say M, and thus write a new function

$$M = H(1, p_2, \ldots, p_n), \qquad \text{for } \mathbf{s} \text{ in } \boldsymbol{N}^0 \qquad (22)$$

* The latter part of this theorem fulfills an earlier promise to show that the Engel curves are continuous.

† See Eggleston, *op. cit.*, Chapter 1, Section 2.

The function H is positive and strictly concave, and is everywhere continuously differentiable in N^0.* Its economic interpretation is that it registers the *minimum* level of income needed, at any set of prices, to achieve a level of *satisfaction* at least equal to that obtaining at $\mathbf{s}^0$. It follows that, throughout N^0, income M is uniquely given by the function H for any price-set $\mathbf{p}$, so that the choice functions $\mathbf{f}$ become functions of prices alone in N^0. It will be convenient to mark this explicitly by introducing a new set of n functions $\mathbf{g}$, *defined only on* $\mathbf{N}^0$, and given by the identity

$$\mathbf{g}(\mathbf{p}) \equiv \mathbf{f}(\mathbf{p}, M), \qquad \text{for } (\mathbf{p}, M) \text{ in } N^0 \tag{23}$$

(In technical terms, $\mathbf{g}$ is the *restriction* of $\mathbf{f}$ to N^0.) It follows also from the existence of H that we can refer unambiguously to the **situation p** in N^0. By the budget identity we have

$$M \equiv \mathbf{pg}(\mathbf{p})$$

which from (22) leads to

$$H(\mathbf{p}) \equiv \mathbf{pg}(\mathbf{p}) \tag{24}$$

Note that there is no need to write "for $\mathbf{p}$ in N^0" since $\mathbf{g}$ is only *defined* for $\mathbf{p}$'s in that neighborhood on W^0.

Now H is continuously differentiable, as are the p_i themselves, but unfortunately it does *not* follow from (24) that each of the g_i is continuously differentiable, or even differentiable. We know from D20, however, that the f_i are continuous everywhere, so the g_i must be continuous, and from the concavity of W^0 that their behavior is reasonably regular. So we impose *very* little further restriction if we make the

Supplementary Assumption of Regularity. Each choice function f_i is continuously differentiable in S.

This assumption implies that the g_i are continuously differentiable, and so that the partial derivatives $D_j\mathbf{g}(\mathbf{p})$ exist and are continuous, for each j. From (24), the $D_jH(\mathbf{p})$—which also exist and are continuous, by the concavity of W^0—are given by the identity

$$D_jH(\mathbf{p}) \equiv g_j(\mathbf{p}) + \mathbf{p}D_j\mathbf{g}(\mathbf{p}), \qquad j = 1, 2, \ldots, n \tag{25}$$

We now demonstrate that the term $\mathbf{p}D_j\mathbf{g}(\mathbf{p})$ in (25) is actually zero. Let $\mathbf{p}$ be any situation in N^0, and let $\mathbf{p}^1$ in N^0 be a situation obtained from $\mathbf{p}$

* See Theorem 1.12 (pp. 6–7) of H. Busemann: *Convex Surfaces* (Interscience, New York, 1958). A function F defined on a convex set Y is said to be *concave* if, for any $\mathbf{y}^1$ and $\mathbf{y}^2$ in Y, and for $0 < k < 1$, we have $F((1-k)\mathbf{y}^1 + k\mathbf{y}^2) \geqq (1-k)F(\mathbf{y}^1) + kF(\mathbf{y}^2)$. It is *strictly* concave if only strict inequality holds in this relation. In geometrical terms and in one dimension, this corresponds to the graph of the function lying everywhere above the chord joining any two of its points.

Note that if Y were not convex, it would not necessarily contain the vector $(1-k)\mathbf{y}^1 + k\mathbf{y}^2$. In our case the convex set in question is, of course, the price space P, or rather, that cross-section of it which corresponds to $p_1 \equiv 1$.

by a simple price change $\Delta p_j > 0$, so that $(\mathbf{p}^1 - \mathbf{p}^0) \equiv (0, 0, \ldots, \Delta p_j, \ldots, 0)$. Then $\mathbf{x}$ $(=\mathbf{g}(\mathbf{p}))$ minimizes the income needed to stay in N^0 at prices $\mathbf{p}$, so that $\mathbf{px} \leqq \mathbf{px}^1$. Similarly, $\mathbf{x}^1$ minimizes the income needed to stay in N^0 at prices $\mathbf{p}^1$, so that $\mathbf{p}^1\mathbf{x}^1 \leqq \mathbf{p}^1\mathbf{x}$. From the first inequality, $\mathbf{p}(\mathbf{x}^1 - \mathbf{x}) \geqq 0$, and from the second, $\mathbf{p}^1(\mathbf{x}^1 - \mathbf{x}) \leqq 0$. Then, dividing each expression by Δp_j, we have

$$\sum p_i \frac{\Delta x_i}{\Delta p_j} \geqq 0 \tag{26a}$$

where $\Delta x_i \equiv x_i^1 - x_i^0$, and

$$\sum p_i \frac{\Delta x_i}{\Delta p_j} + \Delta p_j \frac{\Delta x_i}{\Delta p_j} \leqq 0 \tag{26b}$$

Then if we let Δp_j tend to zero, so that $\mathbf{p}^1$ tends to $\mathbf{p}$, the continuous differentiability of the f_i implies that the limit of $\Delta x_i/\Delta p_j$ is actually the jth partial derivative of f_i evaluated at $\mathbf{p}$, or $D_j f_i(\mathbf{p})$ or—equivalently—$D_j g_i(\mathbf{p})$. Moreover, the second term on the left of (26b) tends to zero faster than Δp_j, for the same reason. Therefore, (25a) and (25b) together imply that, in the limit,

$$\mathbf{p} D_j \mathbf{g}(\mathbf{p}) \equiv 0 \tag{27}$$

It then follows immediately from (25) and (27) that

$$D_j H(\mathbf{p}) \equiv g_j(\mathbf{p}) \equiv x_j(\mathbf{p}), \qquad j = 1, 2, \ldots, n \tag{28}$$

Now, by assumption, the g_j are each continuously differentiable, so that this must also be true for the functions on the left-hand sides of the *identities* (28). Then differentiating both sides of (28) with respect to any price p_i, we get the *equations*

$$D_i(D_j H(\mathbf{p})) = D_i g_j(\mathbf{p}), \qquad i, j = 1, 2, \ldots, n \tag{29}$$

where $D_i(D_j H(\mathbf{p}))$ signifies the *second-order mixed partial derivative* of H, evaluated at $\mathbf{p}$, which is often written $\partial^2 H/\partial p_i \partial p_j$.

Since the g_j are continuously differentiable, the right-hand sides of (29) are always continuous functions of $\mathbf{p}$ in N^0, and therefore so are the left-hand sides. Hence by Young's theorem* we have

$$D_i(D_j H(\mathbf{p})) = D_j(D_i H(\mathbf{p})), \qquad i, j = 1, 2, \ldots, n \tag{30}$$

so that, from (29) and (30) we can conclude that

$$D_i g_j(\mathbf{p}) = D_j g_i(\mathbf{p}), \qquad i, j = 1, 2, \ldots, n \tag{31}$$

* See Courant, *op. cit.*, pp. 55–57. Note that, even if the $\mathbf{g}$ were not continuously differentiable, the fact that H is concave implies that it has a *second* differential "almost everywhere" (i.e., except possibly for a denumerable number of **situations**), so that it very nearly satisfies the requirements for Young's theorem (see Busemann *op. cit.*, p. 24 for these "twice differentiability" properties of convex (or concave) functions).

Let us investigate these equations of symmetry a little more closely. Suppose that at $\mathbf{p}$ we introduce a simple price change Δp_j and compensate this exactly by a change ΔM_j in income. Then the effect of the change Δp_j on the amount of x_i bought can be thought of as composed of two movements, as revealed by the choice function $x_i = f_i(p_1, p_2, \ldots, p_n, M)$. The first is the *direct* effect of the (uncompensated) change Δp_j, a change that might well take the consumer outside of N^0 from S^0; the second movement is that brought about by the compensating change in income ΔM_j; this brings the consumer back into N^0, and, of course, affects the amounts of x_i purchased, as shown by the appropriate Engel curve. Now if Δp_j is small enough, say equal to dp_j (with a consequent compensation dM_j), we can obtain a formula for the change dM_j by utilizing the fact, as yet unused, that H is differentiable, so that

$$dM = dH(\mathbf{p}) \equiv \mathbf{D}H(\mathbf{p})\mathbf{dp} \tag{32}$$

where $\mathbf{dp}$ is a vector of small price changes. For a *simple* price change dp_j, (32) reduces to

$$dM_j = D_jH(\mathbf{p})dp_j$$

which from (28) implies that

$$dM_j = x_j(\mathbf{p})dp_j \tag{33}$$

Now each f_i is differentiable, by assumption, so that we can write the *total* effect on the amount of x_i demanded, caused by a *general* change $(dp_1, dp_2, \ldots, dp_n, dM)$ from $\mathbf{p}$ (not necessarily in N^0), as

$$dx_i = df_i(p) \equiv \mathbf{D}f_i(\mathbf{p})\mathbf{dp} + D_M f_i(\mathbf{p})dM, \qquad i = 1, 2, \ldots, n \tag{34}$$

where $\mathbf{D}f_i(\mathbf{p})$ is the vector of partial derivatives of f_i with respect to prices, and $D_M f_i(\mathbf{p})$ the "scalar" partial derivative of f_i with respect to income, all evaluated at $\mathbf{p}$. For a simple price change dp_j accompanied by an income change dM, (34) reduces to

$$dx_i = df_i(\mathbf{p}) \equiv D_j f_i(\mathbf{p})dp_j + D_M f_i(\mathbf{p})dM, \qquad i = 1, 2, \ldots, n$$

or

$$\frac{dx_i}{dp_j} = D_j f_i(\mathbf{p}) + D_M f_i(\mathbf{p})\frac{dM}{dp_j}, \qquad i = 1, 2, \ldots, n \tag{35}$$

Now if the change in income dM is actually the *compensating* income change dM_j, we can substitute from (33) for dM/dp_j in (35) and obtain

$$\frac{dx_i}{dp_j} = D_j f_i(\mathbf{p}) + D_M f_i(\mathbf{p})x_j(\mathbf{p}), \qquad i = 1, 2, \ldots, n \tag{36}$$

Since dp_j is a simple price change, and since dM_j takes one back into N^0, it follows that the ratio dx_i/dp_j is actually equal to $D_j g_i(\mathbf{p})$, and so from (31) that dx_i/dp_j is equal to dx_j/dp_i. Hence (36) implies that

$$D_j f_i(\mathbf{p}) + D_M f_i(\mathbf{p}) x_j(\mathbf{p}) = D_i f_j(\mathbf{p}) + D_M f_j(\mathbf{p}) x_i(\mathbf{p}), \qquad i, j = 1, 2, \ldots, n \tag{37}$$

These are the famous *Slutsky equations*. They state, in economic terms, that if a "compensated" change is made in the price p_i, then its effect on the quantity of x_j demanded is *exactly* the same in magnitude as the effect on the quantity of x_i demanded which is brought about by a compensated change in the price p_j (in the same direction as that of p_i); and this holds for any pair of commodities i and j. We record this as

THEOREM D22. Assuming C1 to C7, and that each choice function is continuously differentiable, then the Slutsky equations

$$D_j f_i(\mathbf{p}^0) + D_M f_i(\mathbf{p}^0) x_j(\mathbf{p}^0) = D_i f_j(\mathbf{p}^0) + D_M f_j(\mathbf{p}^0) x_i(\mathbf{p}^0), \qquad i, j = 1, 2, \ldots, n$$

hold at any **situation** $\mathbf{s}^0$.*

Before coming to the last—and most important—properties of the choice functions, let us quickly fulfill another earlier promise, and prove

THEOREM D23. The set of choice functions f_i is functionally independent in N^0.

PROOF: Since there is a one-to-one correspondence between the space $\mathbf{X}^+$ and the $\boldsymbol{S}$, and the f_i are continuously differentiable, it follows from the inverse function theorem† that the determinant of the Jacobian matrix $J_{\mathbf{f}}(\mathbf{p})$ is not zero at any $\mathbf{p}$ in N^0. But since we know that the vanishing of this determinant is a necessary and sufficient condition for the functional dependence of the $\mathbf{f}$ at $\mathbf{p}$,‡ it follows that they are independent throughout N^0. *Q.E.D.*

The most important properties of the $\mathbf{f}$ derive from the fact that they are strictly concave functions. In assuming that the $\mathbf{f}$ are continuously differentiable, we have by (28) also assumed that the second-order partial derivatives $D_i(D_j H(\mathbf{p}))$ exist for all i and j, and are continuous throughout N^0.

* Actually it can be demonstrated that C1–C5, C7 and the differentiability condition on the choice functions, *plus* the Slutsky equations, together *imply* C6. This is shown by using a theorem of Frobenius (see Dieudonné, *op. cit.*, pp. 303–7, especially p. 307) to the effect that if (and only if) the Slutsky equations hold, then the *n partial* differential equations $D_i H(\mathbf{p}) = f_i(\mathbf{p}, M)$ will be *integrable* so as to give a unique function H of the type that we have been using. To commit an execrable pun, this implies that the Slutsky equations are an integral part of the theory, being equivalent to C6.

† See Courant, *op. cit.*, pp. 152–53.

‡ See W. Rudin: *Principles of Mathematical Analysis* (New York: McGraw, 1953) Theorem 9.28, pp. 183–86.

Now if we let $D_i(\mathbf{D}H(\mathbf{p}))$ stand for the vector $(D_i(D_1H(\mathbf{p})), D_i(D_2H(\mathbf{p})), \ldots, D_i(D_nH(\mathbf{p})))$, then we can form the *matrix* of all $D_i(D_jH(\mathbf{p}))$ as the collection of n vectors $D_i(\mathbf{D}H(\mathbf{p}))$, where i runs from 1 to n; we will denote this matrix by $\mathbf{D}^2H(\mathbf{p})$.

Now consider the n inner products defined by $D_i(\mathbf{D}H(\mathbf{p}))\mathbf{z}$, for each $i = 1, 2, \ldots, n$, and for *any* n-vector of real numbers $\mathbf{z}$. These n inner products will themselves form a vector $(D_1(\mathbf{D}H(\mathbf{p}))\mathbf{z}, D_2(\mathbf{D}H(\mathbf{p}))\mathbf{z}, \ldots, D_n(\mathbf{D}H(\mathbf{p}))\mathbf{z})$, and this can itself be multiplied by $\mathbf{z}$ to form a scalar quantity. In matrix notation it is written $\mathbf{z}\mathbf{D}^2H(\mathbf{p})\mathbf{z}$, and in Σ-notation as

$$\sum_{i=1}^{i=n} \sum_{j=1}^{j=n} D_i(D_jH(p))z_iz_j.$$

Then it follows from a basic theorem on convex (or concave) functions* that the following theorem is true:

THEOREM D24. A necessary and sufficient condition that H be strictly concave is that, for all $\mathbf{p} \in N^0$, and for any n-vector $\mathbf{z}$ of real numbers, we have

$$\mathbf{z}\mathbf{D}^2H(\mathbf{p})\mathbf{z} < 0 \tag{38}$$

We can derive a whole galaxy of results about the effects of compensated price changes from Theorem D24 by the simple device of putting $\mathbf{z} = \mathbf{dp}$, where $\mathbf{dp}$ is the vector of price changes. We shall leave most of these as exercises for the reader, merely proving the easiest result. For a simple price change dp_j, (38) implies that

$$D_j(D_jH(\mathbf{p}))(dp_j)^2 < 0, \qquad j = 1, 2, \ldots, n$$

which from (29) has the consequence

$$D_jg_j(\mathbf{p})(dp_j)^2 < 0, \qquad j = 1, 2, \ldots, n \tag{39}$$

Since in N^0, $D_jg_j(\mathbf{p})$ equals dx_j/dp_j, we conclude from (39) that

$$dx_jdp_j < 0, \qquad j = 1, 2, \ldots, n \tag{40}$$

Equation (40) states that the effect of a compensated simple price change dp_j on the quantity demanded of x_j is always in the direction opposite to the price change itself; this is our old friend, "the substitution effect is negative," in a new guise—a sheep in wolf's clothing.

Theorem D24, which is so comprehensive in its scope (in this regard being very much akin to its "finitistic" counterpart D17), is the last demand theorem that we shall prove. We have thus completed our program of deriving many important restrictions on individual choice functions from a short set of axioms on individual choice behavior, and now turn, in the next

* See Eggleston, *op. cit.*, pp. 51–52. The scalar $\mathbf{z}\mathbf{D}^2H(\mathbf{p})\mathbf{z}$ is called a *quadratic form* in $\mathbf{z}$; if it obeys (38), it is called *negative definite*.

chapter, to some problems of aggregating individual preference and choice structures.

NOTES ON THE LITERATURE

A. The "ordinal preference" approach to demand theory has its classical expressions in H. Schultz: *The Theory and Measurement of Demand* (Chicago U.P., Chicago, Ill., 1938); J. R. Hicks: *Value and Capital* (Oxford U.P., New York, 1939), Part I; P. A. Samuelson: *Foundations of Economic Analysis* (Harvard, Cambridge, Mass., 1947), Chapter 5; and H. Wold: *Demand Analysis* (Wiley, New York, 1953).

The "composite commodity" construction may be found in Hicks, *op. cit.*, pp. 33–34 and 312–13, and also in J. R. Hicks: *A Revision of Demand Theory* (Oxford U.P., New York, 1956) 36–37.

B. (***i***) The theory of choice behavior, or of "revealed preference," was founded in 1938–39 by Samuelson; the most convenient summary of this early development is his *Foundations* . . . , 107–16, and 146–63. The present approach to the preliminary axioms uses the simple method of proof presented in the same author's "Consumption Theorems in Terms of Over-Compensation Rather than Indifference Comparisons," *Economica*, 20, 1953, pp. 1–9.

(***ii***) There are many excellent books on vectors and matrices. A particularly good example is P. R. Halmos: *Finite Dimensional Vector Spaces* (2nd ed., Van Nostrand, Princeton, N.J., 1958).

(***iii***) The problem of establishing that the two axiom systems are "equivalent" was first tackled by H. S. Houthakker: "Revealed Preference and the Utility Function," *Economica*, 17, 1950, 159–74, though valuable earlier work had been done by I. M. D. Little: "A Reformulation of the Theory of Consumer's Behaviour," *Oxford Economic Papers*, N.S., 1, 1949, 90–99. The whole topic is summarized by P. A. Samuelson: "The Problem of Integrability in Utility Theory," *Economica*, 17, 1950, 355–85, and by R. G. D. Allen: "The Substitution Effect in Value Theory," *Economic Journal*, 60, 1950, 675–85.

The present approach has been influenced most by the work of H. Uzawa, though there are some differences (see his "Preference and Rational Choice in the Theory of Consumption," which is Chapter 9 of *Mathematical Methods in the Social Sciences, 1959: Proceedings of the First Stanford Symposium*, ed. by K. Arrow, S. Karlin, and P. Suppes (Stanford U.P., Stanford, Calif., 1960), 129–50).

The relation Q was introduced informally by Houthakker (*op. cit.*) and was formalized first by H. Rose: "La preferenza rivelata; condizione essenziali per un ordinamento completo," *L'Industria*, 1957, 643–52; this paper also contains proofs of Theorems D1 to D3. Examples have been presented by D. Gale ("A Note on Revealed Preference," *Economica*, 27, 1960, 348–54), and by P. Newman ("A Supplementary Note on Complete Ordering and Revealed Preference," *Review of Economic Studies*, 27, 1960, 202–5) to show that in general the asymmetry of Q is not implied by the asymmetry of C. But in two dimensions these statements are actually fully *equivalent*; the first valid proof of this was given by H. Rose: "Consistency of Preference: The Two-Commodity Case," *Review of Economic Studies*, 25, 1958, 124–25.

The reader who is curious to learn about the role of "accessibility" in thermodynamics should first consult Max Born's: *The Natural Philosophy of Cause and Chance* (Oxford U.P., New York, 1949) Chapter 5 and 143–46; and then follow up with these references: I. N. Sneddon: *Elements of Partial Differential Equations* (McGraw, New York, 1957), 33–42; and L. A. Turner: "Simplification of Carathéodory's Treatment of Thermodynamics," I and II, *American Journal of Physics*, 28, 1960, 781–86, and 30, 1962, 506–8. From the economist's point of view, perhaps the most interesting treatments are by P. T. Landsberg in *Thermodynamics* (Interscience, New York, 1961) Chapter 2, and—especially—in "On Suggested Simplifications of Carathéodory's Thermodynamics," *Physica Status Solidi*, Band 1, Heft 2, 1961, 120–26. The original paper by C. Carathéodory is in *Mathematische Annalen*, 67, 1909, p. 355 *ff*.

(*iv*) I. M. D. Little has consistently laid stress on the "equivalence," rather than equivalence, of the two axiom systems—basically for the reasons mentioned in the text. (See his *A Critique of Welfare Economics* (2nd ed., Oxford U.P., New York, 1957), Chapter 2 and Appendix 2.)

C. (*i*) The discussion here is based partly on that of Samuelson (in the *Foundations* . . . , and in the 1953 *Economica* paper), but also on that of T. Yokoyama: "A Logical Foundation of the Theory of Consumer's Demand," *Osaka Economic Papers*, 2, 1953, 71–79.

(*ii*) The idea that the **situation** space is dual to the commodity space X^+ is implicit in Samuelson's work, and was briefly made explicit by N. Georgescu-Roegen: "Choice and Revealed Preference," *Southern Economic Journal*, 21, 1954, 119–30, especially p. 129 (see also Uzawa, *op. cit.*, and S. N. Afriat: "Preference Scales and Expenditure Systems," *Econometrica*, 30, 1962, 305–23).

This derivation of the "continuous" demand theorems owes much to L. W. McKenzie: "Demand Theory Without a Utility Index," *Review of Economic Studies*, 24, 1957, 185–89, and to the mathematical appendix by H. Uzawa to a paper on "Demand Analysis" by A. P. Lerner in *American Economic Review*, 52, 1962, 797–801. See also S. Karlin: *Mathematical Methods and Theory in Games, Programming and Economics*, Volume I, (Addison-Wesley, Reading, Mass., 1959), Chapter 8, Section 8.6, 265–73. The original paper by E. Slutsky was in the *Giornale degli Economisti* for 1915; an English translation is available in *Readings in Price Theory* (ed. by K. Boulding and G. Stigler), American Economic Association Series (Irwin, Homewood, Ill., 1952).

7

THE AGGREGATION OF PREFERENCES AND CHOICES

A. INTRODUCTION: INDIVIDUAL STRUCTURES AND GROUP STRUCTURES

All of the analysis that has gone before has referred to *individual* preference structures and choice structures,* and not to structures applicable to groups of people. Although we were not very specific about exactly what we meant by an "individual," the use of the Adam and Eve fable indicated that we were indeed thinking of individual persons rather than of an individual family or household. Since everyday experience tells us that in most families there is a good deal of opposition of preferences—what Samuelson has nicely called "the Dr. Jekyll and Mrs. Jekyll problem"—it follows that to postulate the existence of a *consistent* preference or choice structure for a kinship group is quite a bold step, not to be undertaken without considerable further investigation. And the reservations that apply for a family hold with even greater force for larger and less well-knit groups, such as regions and nations.

Yet for many purposes, both practical and pedagogic, it is extremely useful to reason *as if* a group did obey a set of preference (or behavior) axioms such as that in Chapter 2 (or Chapter 6). In the theory of demand, for example, it is often convenient to regard the *household* as displaying consistency of choice, since much of the data for demand analysis takes this unit as the basic locus of decision, and not the individual person. Similarly, if we could postulate the existence of a consistent preference structure for a nation, with the same aplomb with which we did so for an individual, then the analysis of Chapters 3–5 could be taken over, without any change except of terminology (Africa and Europe, rather than Adam and Eve), as the basis for a theory of international exchange of commodities.

In this brief final chapter we shall touch on some of the methodological

* Since we will often have in mind fields of choice more general than a commodity space, the term "preference structure," as used in this chapter, should usually be thought of as one that satisfies only the *general* axioms PI to PIII rather than the more restrictive set of PI–PVII.

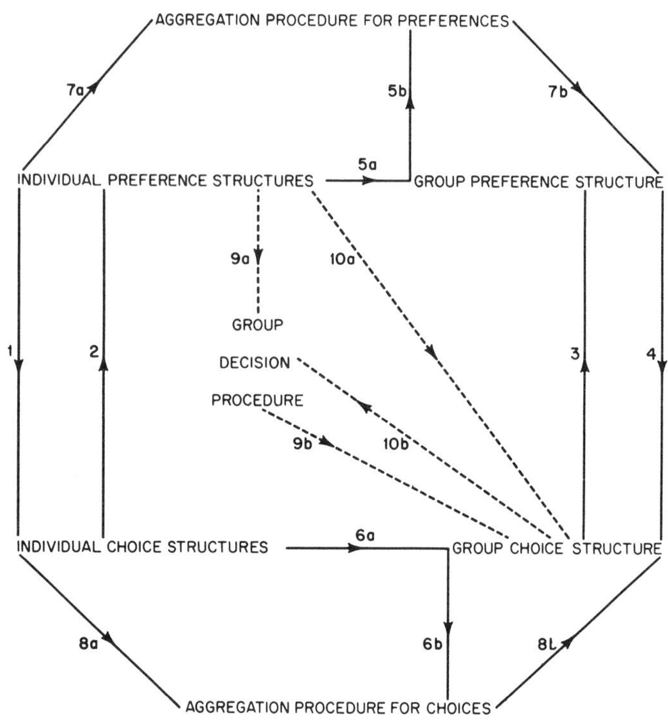

Fig. 7.1

and analytical problems involved in going over from a set of individual preference orderings or choice orderings to a group ordering. Even this very short treatment should bring out the characteristic flavor of these problems, several of which lie on its borders with welfare economics and with econometrics rather than in exchange theory proper.

It is a considerable aid to clarity of thought if we set out a schematic outline in Fig. 7.1, which provides a convenient framework within which to discuss the various types of problem.

The first two routes (1 and 2) of this diagram have already been explored in the last chapter, where we showed that the axioms for choice behavior that we adopted were "equivalent" to the axioms for preferences set out in Chapter 2. Hence if we took an excursion on Routes 1 and 2 in succession we would end up at essentially the same starting point, and similarly for a trip on 2 and 1. If a consistent *group* preference structure and a consistent *group* choice structure existed, each obeying the relevant axiom system, then the same statements could be made about Routes 3 and 4.*

* If the underlying field of choice is not a commodity space, then of course the concepts of preference structure and choice structure would have to be interpreted differently; and these statements in the text then need not be true. "Equivalence"—or equivalence—of preference and choice structures would have to be proved or disproved in each particular case.

In order to discuss the other routes, we first have to say what is meant by an *aggregation procedure*. This is essentially a kind of social machine, into which are fed, as inputs into the hopper, the individual preference (R) or choice (R^C) orderings, and out of which emerges—as output—some kind of group preference or choice structure.

Route 5 describes the following situation: each individual has a preference structure of the usual type, *and so does the group*. We then inquire, as shown by 5b, what class of aggregation procedures for preferences exists that will effect this transition from a collection of consistent individual structures to one consistent group structure. Route 6 indicates a similar problem for aggregation procedures for choices.

With Route 7 we pose a problem that is perhaps more straightforward, and ask: given (a) the individual structures of usual type, and (b) a *prescribed* aggregation procedure, what kind of group structure results? In particular, is it consistent? An analogous question for choices is shown by Route 8.

Routes 9 and 10 do not belong in exchange theory at all, which is why they are shown in broken lines. Here we do not have an aggregation procedure interposed between the individual structures and the group but actual *group decision procedures*—a quite different type of animal—of which the leading species is the class of voting systems. The essential aspect of a group decision procedure is that the persons involved realize that what emerges from their actions is *not* a series of individual choices (which would then be aggregated in some way or other, as in Route 8) but actually a group *decision*. The decision procedure specifies in detail what group decision follows from what individual actions, and these rules are known in advance (or should be) to all the participants.

By contrast, the idea of aggregating individual preferences to a group preference structure (Route 7) is entirely a mental construct on the part of the theorist, for whoever actually observed a *group* preference structure (leaving aside such mystical concepts as the General Will)? If a consistent group preference structure can justifiably be postulated, based on the individual structures and the aggregation procedure, then the theorist can reason that the group acts *as if* it were maximizing its satisfaction subject to the bounds of its attainable set. In a group decision procedure, on the other hand, there *is* no attainable set in the usual sense, for the decision is taken direct from the individuals' preferences, as revealed through the "voting" procedure. Two different procedures of this type may well produce two different group decisions, even with the same pattern of individual preferences each time; we are in fact familiar with this phenomenon from the consideration of different types of voting arrangements, such as in the comparison of simple majority voting with proportional representation.

There is no guarantee, of course, that a group decision procedure will produce *consistent* group choices; this is seen even in almost the simplest example of majority voting. Let the field of choice consist of three alternatives (x, y, z) and let there be three individuals (A, B, C) in the group. Suppose that the rankings are as follows (using "P" for strict preference):

For A: xP_Ay, yP_Az, so that xP_Az.
For B: yP_Bz, zP_Bx, so that yP_Bx.
For C: zP_Cx, xP_Cy, so that zP_Cy.

If the proposed group decision procedure is majority voting, and the members vote in accordance with their preferences, then the group will decide for x against y in a pairwise choice, and for y against z in a similar situation. Therefore one might well want to say that the group (sequentially) chooses x over z; but in an actual contest of x with z, the group would decide on z.*

Far more important for our restricted purposes, however, is the observation that group decision procedures essentially involve *decisons under uncertainty*. For with a given finite number of participants—and the number must necessarily *be* finite—there is always open the possibility that it might "pay," in the sense of maximizing expected utility, for any voter not to vote his preferences but to dissemble in some way. Thus suppose that there is a political election at which Smith, Brown, and Jones are candidates, and that the voter, John Doe, prefers Brown to Smith, and both of them to the infinitely detestable Jones (consider a moderately right-wing member of a center party contemplating a candidate of the extreme left). Unhappily for Doe, he believes that Brown has a small chance of being elected and that Jones has a large chance; as much the lesser of two evils, therefore, he throws his weight behind Smith. Thus he does not vote in accord with his preferences, *for he is not acting under certainty but under uncertainty*, so that it is rational for him to act so as to maximize expected utility, and not as though the probability weight of each outcome were equal, which would generally be implied by voting "straightforwardly."

There is a curious consequence of this behavior, however. Suppose that Smith were in fact elected, but that before he could take office, Jones died; and that, in accord with the electoral rules (the "group decision procedure"), a new election was held with no new candidates. Then, if many voters felt like John Doe, it is quite possible that Brown would now win, even if there were no change of basic preferences. Thus the deletion of one element from the field of choice, although it were not the group decision, might nevertheless result in a *new* group decision, even with constant preferences.

* The reader will probably have noticed that this famous "Paradox of Voting" has much in common with Kenneth May's marriage partner example that was referred to in Section C(ii) of Chapter 2. This is not surprising, for as May himself pointed out in the article cited, the problem for an individual of arriving at a consistent ranking of the whole commodity space, when many criteria are present, is very closely analogous to the problems of aggregating individual preferences to a consistent group structure. In this connection, the reader should remember that the full quotation from Walt Whitman, a fragment of which was given in 2 C(ii), is: "Do I contradict myself? Very well then, I contradict myself. I am large, and I contain multitudes."

To many people this example has seemed paradoxical, to be ruled out by explicit assumption. But we can see that it only appears paradoxical if we neglect the essential fact that the decisions are made in an uncertain situation, brought about by the oligopolistic interdependence, as it were, of the preferences in the group. It is in fact because these problems of group decision (Routes 9 and 10—of which 9 is analogous to 7 and 8, and 10 analogous to 5 and 6) are often confused with the other routes, that we have spent some time on them, even though they do not belong to the category of decisions under certainty, with which we are alone concerned.

Before going on to discuss a few examples of this more restricted class of "certain" problems, let us note an assumption that has been implicit in the analysis so far. This is simply that the field of choice for each person *and* for the group are identical, so that all the orderings concerned are defined over the *same* set. Examination of this assumption will throw further light on the structure of this type of problem.

Suppose that each individual is concerned only with the bundle which he himself would receive, and cares nothing for what other people's preferences are; in other words, in this regard he obeys an axiom system like that of Chapter 2. Then, in trying to formulate a group preference ordering, we are trying to find, as it were, the preference structure of a "representative man" from the group, defined over the relevant set of alternatives. If each individual in the group G faces the same field of choice $\boldsymbol{X}$, then there is no doubt that the "representative man's" preference structure, if it exists, is also defined over $\boldsymbol{X}$.

But what if each person i has a different field of choice $\boldsymbol{X}_i$, the sets possibly overlapping to some extent, but each distinctly different? What is then the appropriate "representative" field of choice? The answer is fairly obvious: it is the smallest field which contains each of the individual fields of choice; in the technical terms of Section B(ii) below, it is the *union* of the various sets of alternatives.

We could now regard *each* individual i as having a preference ordering defined over this union set, being extended from its original domain $\boldsymbol{X}_i$ by the simple device of ignoring, "preferentially" speaking, any goods in the union but not in $\boldsymbol{X}_i$. In this way we can extend the theory so as to satisfy the implicit assumption of identical $\boldsymbol{X}$'s, at least formally. But we do not *have* to satisfy the assumption; it is only a little more difficult to construct theories on the basis of different individual $\boldsymbol{X}_i$'s; we shall not do so in this brief discussion.

Now suppose that each individual were influenced not only by his preferences for what he might get but also by the bundles that the other members of the group do get. Thus if $\mathbf{x}^j$ is any bundle in the jth individual's "personal" field of choice $\boldsymbol{X}^j$, the ith individual is influenced in his ordering not only by the nature of his personal bundle $\mathbf{x}^i$, but also by each of the other bundles $\mathbf{x}^j$. Then his (complete) ordering R_i is defined not merely over all possible vectors $\mathbf{x}^i$ but over *all possible sets* of vectors $(\mathbf{x}^1, \mathbf{x}^2, \ldots, \mathbf{x}^m)$ where $\mathbf{x}^j \in X^j$, and there are m individuals in the group. The space of all possible sets of vectors is called the *product space* of the sets X^j, and written $X^1 \times X^2 \times \ldots \times X^j \times \ldots \times X^m$. If each X^j is identical, say to X, then the product space for the group may be written $(X)^m$, and the sets of vectors become $n \times m$ *matrices*, where n is the dimension of X.*

In these cases, each individual's domain for his ordering relation is the product space, and so is that of the representative man of the group, should he exist; he can therefore be thought of as some kind of consensus function giving expression to the group's ideas of how bundles should be distributed to everybody. Such an idea underlies the discussion in the next section. In any event, we must always be quite aware of just what individual orderings on just what fields of choice are being aggregated. In aggregation theory, no less than in any other branch of economic theory, it helps a great deal to know *exactly* what problem is under discussion.

B. THE EXISTENCE OF AGGREGATION PROCEDURES FOR PREFERENCES

(i) Statement of the Problem

In this section we will tackle some of the problems posed by Route 5 namely: Given a set of individual preference structures, each defined on a set of alternatives X, and given also a group preference structure, does there exist any aggregation procedure that will link the two types of structure? To restrict the problems to manageable proportions, we shall follow the trail blazed by Arrow, and impose some "reasonable" conditions on the nature of the aggregation procedure. We shall list these constraints in order, following each with brief comments about its reasonableness.

Condition 1. (Range) The group preference ordering R shall be defined for every possible profile $(R_1, R_2, \ldots, R_m)$ of the individual preference orderings R_i.

This means that, no matter how odd the R_i—provided that they *are* complete weak orderings—the group ordering R must somehow take them into account.

Condition 2. (Unanimity) If for two alternatives $\mathbf{x}$ and $\mathbf{y}$ in the space of alternatives X, we have $\mathbf{x}R_i\mathbf{y}$ for each i, then $\mathbf{x}R\mathbf{y}$.†

This assumption is so reasonable as not to require comment.

* This notation implies that the jth field of choice is actually a vector (commodity) space; but it is not difficult to devise notation for the product spaces of more general fields of choice.

† In order to economize on subscripts and superscripts, we shall here denote various alternatives in X by $\mathbf{x}$, $\mathbf{y}$, and $\mathbf{z}$, rather than the more usual $\mathbf{x}^1$, $\mathbf{x}^2$, ... This will perhaps help to reinforce the warning that X need not be a commodity space.

Condition 3. (Nondictatorship) For each individual i there is some pair of alternatives $\mathbf{x}$ and $\mathbf{y}$ such that, when $\mathbf{x}P_i\mathbf{y}$, and, for *every* other individual j, $\mathbf{y}P_j\mathbf{x}$, then the group ordering is $\mathbf{y}R\mathbf{x}$.

This nondictatorship condition is not very strong, for it merely states that no individual should be decisive on *every* issue, regardless of the wishes of the rest of the group. Indeed, it is not strong enough, for the result that we wish to prove—to be announced later—cannot be obtained for the general case of more than three alternatives when Condition 3 is adopted. The trouble is this: few dictators in the real world, even of the Hitler-Stalin variety, enjoy the kind of power that is excluded by Condition 3. But most of us would feel that there was still something oppressive about the structure of a group which allowed one man (or one woman) to be decisive on *almost* all of the issues confronting it. So we have to strengthen Condition 3 a little to exclude this kind of incomplete dictatorship, if the theorem proved by Arrow is to be generally valid. Since we shall only give a proof for the case of three alternatives, however, where the problem does not arise, we will leave Condition 3 as it stands.

Condition 4. (Binary choice) Let $(R'_1, R'_2, \ldots, R'_i, \ldots, R'_m)$ and $(R''_1, R''_2, \ldots, R''_i, \ldots, R''_m)$ be two possible profiles of individual orderings, and let them *agree* concerning the pair of alternatives $\mathbf{x}$ and $\mathbf{y}$ (i.e., $\mathbf{x}R'_i\mathbf{y} \equiv \mathbf{x}R''_i\mathbf{y}$ for each i). Then the associated group orderings R' and R'' must *agree* concerning $\mathbf{x}$ and $\mathbf{y}$ (i.e., $\mathbf{x}R'\mathbf{y}$ if and only if $\mathbf{x}R''\mathbf{y}$).

This seemingly innocuous condition has a quite different logical status from the others, and indeed refers to a problem that has not been dealt with at all in this book. For it lays down a powerful constraint on the behavior of the group ordering R when one or more of the individual preference orderings *changes*; in common parlance, it is a condition designed to cope with *changes in tastes.** As such, it sounds reasonable enough; but in all such situations, we can best judge an assumption by its consequences, and its consequences are quite startling.

For Arrow demonstrated that, when there are only three alternatives, there exists NO aggregation procedure linking individual preference structures to a group structure which would satisfy the four conditions; and if Condition 3 is altered suitably, this conclusion holds for *any* number of alternatives in the field of choice. In B(iii) we shall give a proof of the first result, and there it will be apparent that Condition 4 plays the crucial role.

The main concern of this chapter is with methodological problems, so that we shall not stop to examine the implications of Arrow's theorem for welfare economics, a topic on which there has been a lively controversy. For our purposes, it is sufficient to note it as an important example of the

* The Smith-Brown-Jones example of the last section is often quoted as a case that is ruled out by Condition 4. But the discussion there made it clear that in fact the example has nothing to do with the present situation, for it involved choice under uncertainty, and here we are concerned only with choice under certainty.

truth that to embark on Route 5 is not a trivial journey; the existence of a suitable aggregation procedure for preferences must be proved—or, as in this case, disproved—for each set of individual and group structures that we postulate. In point of fact, the existence of an aggregation procedure has been proved several times for various sets of subsidiary conditions different from those of Arrow.

(ii) A Digression on Sets

The proof of Arrow's Theorem that we shall give is quite elementary but involves a few simple ideas about sets which we have not had occasion to formalize earlier in the book; so we take this opportunity to do so. A *set* is any collection of objects whatever, but for the purposes at hand, it is useful to regard the objects in any set as having one or more properties in common. In our discussion, we shall deal only with sets of alternatives and sets of people. The objects in any set are called its *members*, or its *elements* and, as we saw in the last chapter, we denote the statement: "$\mathbf{x}$ is a member of the set X" by $\mathbf{x} \in X$ and its negation by $\mathbf{x} \notin X$.

Let X and Y be two sets; then the set $\{\mathbf{x}: \mathbf{x} \in X \textit{ or } \mathbf{x} \in Y\}$ is the set of all elements belonging to *either* of the two sets, and is called the *union* of X and Y, usually written $X \cup Y$. For the same two sets, the set $\{\mathbf{x}: \mathbf{x} \in X \text{ and } \mathbf{x} \in Y\}$ is the set of elements common to both, and is called the *intersection* of X and Y, written $X \cap Y$.

Now $\cup$ and $\cap$ are operations on pairs of sets, and must result in sets themselves. But what if X and Y have *no* elements in common? How is the expression $X \cap Y$ then to be interpreted as a set? This difficulty is overcome by introducing the *empty set*, denoted by $\varnothing$, which is defined to be the set that has no members at all.* Such an apparently bizarre concept is most useful; for example, we can now say that two sets X and Y are *disjoint* if (and only if) $X \cap Y = \varnothing$.

If it is true that every element of Y is also an element of X, then we say that Y is a *subset* of X, and write $Y \subset X$. If $Y \subset X$, then the *complement of Y in X* is the set $\{\mathbf{x}: \mathbf{x} \in X \text{ and } \mathbf{x} \notin Y\}$, i.e., all those in X but not in Y; it is written $\mathscr{C}(Y)$, where the "containing" set X is understood. If $\mathscr{C}(Y)$ is not the empty set, then Y is called a *strict* subset of X; if $\mathscr{C}(Y) = \varnothing$, then we have also that $\mathscr{C}(X)$ in Y is equal to $\varnothing$, so that $X \subset Y$, and actually $X = Y$.

Finally, let us note that a *partition* of a set X is a division of X into a finite number of disjoint subsets $X^1, X^2, \ldots, X^r$, so that $X^i \cap X^j = \varnothing$ for $i \neq j$, and $X^1 \cup X^2 \cup \ldots \cup X^r = X$. With these few tools of elementary set theory, plus the concepts of preference orderings used in Chapter 2, we can give a simple proof, due to Inada, of Arrow's Theorem.

* It can very easily be proved that there is only one empty set, so that we can talk about *the* empty set, but the proof will not be given here.

(iii) A Nonexistence Theorem for Aggregation Procedures

We shall prove the following version of

ARROW'S THEOREM. *If* (a) each of a finite number m of individuals has a complete preference ordering R_i of a set of alternatives X; (b) there exists a complete group preference ordering R of X; and (c) X consists of only three alternatives, *then* no aggregation procedure exists which satisfies Conditions 1–4 above.

PROOF: Let the elements of X be $\mathbf{x}$, $\mathbf{y}$, and $\mathbf{z}$, and let the set of m individuals be denoted by G (for "group"). Define a group of individuals $G_{\mathbf{xy}}$ *to be decisive for* $\mathbf{x}$ *against* $\mathbf{y}$ if, whenever $\mathbf{x}P_i\mathbf{y}$ for each $i \in G_{\mathbf{xy}}$, and $\mathbf{y}P_j\mathbf{x}$ for each $j \in \mathscr{C}(G_{\mathbf{xy}})$ (in G), then the group ordering is $\mathbf{x}P\mathbf{y}$. We write $G_{\mathbf{yz}}$ and $G_{\mathbf{xz}}$ for sets defined in a similar way.

In order to make $G_{\mathbf{xy}}$ a useful tool of analysis, we have to show that it is nonvacuous, i.e., that $G_{\mathbf{xy}}$ is not the empty set. Suppose that it were. Then for *all* individuals j, $\mathbf{y}P_j\mathbf{x}$; but since $G_{\mathbf{xy}}$ is by definition decisive, $\mathbf{x}P\mathbf{y}$; and this contradicts Condition 2. Hence $G_{\mathbf{xy}}$ has at least one member.

Usually there will be *more* than one such decisive set $G_{\mathbf{xy}}$ for $\mathbf{x}$ against $\mathbf{y}$, so let us define the class of *minimal decisive sets for* $\mathbf{x}$ *against* $\mathbf{y}$ by the condition: for no $G_{\mathbf{xy}}$ do we have $G_{\mathbf{xy}} \subset \bar{G}_{\mathbf{xy}}$, where $\bar{G}_{\mathbf{xy}}$ is any such minimal decisive set; note that $G_{\mathbf{xy}}$ need not be a strict subset.

The theorem is proved by the reiterated use of the following subsidiary result or (as such results are often called),

Lemma: If an individual $k \in \bar{G}_{\mathbf{xy}}$ changes his ordering from $\mathbf{x}P_k\mathbf{y}$ to $\mathbf{y}P_k\mathbf{x}$, and the preferences of each individual $j \in \mathscr{C}(\bar{G}_{\mathbf{xy}})$ were, and remain, $\mathbf{y}P_j\mathbf{x}$, then the group ordering of $\mathbf{x}$ and $\mathbf{y}$ changes from $\mathbf{x}P\mathbf{y}$ to $\mathbf{y}R\mathbf{x}$.*

PROOF: Suppose that the result were false; then because R is a complete weak ordering $\sim(\mathbf{y}R\mathbf{x})$ implies $\mathbf{x}P\mathbf{y}$. Let the complement of k in $\bar{G}_{\mathbf{xy}}$ be denoted by $\bar{K}_{\mathbf{xy}}$. Then for each i in $\bar{K}_{\mathbf{xy}}$ we have $\mathbf{x}P_i\mathbf{y}$, by definition; and for each j in the complement of $\bar{K}_{\mathbf{xy}}$ with respect to G, we have $\mathbf{y}P_j\mathbf{x}$; and the group ordering is $\mathbf{x}P\mathbf{y}$. But this string of assertions implies that $\bar{K}_{\mathbf{xy}}$ is decisive for $\mathbf{x}$ against $\mathbf{y}$; moreover, by construction $\bar{K}_{\mathbf{xy}}$ is a *strict* subset of $\bar{G}_{\mathbf{xy}}$. These two statements together contradict the definition of $\bar{G}_{xy}$ as a *minimal* decisive set for $\mathbf{x}$ against $\mathbf{y}$. *Q.E.D.*

Let us now return to the proof of the theorem. If we consider any two minimal decisive sets, say $\bar{G}_{\mathbf{xy}}$ and $\bar{G}_{\mathbf{xz}}$, then there are five possible different ways in which they may be related. The proof takes each of these possibilities in turn, and proves that each one leads to a contradiction, so that the

* Note that the hypotheses of this lemma refer precisely to a *change of tastes* by an individual, and therefore enable the crucial Condition 4 to be used strategically in the proof of the theorem.

assumption that there exists an aggregation procedure satisfying Conditions 1–4 is shown to be untenable.

The five possibilities are:

(a) $\bar{G}_{\mathbf{xy}} \cap \bar{G}_{\mathbf{yz}}$ is the empty set, so that the two subgroups of individuals are disjoint, having no members in common.

(b) $\bar{G}_{\mathbf{xy}} \subset \bar{G}_{\mathbf{yz}}$ and $\bar{G}_{\mathbf{xy}} \neq \bar{G}_{\mathbf{yz}}$, so that every member of $\bar{G}_{\mathbf{xy}}$ is also a member of $\bar{G}_{\mathbf{yz}}$, but the two subgroups are not identical.

(c) $\bar{G}_{\mathbf{yz}} \subset \bar{G}_{\mathbf{xy}}$ and $\bar{G}_{\mathbf{yz}} \neq \bar{G}_{\mathbf{xz}}$, which is the reverse case to (b).

(d) $(\bar{G}_{\mathbf{xy}} \cup \bar{G}_{\mathbf{yz}} \neq \bar{G}_{\mathbf{xy}})$ and $(\bar{G}_{\mathbf{xy}} \cup \bar{G}_{\mathbf{yz}} \neq \bar{G}_{\mathbf{yz}})$, so that the subgroups have members in common, but each has at least one member that does not belong to the other set.

(e) $\bar{G}_{\mathbf{xy}} = G_{\mathbf{yz}}$, whose meaning is obvious.

(a) $\bar{G}_{\mathbf{xy}} \cap \bar{G}_{\mathbf{yz}} = \varnothing$.

In this case the whole group may be partitioned into three subgroups, $\bar{G}_{\mathbf{xy}}$, $\bar{G}_{\mathbf{yz}}$, and $\mathscr{C}(\bar{G}_{\mathbf{xy}} \cup \bar{G}_{\mathbf{yz}})$ in G. The first two sets are not empty, by an earlier result, but the latter may be. Let us suppose, as is quite compatible with our assumptions, that the individuals in each of these three sets have the following specific rankings (remember that, by Condition 1, R must be defined for *all possible* profiles of individual orderings):

For all individuals i in $\bar{G}_{\mathbf{xy}}$: $\mathbf{z}P_i\mathbf{x}$ and $\mathbf{x}P_i\mathbf{y}$.
For all individuals i in $\bar{G}_{\mathbf{yz}}$: $\mathbf{y}P_i\mathbf{z}$ and $\mathbf{z}P_i\mathbf{x}$.
For all individuals i in neither: $\mathbf{z}P_i\mathbf{y}$ and $\mathbf{y}P_i\mathbf{x}$.

Then since $\bar{G}_{\mathbf{xy}}$ and $\bar{G}_{\mathbf{yz}}$ *are* decisive, $\mathbf{x}P\mathbf{y}$ and $\mathbf{y}P\mathbf{z}$, so that $\mathbf{x}P\mathbf{z}$, because R is a complete weak ordering. On the other hand, for each P_i we have $\mathbf{z}P_i\mathbf{x}$, so that by Condition 2, $\mathbf{z}P\mathbf{x}$. This is a contradiction. *Q.E.D.* Note that the proof does not actually assume that $\mathscr{C}(\bar{G}_{\mathbf{xy}} \cup \bar{G}_{\mathbf{yz}})$ in G *has* any members.

(b) $\bar{G}_{\mathbf{xy}} \subset \bar{G}_{\mathbf{yz}}$ and $\bar{G}_{\mathbf{xy}} \neq \bar{G}_{\mathbf{yz}}$.

The set G can again be partitioned into three disjoint subsets (the last possibly empty), and again we make specific assumptions about the orderings:

For all i in $\bar{G}_{\mathbf{xy}}$: $\mathbf{x}P_i\mathbf{y}$ and $\mathbf{y}P_i\mathbf{z}$.
For all i in $\bar{G}_{\mathbf{yz}}$ but not in $\bar{G}_{\mathbf{xy}}$: $\mathbf{y}P_i\mathbf{z}$ and $\mathbf{z}P_i\mathbf{x}$.
For all i in the rest of G: $\mathbf{z}P_i\mathbf{y}$ and $\mathbf{y}P_i\mathbf{x}$.

Then $\mathbf{x}P\mathbf{y}$ and $\mathbf{y}P\mathbf{z}$, so that $\mathbf{x}P\mathbf{z}$. Suppose that one member $j \in \bar{G}_{\mathbf{xy}}$, changes his ordering to $\mathbf{y}P_j\mathbf{x}$ and $\mathbf{x}P_j\mathbf{z}$, and that another individual k, belonging to the complement of $\bar{G}_{\mathbf{xy}}$ in $\bar{G}_{\mathbf{yz}}$, changes to $\mathbf{z}P_k\mathbf{y}$ and $\mathbf{y}P_k\mathbf{x}$. Then, by the lemma, the first change results in $\mathbf{z}R\mathbf{y}$, and the second change in $\mathbf{y}R\mathbf{x}$, so that now $\mathbf{z}R\mathbf{x}$, by the fact that R is an ordering. But the rankings of $\mathbf{x}$ *relative to* $\mathbf{z}$ remain exactly as they were before the turncoats changed their minds. Therefore, by Condition 4, the *group* ordering of **x** relative to **z** should remain unchanged as well. But it did not, for previously it was $\mathbf{x}P\mathbf{z}$ and now it is $\mathbf{z}R\mathbf{x}$, which is the negation of $\mathbf{x}P\mathbf{z}$; thus we have found a set of orderings and a change in those orderings, for which case (b) leads to a contradiction. Since by Condition 1 the group relation R must be defined for *all* profiles, we therefore have to reject case (b). *Q.E.D.*

(c) $\bar{G}_{\mathbf{yz}} \subset \bar{G}_{\mathbf{xy}}$ and $\bar{G}_{\mathbf{xy}} \neq \bar{G}_{\mathbf{yz}}$.

This demonstration is left to the reader, since—*mutatis mutandis*—it is the same as that for case (b).

(d) $(\bar{G}_{\mathbf{xy}} \subset \bar{G}_{\mathbf{yz}} \neq \bar{G}_{\mathbf{xy}})$ and $(\bar{G}_{\mathbf{xy}} \cup \bar{G}_{\mathbf{yz}} \neq \bar{G}_{\mathbf{yz}})$.

The whole group G may be partitioned into four subsets (the last possibly empty), and the following specific rankings assumed in them:*

For all i in $\bar{G}_{\mathbf{xy}} \cap \bar{G}_{\mathbf{yz}}$: $\mathbf{x}P_i\mathbf{y}$ and $\mathbf{y}P_i\mathbf{z}$.
For all i in $\bar{G}_{\mathbf{xy}}$ and not in $\bar{G}_{\mathbf{yz}}$: $\mathbf{z}P_i\mathbf{x}$ and $\mathbf{x}P_i\mathbf{y}$.
For all i in $G_{\mathbf{yz}}$ and not in $\bar{G}_{\mathbf{xy}}$: $\mathbf{y}P_i\mathbf{z}$ and $\mathbf{z}P_i\mathbf{x}$.
For all i in none of these: $\mathbf{z}P_i\mathbf{y}$ and $\mathbf{y}P_i\mathbf{x}$.

Since $\bar{G}_{\mathbf{xy}}$ and $\bar{G}_{\mathbf{yz}}$ are decisive, we have $\mathbf{x}P\mathbf{y}$ and $\mathbf{y}P\mathbf{z}$, so that $\mathbf{x}P\mathbf{z}$. Suppose that an individual j in the second set changes his tastes from $\mathbf{z}P_j\mathbf{x}$ and $\mathbf{x}P_j\mathbf{y}$, to $\mathbf{z}P_j\mathbf{y}$ and $\mathbf{y}P_j\mathbf{x}$. Then, by the lemma, $\mathbf{y}R\mathbf{x}$. Similarly, let an individual k in the third set change from $\mathbf{y}P_k\mathbf{z}$ and $\mathbf{z}P_k\mathbf{x}$, to $\mathbf{z}P_k\mathbf{y}$ and $\mathbf{y}P_k\mathbf{x}$. Then using the lemma again, we have $\mathbf{z}R\mathbf{y}$ so that, with these individual changes, the resulting changes in the group ordering yield $\mathbf{z}R\mathbf{x}$ (from $\mathbf{z}R\mathbf{y}$ and $\mathbf{y}R\mathbf{x}$). But the previous ordering was $\mathbf{x}P\mathbf{z}$, and no individual has altered his ranking of **x** relative to **z**. By Condition 4, therefore, the group ordering of **x** relative to **z** should not have changed either, but it did. It follows that, arguing as in case (b), we must reject case (d), for we can find a set of orderings, and a pattern of changes in tastes, that violate Condition 4. *Q.E.D.*

(e) $G_{\mathbf{xy}} = \bar{G}_{\mathbf{yz}}$.

Suppose that in this case the rankings were as follows:

For all i in $\bar{G}_{\mathbf{xy}}$: $\mathbf{x}P_i\mathbf{y}$ and $\mathbf{y}P_i\mathbf{z}$.
For all i in $\mathscr{C}(\bar{G}_{\mathbf{xy}})$ in G: $\mathbf{z}P_i\mathbf{y}$ and $\mathbf{y}P_i\mathbf{x}$.

Then we have $\mathbf{x}P\mathbf{y}$ and $\mathbf{y}P\mathbf{z}$, since the group of individuals $\bar{G}_{\mathbf{xy}}$ is decisive for **y** against **z** as well; hence $\mathbf{x}P\mathbf{z}$, and the set $\bar{G}_{\mathbf{xy}}$ is also a $G_{\mathbf{xz}}$. It follows that $\bar{G}_{\mathbf{xz}} \subset \bar{G}_{\mathbf{xy}}$.

Now suppose that $\bar{G}_{\mathbf{xy}}$ contains more than one member, and let one of these members j change to $\mathbf{x}P_j\mathbf{z}$ and $\mathbf{z}P_j\mathbf{y}$, and simultaneously another member k change to $\mathbf{y}P_k\mathbf{x}$ and $\mathbf{x}P_k\mathbf{z}$; and let no one else change. Then it follows from the lemma that $\mathbf{z}R\mathbf{y}$ and $\mathbf{y}R\mathbf{x}$, since $\bar{G}_{\mathbf{xy}}$ is minimally decisive

* The reader should check that each of these rankings is compatible with the definitions of the subgroups as minimal decisive sets.

for $\mathbf{x}$ against $\mathbf{y}$, and for $\mathbf{y}$ against $\mathbf{z}$. Hence $\mathbf{z}R\mathbf{x}$. But no ranking of $\mathbf{x}$ relative to $\mathbf{z}$ has changed, so that by Condition 4 we should have not $\mathbf{z}R\mathbf{x}$ but $\mathbf{x}P\mathbf{z}$, as before. This is a contradiction, and therefore $\bar{G}_{\mathbf{xy}}$ can have only one member.

But since $\bar{G}_{\mathbf{xz}}$ is not empty, and such that $\bar{G}_{\mathbf{xz}} \subset \bar{G}_{\mathbf{xy}}$, it follows that $\bar{G}_{\mathbf{xz}}$ also has only one member; and so one particular individual is the sole member of each of the subgroups $\bar{G}_{\mathbf{xy}}$, $\bar{G}_{\mathbf{xz}}$, and $\bar{G}_{\mathbf{yz}}$. This individual is therefore a dictator in the sense of Condition 3, and his existence is not permitted by that constraint. Hence case (e) leads to a contradiction as well. *Q.E.D.*

And this concludes the whole proof of the theorem. Notice the powerful role assumed by Condition 4, which is the chief tool used in cases (b) to (e). Notice also how an easy, if lengthy, use of very elementary tools proved a result of some importance, and certainly of some surprise value, judging by the reception accorded to Arrow's Theorem. This proof by Inada is remarkable for its very effective exploitation of what might be called a "variational" technique in the theory of ordering relations. By varying one (or more) person's ordering at each stage, Condition 4 is allowed full scope, and the required contradictions are obtained in a very simple way.

Let us now turn from these problems of Route 5 and concentrate briefly on the apparently more straightforward Route 7 and its analogue for choices, Route 8.

C. THE CONSTRUCTION OF GROUP PREFERENCE AND GROUP CHOICE STRUCTURES

(i) An Example of an Inconsistent Group Preference Structure

Consider a commodity space $\boldsymbol{X}$, and a group of individuals G, each of whom has a preference ordering R_i dependent solely on the amounts of goods in the bundle $\mathbf{x}^i$ which he himself receives. Let us try the obvious aggregation procedure which consists simply of adding, for any allocation of goods among the group G, the various quantities of commodities, and asking if there exists a group preference structure defined for these commodity totals. It is then not difficult to show, by means of the implicit function theorem (see the references in Chapter 6, Section C(ii)), that such a structure only exists if each Engel curve in the *commodity space* is a ray through the origin, different for different price-sets but actually identical for each individual. This condition is so enormously restrictive, implying extreme identity of individual tastes, that it effectively closes this simple avenue of approach to the aggregation problem.

So let us try another tack, employing a more subtle aggregation procedure. In Figs. 7.2(a) and (b) we present two diagrams which are again "dual"

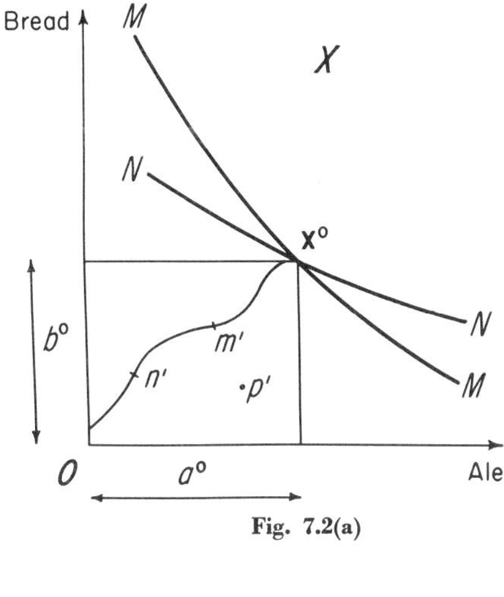

Fig. 7.2(a)

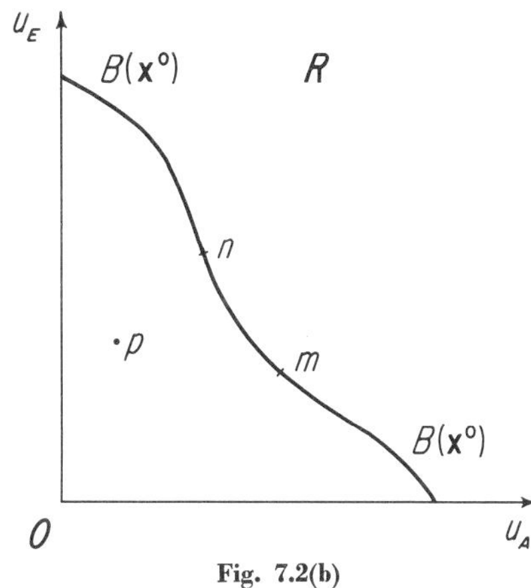

Fig. 7.2(b)

to each other—as were Figs. 6.5(a) and (b)—but in a quite different sense of the word "duality," one that is more akin to its use in projective geometry.

Suppose that there were only two individuals in G and only two commodities in $\mathbf{X}$; then we can return to the familiar shooting script for the Adam and Eve parable. In Fig. 7.2(a) we plot on each axis the *total* amount of ale and bread, respectively, allotted to the two individuals together. These totals can, of course, be allocated in infinitely many different ways; at $\mathbf{x}^0$, for example, the Edgeworth box whose dimensions are (a^0, b^0) represents a double-infinity of ways of allocating the totals a^0 and b^0 among the two persons.

But, as we saw in Chapter 3, there is only a *single* infinity of ways of making these allocations "efficiently," i.e., in such a way that, for a given level of Adam's satisfaction (or of Eve's), the highest possible level of Eve's satisfaction (or Adam's) is secured. This single parameter locus is of course the *efficiency locus* (*not* the contract curve), which in 2(a) is the curve joining **O** to $\mathbf{x}^0$. Each point on this locus corresponds to the highest possible level for a given representation u_E (for Eve) that is consistent with a given level of Adam's representation u_A.

This situation is also depicted in Fig. 7.2(b), which measures the representation levels on each axis, and where the satisfaction boundary curve $B(\mathbf{x}^0)$ that is associated with $\mathbf{x}^0$, corresponds to the representation levels along the efficiency locus of $\mathbf{x}^0$'s box. Since each representation is arbitrary up to a strictly increasing order-preserving transformation, we cannot give $B(\mathbf{x}^0)$ any unambiguous curvature, and in particular its convexity or concavity has no meaning; nor need it even stay in the positive quadrant, though for simplicity we have drawn it so. The only restriction on its shape is that it must slope downwards from left to right, corresponding to the sex war that is played out along the efficiency locus of $\mathbf{x}^0$'s box.

Hence to any *point* $\mathbf{x}^0$ in the (total) commodity space $\boldsymbol{X}$ there corresponds a *curve* in the "representation space" $\boldsymbol{R}$. A point such as m' in $\mathbf{x}^0$'s box corresponds to a point m on $B(\mathbf{x}^0)$, and—assuming the usual orientation of the preference maps in the box—the point n', which is a better position than m' for Eve in Fig. 7.2(a), corresponds to a point n in Fig. 7.2(a). An "inefficient" point like p' in 2(a) corresponds to a point p *within* the boundary (or frontier) $B(\mathbf{x}^0)$ in 2(b).

Now consider any *point*, such as m, in $\boldsymbol{R}$. This indicates—for any choice of representations u_A and u_E—a given level of well-being for each individual, and can be achieved if the vector of "totals" $\mathbf{x}^0$ is allocated in the way indicated by m' in $\boldsymbol{X}$. But it can *also* be achieved if some *other* vector of "totals" $\mathbf{x}^1$ (not shown) is allocated in a different way, say m''; e.g., we can have a set of commodity totals very slightly different to $\mathbf{x}^0$ allocated in a way very slightly different to m', and then by the continuity axioms we could get satisfaction levels equal to those at m. Therefore, corresponding to each point m on $B(\mathbf{x}^0)$ there will be a whole locus, or *curve* MM of points in $\boldsymbol{X}$ which indicate the totals that, when "efficiently" allocated, can achieve the satisfaction levels ruling at m; and MM will of course go through $\mathbf{x}^0$. It is not difficult to prove that, given the axiom system, this curve must also be convex, just like an individual's ordinary indifference curve.

But it fails to share another important property possessed by individual indifference curves, namely, that to each point in $\boldsymbol{X}$ there is just one individual curve. For consider the point n on $B(\mathbf{x}^0)$. In exactly the same way that we deduced the existence of a convex locus MM in $\boldsymbol{X}$ showing the minimum totals of goods needed to achieve the satisfaction levels represented by m, so we can deduce a similar convex locus NN in $\boldsymbol{X}$ showing the same thing for the satisfaction levels ruling at n. And because m and n are both achievable by the totals $\mathbf{x}^0$, distributed in different ways (but each of them "efficient"), it follows that NN goes through $\mathbf{x}^0$ as well.

Thus each point in X corresponds to a curve in R and, dually, each point in R corresponds to a curve in X. It follows that there is no one group indifference curve, in this sense, at $\mathbf{x}^0$, and that in particular there is no unique slope which we could then confront with a group-attainable set to determine a definite group choice. So even this sophisticated method of "adding" individual preferences, by means of the box construction, fails to produce a consistent group preference ordering.

A number of ways of escaping from these problems by means of a "social welfare function" have been proposed, but they lie outside the self-imposed terms of reference of this brief discussion.

(ii) Individual Choice Functions and Group Choice Functions

Finally, and in great brevity, let us note one or two properties of group choice functions. Let us consider any commodity, say x_k, and obtain its market demand function by adding up, for each set of market prices (the same for everybody), and for each person's income M_i, the amount of x_k that the individual i would demand. Provided that individual demands for a commodity do not depend on the amounts that *other* people are buying, as might happen (almost by definition) in the case of "fashion" goods, this aggregation procedure can always be carried out.

But it will not give us a group function analogous to the individual demand functions. There we have n money prices, and one income term; for a market demand function there are still only n money prices, but there are m income terms, one for each member of the market group. The discussion in (i) above has indicated that we cannot write group demand as a unique function of market prices and *group* income, except under very special conditions. If the group choices obeyed the Weak Axiom of Revealed Preference, for example, then such a group choice function would exist; and it is possible to give other conditions on the group choices which would in turn imply the Weak Axiom, C4.* But these are all very special restrictions, and, in general, market demand is a function of income distribution as well as of income totals.

The market demand functions that do always exist, however, have quite nice properties. In particular, they share all the properties regarding the effects of price changes that were deduced for individual functions in Section C of Chapter 6. If price p_j rises in a simple price change, then the market substitution effect on x_j will go in the opposite direction, as before, and—as before—little can be said about the group income effect of the price change. It is perhaps more likely that this income effect will be fairly well-behaved, since the existence of a large group of individual income effects will

* For example, Finn has showed that if market versions of C1 to C3 hold, and if no commodity is an "inferior" good (from the viewpoint of the group as a whole), *then* C4, the Weak Axiom, is satisfied for the group.

tend to iron out the consequences of very idiosyncratic effects through some kind of law of large numbers, but there are no guarantees about it.

If we are interested in the econometric aspects of demand, then, we do not need to worry about the nonexistence of demand functions based on group "income." Only if our interests lie in different directions, say in welfare economics or in problems of the uniqueness of exchange equilibrium, will these difficulties cause us any real concern.

NOTES ON THE LITERATURE

A. The reference to "Dr. Jekyll and Mrs. Jekyll" may be found in P. A. Samuelson: "The Problem of Integrability in Utility Theory," *Economica*, 17, 1950, 355–85, while references to early papers on the paradox of voting may be found in Arrow's book cited below.

A discussion of the conditions under which it will pay a voter not to dissemble but to vote in accordance with his preferences is given in R. Farquharson: "Straightforwardness in Voting Procedures," *Oxford Economic Papers*, 8, 1956, 80–89; see also M. Dummett and R. Farquharson: "Stability in Voting," *Econometrica*, 29, 1961, 33–43.

B. Although valuable earlier work had been done by such people as Lewis Carroll and Duncan Black, the first major discussion of the problems of this section (and of some of those in Section A) was by Kenneth Arrow: *Social Choice and Individual Values* (Wiley, New York, 1952). The result cited as Arrow's Theorem is not quite his General Possibility Theorem, since our Conditions 1–4 are not quite equivalent to his Conditions 1–5; but the relationship is sufficiently close to justify the use of his name.

Arrow's work evoked a flood of response. Two papers which sought to establish an existence theorem by weakening Arrow's conditions were those of L. A. Goodman and H. Markowitz ("Social Welfare Functions Based on Individual Rankings," *American Journal of Sociology*, 58, 1952, 257–62), and C. Hildreth ("Alternative Conditions for Social Orderings," *Econometrica*, 21, 1953, 81–94). I. M. D. Little, in his review article of Arrow's book (*Journal of Political Economy*, 60, 1952, 422–32), and P. A. Samuelson, in his review of J. de V. Graaff's: *Theoretical Welfare Economics* (*Economic Journal*, 68, 1958, 539–41) have each drawn attention to the different logical status of Condition 4, as prescribing what happens to the group ordering for a change in tastes. Many aspects of the whole discussion are summarized in J. Rothenberg: *The Measurement of Social Welfare* (Prentice-Hall, Englewood Cliffs, N.J., 1961).

The proof of Arrow's Theorem follows closely that given by K. Inada: "Alternative Incompatible Conditions for a Social Welfare Function," *Econometrica*, 23, 1955, 396–99. A demonstration of the incompleteness of Arrow's (and Inada's)proof for the general case of more than three alternatives was given by J. Blau in *Econometrica*, 25, 1957, 302–13, while more recent contributions are by W. Vickrey "Utility Strategy and Social Decision Rules," *Quarterly Journal of Economics*, 74, 1960, 507–35; and by Y. Murakami: "A Note on the General Possibility Theorem of the Social Welfare Function," *Econometrica*, 29, 1961, 244–46; this last paper shows how to modify Arrow's nondictatorship condition so as to make the theorem completely general (see also his paper in *Journal of Economic Behavior*, 1, 1961, 77–84).

For an excellent exposition of the methods of symbolic logic used in the proof, see P. Suppes: *Introduction to Logic* (Van Nostrand, Princeton, N. J., 1957).

C. The brief discussion in (i) is based mainly on P. A. Samuelson: "Social Indifference Curves," *Quarterly Journal of Economics*, 70, 1956, 1–22, and on T. J. Finn: "Some Properties of Group Demand," *International Economic Review*, 3, 1962, 189–205; see also W. Gorman: "Are Social Indifference Curves Convex?" *Quarterly Journal of Economics*, 73, 1959, 485–96; and T. Negishi: "On Social Welfare Function," *Quarterly Journal of Economics*, 77, 1963, 156–58.

A very full discussion of the aggregation of demand functions is contained in H. Wold: *Demand Analysis* (Wiley, New York, 1953), while a succinct account is in J. R. Hicks: *Value and Capital* (2nd ed., Oxford U.P., New York, 1946) 34–35 and 313–14.

INDEX

NAME INDEX

SUBJECT INDEX